Prentice Hall
Foundations of Philosophy

Roderick M. Chisholm	Theories of Knowledge, 3/E
William Dray	Philosophy of History, 2/E
Joel Feinberg	Social Philosophy
William K. Frankena	Ethics, 2/E
Martin P. Golding	Philosophy of Law
Carl Hempel	Philosophy of Natural Science
John H. Hick	Philosophy of Religion, 4/E
Dale Jacquette	Philosophy of Mind
Stephen Nathanson	Economic Justice
Wesley C. Salmon	Logic, 3/E
Richard Taylor	Metaphysics, 4/E

Tom L. Beauchamp, Editor
Monroe Beardsley and Elizabeth Beardsley, Founding Editors

EPISTEMOLOGY

Richard Feldman

University of Rochester

Upper Saddle River, New Jersey 07458

Library of Congress Cataloging-in-Publication Data

Feldman, Richard
  Epistemology / Richard Feldman.
    p. cm. — (Prentice-Hall foundations of philosophy series)
  Includes bibliographical references and index.
  ISBN 0-13-341645-3
  1. Knowledge, Theory of. I. Title. II. Series.

  BD161.F385 2003
  121—dc21

                                        2002042533

VP, Editorial Director: Charlyce Jones Owen
Senior Acquisition Editor: Ross Miller
Assistant Editor: Wendy Yurash
Editorial Assistant: Carla Worner
Sr. Managing Editor: Jan Stephan
Production Liaison: Fran Russello
Project Manager: Rebecca Giusti, Clarinda Publication Services
Prepress and Manufacturing Buyer: Brian Mackey
Art Director: Jayne Conte
Cover Designer: Kiwi Design
Marketing Manager: Chris Ruel
Marketing Assistant: Kimberly Daum

This book was set in 10/12 Baskerville by The Clarinda Company.
The cover was printed by Phoenix Color Corp.

© 2003 by Pearson Education, Inc.
Upper Saddle River, New Jersey 07458

Printed in the United States of America

10   9   8   7   6

ISBN   0-13-341645-3

Pearson Education LTD., London
Pearson Education Australia Pte, Limited., Sydney
Pearson Education Singapore, Pte. Ltd.
Pearson Education North Asia Ltd., Hong Kong
Pearson Education Canada, Ltd., Toronto
Pearson Educacion de Mexico, S.A. de C.V.
Pearson Education Japan, Tokyo
Pearson Education Malaysia, Pte. Ltd.
Pearson Education, Upper Saddle River, New Jersey

Contents

Foundations of Philosophy

Many of the problems of philosophy are of such broad relevance to human concerns, and so complex in their ramifications, that they are, in one form or another, perennially present. Though in the course of time they yield in part to philosophical inquiry, they may need to be rethought by each age in the light of its broader scientific knowledge and deepened ethical and religious experience. Better solutions are found by more refined and rigorous methods. Thus, one who approaches the study of philosophy in the hope of understanding the best of what it affords will look for both fundamental issues and contemporary achievements.

Written by a group of distinguished philosophers, the *Foundations of Philosophy Series* aims to exhibit some of the main problems in the various fields of philosophy as they stand at the present stage of philosophical history.

While certain fields are likely to be represented in most introductory courses in philosophy, college classes differ widely in emphasis, in method of instruction, and in rate of progress. Every instructor needs freedom to change his course as his own philosophical interests, the size and make-up of his classes, and the needs of his students vary from year to year. The volumes in the Foundations of Philosophy Series—each complete in itself, but complementing the others—offer a new flexibility to the instructor, who can create his own textbook by combining several volumes as he wishes, and can choose different combinations at different times. Those volumes that are not used in an introductory course will be found valuable, along with other texts or collections of readings, for the more specialized upper-level courses.

Tom L. Beauchamp, Editor
Elizabeth Beardsley and Monroe Beardsley, Founding Editors

Acknowledgments

I wish to express my indebtedness to a great many people with whom I have discussed epistemological issues. I first learned about epistemology when I sat in on the lectures in an epistemology course taught by my brother, Fred Feldman. That course initiated what has become an enduring interest and also taught me much of what I know about how to do philosophy. My interest and understanding were greatly enhanced by a series of seminars with Herbert Heidelberger and Roderick Chisholm. I would not have been able to write this book were it not for what I have learned from countless discussions of philosophy with John Bennett, David Braun, Stewart Cohen, Jonathan Vogel, Ed Wierenga, and especially Earl Conee. Todd Long, Dan Mittag, Nathan Nobis, Jim Pryor, Bruce Russell, Harvey Siegel, and Matthias Steup all gave me helpful comments on some or all of the manuscript. Many students, who endured courses making use of preliminary drafts, have provided useful guidance.

And thanks also to Andrea, for helping me to persevere, and for everything else as well.

CHAPTER ONE

Epistemological Questions

The theory of knowledge, or epistemology, is the branch of philosophy that addresses philosophical questions about knowledge and rationality. Epistemologists are primarily interested in questions about the nature of knowledge and the principles governing rational belief. They are less focused on deciding whether there is knowledge or rational belief in specific, actual cases. Thus, for example, it is not the epistemologist's business to rule on whether it is now reasonable to believe that there is life on other planets. That is primarily the job of astronomers and cosmologists. It is the epistemologist's business to try to develop a general theory stating the conditions under which people have knowledge and rational beliefs. One can then go on to apply that more general theory to the specific case of the belief in life on other planets, but to do so is to go beyond the central epistemological issues. Although in the course of examining the philosophical questions it is customary to think about many specific examples, this is mainly to illustrate the general issues. The point of this chapter is to identify some of the central theoretical issues epistemology addresses.

A good way to begin is to look at the things we ordinarily say and think about knowledge and rationality. By systematizing and reflecting on them, we will arrive at a set of questions and puzzles. Thus, we will begin by stating in a systematic way some commonly (but not universally) held ideas about what we know and how we know these things. We will call this collection of ideas *The Standard View*. In this chapter we will identify some of the central claims of *The Standard View*. In Chapters 2 through 5, we will attempt to spell out in detail the implications of *The Standard View* and to state its answers to some of the central questions. Then, in Chapters 6 though 9, we will turn to several challenges and objections to *The Standard View*. Thus, the general aim of this book is to provide a better understanding of our commonsense views about knowledge and rationality and to see to what extent those views can withstand criticism.

I. THE STANDARD VIEW

In the ordinary course of events, people claim to know many things and they attribute knowledge to others in a variety of cases. We will give examples below. The claims to knowledge with which we are concerned are not unreflective or outlandish. Rather, they are sensible and considered judgments. Thus, the list that follows reflects a set of thoughts about knowledge and rationality that many people are likely to arrive at if they reflect honestly and carefully about the topic. You may not agree with every detail of the view to be described, but it is fair to say that it accurately captures reflective common sense.

A. What We Know

Most of us think we know quite a lot. The following list identifies some general categories of these things and gives examples of each. The categories may overlap, and they are far from precise. Still, they give us a good idea of the sorts of things we can know.

a. Our immediate environment:
     "There's a chair over there."
     "The radio is on."
b. Our own thoughts and feelings:
     "I'm excited about the new semester."
     "I'm not looking forward to filling out my tax forms."
c. Commonsense facts about the world:
     "France is a country in Europe."
     "Many trees drop their leaves in the fall."
d. Scientific facts:
     "Smoking cigarettes causes lung cancer."
     "The earth revolves around the sun."
e. Mental states of others:
     "My neighbor wants to get his house painted."
     "That person over there who is laughing hard found the joke he just heard funny."
f. The past:
     "George Washington was the first president of the United States."
     "President Kennedy was assassinated."
g. Mathematics:
     "2 + 2 = 4"
     "5 · 3 = 15"
h. Conceptual truths:
     "All bachelors are unmarried."
     "Red is a color."

i. Morality:
    "Gratuitous torturing of infants is wrong."
    "There's nothing wrong with taking a break from work once in a while."
j. The future:
    "The sun will rise tomorrow."
    "The Chicago Cubs will not win the World Series next year."[1]
k. Religion:
    "God exists."
    "God loves me."

There are, of course, many things in each of these categories that we do not know. Some facts about the distant past are irretrievably lost. Some facts about the future are, at least for now, beyond us. Some of the areas of knowledge on the list are controversial. You may have doubts about our knowledge in the areas of morality and religion. Still, the list provides a fair sampling of the sorts of things we typically claim to know.

Thus, the first thesis within *The Standard View* is

SV1.   We know a large variety of things in categories (a)–(k).

B. Sources of Knowledge

If (SV1) is right, then there are some ways we come to know the things it says we know; there are some sources for our knowledge. For example, if we know about our immediate environment, then perception and sensation play a central role in acquiring this knowledge. Memory obviously is crucial in our knowledge of the past and also in certain aspects of our knowledge of current facts. For example, my knowledge that the tree that I see through my window is a maple relies on my perception of the tree and my memory of the way maples look. Another source of much of our knowledge is the testimony of others. Testimony is not here restricted to statements made on the witness stand under oath. It is much broader than that. It includes what other people tell you, including what they tell you on television or in books and newspapers.

Three other sources of knowledge deserve brief mention here as well. If perception is our awareness of external things through sight, hearing, and the other senses, then perception does not account for our knowledge of our own internal states. You may now know that you feel sleepy, or that you are thinking about what you will do on the weekend. But this is not by means of perception in the sense just given. It is, rather, introspection. So this is another potential source of knowledge.

Next, sometimes we know things by reasoning or inference. When we know some facts and see that those facts support some further fact, we can come to know that further fact. Scientific knowledge, for example, seems to arise from inferences from observational data.

Finally, it seems that we know some things simply because we can "see" that they are true. That is, we have the ability to think about things and to discern certain simple truths. Though this is a matter of some controversy, our knowledge of elementary arithmetic, simple logic, and conceptual truths seems to fall into this category. For lack of a better term, we will say that we know these things by means of *rational insight*.

Our list of sources of knowledge, then, looks like this:

a. Perception
b. Memory
c. Testimony
d. Introspection
e. Reasoning
f. Rational insight

No doubt in many cases we rely for our knowledge on some combination of these sources.

The Standard View holds that we can gain knowledge from these sources. It does not say that these sources are perfect. No doubt they are not. Sometimes our memories are mistaken. Sometimes our senses mislead us. Sometimes we reason badly. Still, according to *The Standard View*, we can get knowledge by using these sources.

Whether the list of sources of knowledge ought to be expanded is a matter of some controversy. Perhaps some people would add religious or mystical insight to the list. Perhaps others think that there are forms of extrasensory perception that we should add. However, these are issues about which there is greater disagreement. To add them to the list, then, might make the list look less like something deserving the name "*The Standard View.*" Thus, we will not add them here. Others might want to add science to the list of sources of knowledge. Although it may be unobjectionable to do so, science is probably best seen as a combination of perception, memory, testimony, and reasoning. Thus, it may not be necessary to add it to the list.

Thus, the second thesis in *The Standard View* is

SV2.   Our primary sources of knowledge are (a)–(f).

The Standard View, then, is the conjunction of (SV1) and (SV2).

II. DEVELOPING THE STANDARD VIEW

Numerous questions arise once we reflect on *The Standard View*. These questions constitute the primary subject matter of epistemology. This section identifies some of those questions.

If some cases fall into the category of knowledge and others are excluded from that category, then there must be something that differentiates these two groups of things. What is it that distinguishes knowledge from the lack of knowledge? What does it take to know something? This leads to the first question:

Q1.   Under what conditions does a person know something to be true?

One might think that it is a matter of how sure a person feels about something or whether there is general agreement about the matter. As we will see, these are not good answers to (Q1). Something else distinguishes knowledge from its opposite. (Q1), it turns out, is surprisingly hard, controversial, and interesting. Working out an answer to it involves thinking through some difficult issues. This will be the focus of Chapters 2 and 3.

According to many philosophers, an important condition on knowledge is rational or justified belief. To know something requires something along the lines of having a good reason to believe it, or coming to believe it in the right sort of way, or something like that. You do not know something if you are just guessing, for example. This leads us to a second question, one that has been central to epistemology for many years:

Q2.　Under what conditions is a belief justified (or reasonable or rational)?

And this will lead us to further questions about the alleged sources of knowledge. How do these faculties enable us to satisfy the conditions of knowledge? How could they yield epistemic justification? This will be the focus of Chapters 4 and 5, as well as parts of Chapters 7–9.

Our beliefs obviously play a central role in determining our behavior. You will behave very differently toward your neighbor if you believe that she is a trustworthy friend rather than a dishonest enemy. Given the ability of beliefs to affect our behavior, it seems clear that your beliefs can affect your life and the lives of others. Depending upon your career and the extent to which others depend upon you, you may have obligations to know about certain things. For example, a medical doctor ought to know about the latest developments in her specialty. Sometimes, however, knowledge can be a bad thing, as when one learns of an apparent friend's disloyalty. These considerations suggest that practical and moral issues interact with epistemological issues in ways that merit examination. Thus,

Q3.　In what ways, if any, do epistemological, practical, and moral matters affect one another?

We will address this question in Chapter 4.

III. CHALLENGES TO THE STANDARD VIEW

Careful philosophical reflection on the questions listed so far, to be carried out in Chapters 2–5, will result in a detailed statement of just what *The Standard View* amounts to. However, as will be evident as we proceed, there are reasons to wonder whether this commonsense view really is correct. We will give these reasons, and the alternative views about knowledge and rationality associated with them, a full hearing in Chapters 6–9. The central ideas behind these doubts are the basis for the remaining questions about *The Standard View.*

A. The Skeptical View

Advocates of *The Skeptical View* contend that we know far less than *The Standard View* says we know. Skepticism constitutes a traditional and powerful philosophical challenge to *The Standard View*. Skeptics think that *The Standard View* is far too charitable and self-indulgent. They think that our confident assertion that we know a lot results from a rather smug self-confidence that is entirely unjustified. As we shall see, some skeptical arguments rely on seemingly bizarre possibilities: Maybe you are just dreaming that you are seeing and hearing the things you think you are seeing and hearing; maybe your life is some sort of computer-generated artificial reality. Other skeptical arguments do not rely on odd hypotheses like these. But all of them challenge our comfortable commonsense view. These considerations prompt the next set of epistemological questions:

> Q4. Do we really have any knowledge at all? Is there any good response to the arguments of the skeptics?

(Q4) asks, in effect, whether the conditions spelled out in response to (Q1) are actually satisfied. Advocates of *The Skeptical View* hold that the answer to each of the questions in (Q4) is "No." They are inclined to deny both (SV1) and (SV2).

B. The Naturalistic View

The methodology traditionally used by epistemologists is primarily conceptual or philosophical analysis: thinking hard about what knowledge and rationality are like, often using hypothetical examples to illustrate the points. However, one might wonder whether we could better study some of these questions scientifically. Many recent philosophers have said that we can. We will call their view *The Naturalistic View* because it emphasizes the role of natural (or empirical or experimental) science. Thus, one way *The Naturalistic View* challenges *The Standard View* has to with the methodology used to support theses (SV1) and (SV2) of *The Standard View*.

The Naturalistic View also leads to a second kind of challenge to *The Standard View*. There is a body of research about the ways people think and reason that is troubling. It shows, or at least seems to show, systematic and widespread errors and confusions in how we think and reason. When confronted with the results of this research, some people wonder whether anything like *The Standard View* can be right.

These considerations lead to our next set of questions:

> Q5. In what ways, if at all, do results in natural science, especially cognitive psychology, bear on epistemological questions? Do recent empirical results undermine *The Standard View*?

C. The Relativistic View

Another challenge to *The Standard View* emerges from considerations of relativism and cognitive diversity. To see the issues here, notice that people's beliefs and their policies for forming beliefs differ widely. For example, some people are willing to believe on the basis of rather little evidence. Some seem to demand a lot of evidence. People also differ in their attitudes toward science. Some people are strong believers in the power of science. They think that the methods of science provide the only reasonable way to learn about the world around us. They sometimes regard others as irrational for believing in such things as astrology, reincarnation, ESP, and other occult phenomena. Defenders of these beliefs sometimes charge their critics with a blind and irrational faith in science. People also differ widely over political, moral, and religious matters. Seemingly intelligent people can find themselves seriously at odds with one another over these issues. There is, then, no doubt that people disagree, often vehemently, about a great many things.

The fact that there is this much disagreement leads some people to wonder whether in each case (at least) one party to the dispute must be unreasonable. A comforting thought to many is that there is room for reasonable disagreement, at least on certain topics. That is, two people can have different points of view, yet each can be reasonable in maintaining his or her own view. Defenders of *The Relativistic View* are inclined to find room for a great deal of reasonable disagreement, whereas defenders of *The Standard View* seemed to be more inclined to think that one side (at least) must be wrong in every dispute.

These considerations about cognitive diversity and the possibility of reasonable disagreements provoke the following questions having to do with epistemological relativism:

> Q6. What are the epistemological implications of cognitive diversity? Are there universal standards of rationality, applicable to all people (or all thinkers) at all times? Under what circumstances can rational people disagree with one another?

The questions raised in (Q1) through (Q6) are among the central problems in epistemology. The chapters that follow will address them.

ENDNOTE

1. Cubs fans may not like this example. But those who follow baseball know that, no matter what happens, the Cubs never win. Neither do the Boston Red Sox.

CHAPTER TWO

The Traditional Analysis of Knowledge

The goal of the next few chapters is to try to get clearer about just what *The Standard View* says and what implications it has. While doing this we will not call into question the truth of *The Standard View*. We will assume that it is basically correct, reserving discussion of challenges to our commonsense view until later.

I. KINDS OF KNOWLEDGE

The Standard View says that we have a good deal of knowledge and it says something about the sources of that knowledge. One central aspect of getting clearer about just what *The Standard View* amounts to is getting clearer on just what it takes knowledge to be. *The Standard View* says that we do have knowledge, but what is knowledge?

A. Some Main Kinds of Knowledge

We use the words "knows" and "knew" in a variety of importantly different kinds of sentences. Here are some examples:[1]

a. Knowing an individual: S knows x.
   "The professor knows J. D. Salinger."
b. Knowing who: S knows who x is.
   "The student knows who J. D. Salinger is."
c. Knowing whether: S knows whether p.
   "The librarian knows whether there is a book by J. D. Salinger in the library."

   d. Knowing when: S knows when A will (or did) happen.
      "The editor knew when J. D. Salinger's book would be published."
   e. Knowing how: S knows how to A.
      "J. D. Salinger knows how to write."
   f. Knowing facts: S knows p.
      "The student knows that J. D. Salinger wrote *The Catcher in the Rye.*"

This list is far from complete. We could add sentences using phrases such as "knows which," "knows why," and so on. But the list we have already will be enough to bring out the main points to be made here.

B. Is All Knowledge Propositional Knowledge?

"Knows that" sentences report that a person knows a certain fact or proposition. These sentences are said to express *propositional knowledge.* One initially plausible idea about the connection between these various ways in which the word "knows" is used is that "knows that" is fundamental and that the others can be defined in terms of it. To see why propositional knowledge is more fundamental than the others, consider how some of the other kinds might be explained in terms of it.

    Consider (c), "knowing whether." Suppose it is true that

   1. The librarian knows whether there is a book by J. D. Salinger in the library.

If (1) is true, then if there is a book by J. D. Salinger in the library, the librarian knows that there is. If, on the other hand, there is no book by him in the library, then the librarian knows that there is not. Whichever proposition is actually true—the proposition that there is a book or the proposition that there is not—the librarian knows it. So, saying (1) is a short way of saying

   2. Either the librarian knows that there is a book by J. D. Salinger in the library or the librarian knows that there is no book by J. D. Salinger in the library.[3]

In this respect, the librarian differs from a patron who does not know whether there is a book by Salinger there. The patron does not know that there is a book there and does not know that there is no book there.

    The point just made about (1) can be generalized. For any person and any proposition, the person knows whether the proposition is true just in case either the person knows that it is true or the person knows that it is not true. A person who does not know whether it is true neither knows that it is true nor knows that it is not.

We can express the point about the connection between (1) and (2) in terms of a general definition, using the letter "S" to stand for a potential knower and "p" to stand for a proposition:

> D1.   S knows whether p = df. Either S knows p or S knows ~p.[4]

Definition (D1) illustrates an important methodological tool: definitions. A definition is correct only if the two sides are equivalent. To check whether the two sides are equivalent, you consider the results of filling in the variables or placeholders with specific instances. In the case of (D1), you fill in the name of a person for S and you replace p by a sentence expressing some proposition. If the definition is correct, in all such cases the two sides will agree: If the left side is true—if the person does know whether the proposition is true—then the right side will also be true—either the person knows that it is true or the person knows that it is not true; if, on the other hand, the left side is not true—if the person does not know whether the proposition is true—then the right side will not be true either. (D1) seems to pass this test: The two sides of the definition do coincide. Thus, we can explain "knowing whether" in terms of "knowing that."

It is also possible to define some of the other kinds of knowledge in terms of propositional knowledge. The definitions are more complicated, but the ideas are still fairly straightforward. Consider "knows when." If you know when something happened (or will happen), then there is some proposition stating the time at which it happened (or will happen) such that you know that proposition to be true. Thus, to say

> 3.   The editor knew when J. D. Salinger's book would be published.

is to say that the editor knew, with respect to some particular time, that Salinger's book would be published at that time, e.g., she knew that it would be published in 1950 or that it would be published in 1951, etc. Those who were less knowledgeable than the editor were not in this position. For them, there was no time such that they knew the proposition that the book would be published at that time.

Again, we can generalize the idea and express it as a definition:

> D2.   S knows when x happens = df. There is some proposition saying that x happens at some particular time and S knows that proposition. (There is some proposition, p, where p is of the form "x happens at t" and S knows p.)

Once again, we have a way to explain one kind of knowledge—knowing when—in terms of propositional knowledge. It is likely that similar approaches will work for knowing which, knowing why, and numerous other sentences about knowledge. The case for propositional knowledge being fundamental looks fairly strong.

However, it is unlikely that all the things we say using the word *knows* can be expressed in terms of propositional knowledge. Consider the first item on our list: "S knows x." You might think that to know someone or something is to have propositional knowledge of some facts about that person or thing. Thus, we might propose

> D3.   S knows x = df. S has propositional knowledge of some facts about x (i.e., for some proposition p, p is about x, and S knows p).

It is likely that anyone you know is someone you know some facts about. But knowing some facts about a person is not sufficient for knowing the person. J. D. Salinger is a reclusive, but well-known, author. Many people do know some facts about him: they know that he wrote *The Catcher in the Rye*. They may know that he does not interact with a great many people. So they know facts about him, but they do not know him. Thus, knowing a person is not the same as knowing some facts about a person.

This shows that definition (D3) is not correct. It also illustrates another important methodological point. The example shows that (D3) is not correct because it is a *counterexample* to (D3): an example showing that the sides of the definition do not always agree—one side can be true when the other is false. A clear-cut counterexample refutes a proposed definition. By revising a definition in response to counterexamples, it is possible to get a better understanding of the concepts under discussion.[5]

The counterexample to (D3) shows not only that (D3) is false but that it is not even on the right track. We cannot make some minor change in order to fix things up. It would not help to add that S knows lots of facts about x, or that S knows important facts about x. You can have that sort of propositional knowledge and still not know the person. Knowing x isn't a matter of knowing facts about x. Instead, it is a matter of being acquainted with x—having met x and perhaps remembering that meeting. No matter how many facts you know about a person, it does not follow that you know that person. Knowing a person or a thing is being acquainted with that person or thing, not having propositional knowledge about the person or thing. So not all knowing is propositional knowing.

Consider next "knowing how." Suppose that there is a former expert skier who, after a serious accident leaves him unable to ski, becomes a successful ski coach. His success as a coach is largely the result of the fact that he is unusually good at explaining skiing techniques to students. Does the coach know how to ski? The answer seems to be "Yes." A plausible explanation of this appeals to the following definition:

> D4a.   S knows how to A = df. If a is an important step in A-ing, then S knows that a is an important step in A-ing.[6]

This seems to show that "knowing how" can be defined in terms of propositional knowledge.

However, other examples suggest a different idea. Consider a young child who begins skiing and does it successfully, without any training or intellectual understanding of what she is doing. She also knows how to ski, but she seems to lack the relevant propositional knowledge. She does not have any explicit conscious understanding of the various steps. She is just able to do it. This example suggests that there is a second meaning to the phrase "knows how." The following definition captures this second meaning:

D4b.   S knows how to A = df. S is able to A.

The ex-skier knows how to ski in the (D4a) sense, but not in the (D4b) sense. Just the reverse is true of the young prodigy. So one kind of knowhow is propositional knowledge, but another kind is not.

C. Conclusion

The attempt to explain all the different kinds of knowledge in terms of propositional knowledge is unsuccessful. The most reasonable conclusion seems to be that there are (at least) three basic kinds of knowledge: (1) propositional knowledge, (2) acquaintance knowledge or familiarity, and (3) ability knowledge (or procedural knowledge).

Even though we cannot explain all knowledge in terms of propositional knowledge, propositional knowledge does have a special status. We can explain several other kinds of knowledge in terms of it. Furthermore, many of the most intriguing questions about knowledge turn out to be questions about propositional knowledge. It will be the focus of this book. And the point of this section is mainly to get clear about the sort of knowledge that is the topic of our study. It is propositional knowledge, or knowledge of facts.

II. KNOWLEDGE AND TRUE BELIEF

What does it take to know a fact? What is propositional knowledge? These are the questions raised by (Q1) in Chapter 1. We will begin our examination of this with a simple, and inadequate, answer. Then we will attempt to build upon this answer.

A. Two Conditions on Knowledge

It is easy to come up with two conditions for knowledge: truth and belief. It is clear that knowledge requires truth. That is, you cannot know something unless it is true. It can never be right to say, "He knows it but it's false." You cannot know that Thomas Jefferson was the first president of the United States. The reason that you cannot know this is that he was not the first president.

People can feel very sure of things that are not true. You might feel sure that Jefferson was the first president. You might think that you remember being taught this in school. But you are mistaken about this. (Or your teacher made a big mistake.) You might even *claim* to know that Jefferson was the first president. But he was not the first president, and you do not know that he was. This is because knowledge requires truth. You know a proposition only if it is true.

There is a possible objection to the claim that knowledge requires truth. It is illustrated by the following example:

Example 2.1: The Mystery Story

You are reading a mystery story. All the clues presented right up to the last chapter indicated that the butler was guilty. You felt sure the butler did it and were surprised when it was revealed in the final scene that the accountant was guilty. After you finish the book you say:

4. I knew all along that the butler did it, but then it turned out that he didn't.

If you are right when you say (4), then it is possible to know things that are not true. You knew that the butler did it, but it was not true that the butler did it. However, even though people sometimes say things such as (4), it is clear that these things are not literally true. You did not *know* all along that the butler did it. What was true all along was that you felt sure that the butler did it, or something like that. By saying (4) you convey, in a slightly colorful way, that you were surprised by the ending. But (4) is not true, and it does not show that there can be knowledge without truth.

A second condition for knowledge is belief. If you know something, then you must believe it or accept it. If you do not even think that something is true, then you do not know it. We are using "belief" in a broad sense here: anytime you take something to be true, you believe it. Believing thus includes hesitant acceptance as well as fully confident acceptance. A good way to think about this is to notice that when you consider a statement, you can adopt any of three attitudes toward it: belief, disbelief, or suspension of judgment. As an analogy, imagine yourself forced to say one of three things about a statement: "yes," "no," or "no opinion." You will say "yes" over a range of cases, including the ones in which you are entirely confident of a statement and the ones in which you merely think the statement is probably true. You will say "no" when you think that the statement is definitely or probably false. And you will say "no opinion" in the remaining cases. Similarly, as we are using the term here, "belief" applies to a range of attitudes. It is contrasted with disbelief, which involves a similar range, and suspension of judgment.

It is clear, then, that knowledge requires belief. If you do not even think that a statement is true, then you do not know that it is true. There is, however, an objection to this claim that deserves consideration. We sometimes talk in ways that contrast knowledge and belief, suggesting that when you know something, you do not believe it. To see this, consider the following example:

Example 2.2:   Knowing Your Name

You have a friend named "John" and you ask him, "Do you believe that your name is 'John'?" He replies:

5.   I do not *believe* that my name is "John"; I *know* that it is.

In saying (5), John seems to be saying that this is a case of knowledge and not a case of belief. The suggestion is that if it is belief, then it is not knowledge. If he is right, then belief is not a condition for knowledge.

However, again, this appearance is misleading. John surely does accept the statement that his name is "John." He does not reject that statement or have no opinion about it. When he says (5), his point is that he does not *merely* believe that his name is "John"; he can say something stronger—that he knows it. And one of the ways we typically proceed in conversations is to avoid saying the weaker or more modest thing when the stronger one is true as well. If your friend were to say to you, "I believe that my name is 'John,'" this would suggest, but not literally say, that he does not know it. There are many other examples of the same phenomenon. Suppose that you are extremely tired, having worked very hard for a long time. Someone asks if you are tired. You might respond by saying something like:

6.   I'm not tired; I'm exhausted.

Taken literally, what you say is false. You *are* tired. The point of your utterance is to emphasize that you are not *merely* tired; you are exhausted. The same thing goes on in (5). By saying (5), John is not really saying that he does not believe the statement. So this example is not a counterexample to the thesis that knowledge requires belief.

We have now found two conditions for knowledge: To know something, you must believe it and it must be true.

B. Knowledge as True Belief

The ideas just presented may suggest that knowledge is true belief; that is,

TB.   S knows p = df. (i) S believes p, and (ii) p is true.

A little reflection should make it clear that (TB) is mistaken. There are lots of times that a person has a true belief but does not have knowledge. Here is a simple counterexample to (TB):

Example 2.3:   Correct Predictions

New York is playing Denver in an upcoming Superbowl. The experts are divided about who will win, and the teams are rated as even. You have a hunch that Denver will win. When the game is finally played, your hunch turns out to have been correct. So you believed that Denver would win, and your belief was true.

In Example 2.3 you believe that Denver will win, and this is true. But you did not know that Denver would win. You just had a guess that turned out to be correct.

Some will say that the fact the belief in Example 2.3 is about the future ruins the example. But we can easily eliminate that feature without undermining the point. Suppose you do not watch the game, but instead go to a long movie. When you get out of the movie, you know that the game is over. You now have a belief about the past, namely that Denver won. And you are right. You still do not know that they won. You are still right as a result of a lucky guess. But now there are no complications having to do with beliefs about the future.

The objections to (TB) are not limited to cases of lucky guesses. Another sort of example will illustrate the heart of the problem with (TB).

Example 2.4:   The Pessimistic Picnic Planner

You have a picnic scheduled for Saturday and you hear a weather forecast that says at the chances that it will rain on Saturday are slightly more than 50%. You are a pessimist, and on the basis of this report you believe confidently that it will rain. And then it does rain. So you had a true belief that it would rain.

You did have a true belief that it would rain, but you lacked knowledge. (When the rain starts, you might say, "I knew it would rain," but you did not really know it.) The reason you did not know in this case is not that you were guessing. Your belief is based on some evidence—the weather report—so it is not simply a guess. But this basis is not good enough for knowledge. What you need for knowledge is something along the lines of very good reasons or a more reliable basis, not just a potentially inaccurate weather report.

Philosophers often say that what is needed for knowledge, in addition to true belief, is *justification* for the belief. Exactly what justification amounts to is a matter of considerable controversy. We will spend a good deal of time later in this book examining this idea. But for now it will suffice to notice that in the examples of knowledge that we put forth in Chapter 1, the believers had extremely good reasons for their beliefs. In contrast, in the counterexamples to (TB), you did not have very good reasons and you could easily have been wrong. What is missing, then, in the counterexamples to (TB) and is present in the examples of knowledge we have described is justification. This leads us to *The Traditional Analysis of Knowledge*.

III. THE TRADITIONAL ANALYSIS OF KNOWLEDGE

The Traditional Analysis of Knowledge (the *TAK*) is formulated in the following definition:

TAK.   S knows p = df. (i) S believes p, (ii) p is true, (iii) S is justified in believing p.

Something along these lines can be found in various sources, perhaps going back as far as Socrates. In Plato's dialogue *Meno,* Socrates says:

> For true opinions, as long as they remain, are a fine thing and all they do is good, but they are not willing to remain long; and they escape from man's mind, so that they are not worth much until one ties them down by (giving) an account of the reason why. . . . After they are tied down, in the first place they become knowledge, and then they remain in place.[7]

According to one possible interpretation of this passage, to be able to give "an account" of an opinion is to have a reason or justification for that opinion. And one idea in the passage is that this is needed in order to have knowledge.[8] We will ignore the additional claim, that knowledge is less likely to "escape" from one's mind than other beliefs.

Similar ideas can be found in the work of many more contemporary philosophers. For example, Roderick Chisholm once proposed that one knows a proposition just in case one believes the proposition, it is true, and the proposition is "evident" for one. And this last condition is understood in terms of how reasonable it is for the person to believe the proposition.[9]

We turn now to a more thorough examination of the three elements of the *TAK*.

A. Belief

To believe something is to accept it as true. When you consider any statement, you are faced with a set of *alternatives:* You can believe it, you can disbelieve it, or you can suspend judgment about it. Recall that we are taking belief to include a range of more specific attitudes, including hesitant acceptance and complete conviction. Disbelief includes a corresponding range of negative attitudes toward a proposition. At any given time, if you consider a proposition, you will end up adopting one of these three attitudes.[10]

For present purposes, think of disbelieving a proposition as being the same thing as believing the negation (or denial) of that proposition. So disbelieving that George Washington was the first president is the same as believing that it is not the case that George Washington was the first president. Suspending judgment about the proposition is to neither believe it nor disbelieve it.[11]

One additional point about belief deserves mention here. Suppose a French child is taught that George Washington was the first president of the United States. Thus, it becomes true that

7. Pierre believes that George Washington was the first president of the United States.

The noteworthy thing here is that (7) can be true even if Pierre does not speak a word of English. He does not have to understand the English sentence "George Washington was the first president of the United States." Presumably, he would express his belief using a French equivalent of this sentence. Pierre's American counterpart, Peter, might believe what Pierre does. Thus,

> 8. Peter believes that George Washington was the first president of the United States.

Peter, we may assume, does not speak a word of French. So Peter and Pierre believe the same thing, even though there is no sentence that they both accept. How can this be?

One way to understand these matters is as follows. Sentences are used to express certain thoughts or ideas. Philosophers use the word *proposition* to refer to these items. The English sentence Peter uses and the French sentence Pierre uses express the same proposition. Belief is fundamentally a relation to a proposition. So (7) can be true because Pierre believes the relevant proposition about George Washington; (8) is true because Peter believes that same proposition. But they would use different sentences to express that proposition.

There are, then, two important points to extract from this: Sentences differ from the propositions they are used to express, and belief is fundamentally an attitude one takes toward propositions.[12]

B. Truth

The second element of the *TAK* is truth. People say many complicated and murky things about truth, but the fundamental idea is very simple. The issue here is not about which things are in fact true. Rather, the question for now is about what it is for something to be true. One simple and widely accepted answer to this is contained in the *correspondence theory of truth*.

The central point of the correspondence theory is expressed in the following principle:

> CT. A proposition is true if and only if it corresponds to the facts (iff the world is the way the proposition says it is). A proposition is false iff it fails to correspond to the facts.[13]

The idea here is extraordinarily simple. It applies to our example about George Washington in the following way. The proposition that George Washington was the first president is true just in case it corresponds to the facts as they actually are. In other words, it is true just in case George Washington was the first president. The proposition is false if he was not the first president. This should come as no surprise. The principle applies in analogous ways to other propositions.

It will be helpful to spell out a few consequences of (CT) and to mention a few things that are not consequences of (CT).

1) Whether a proposition is true or false does not depend in any way upon what anyone believes about it. For example, our beliefs about George

Washington have no bearing on the truth value (i.e., truth or falsity) of the proposition that George Washington was the first president. The actual facts of the case determine its truth value.

2) Truth is not "relative." No single proposition can be "true for me but not true for you." I might believe a proposition that you disbelieve. In fact, this is almost surely the case. Any two people will almost surely disagree about something. However, if there is a proposition they disagree about, then the truth value of that proposition is determined by the facts.

3) (CT) does not legitimize any kind of dogmatism or intolerant attitude toward people who disagree with you. Some people dismiss without consideration anyone who disagrees with them. That is a nasty and unreasonable way to treat others. However, if we disagree about something, then, trivially, I think that I am right and that you are wrong. If, for example, you think that Thomas Jefferson was the first president and I think that it was George Washington instead, then I think that you are wrong about this and you think that I am wrong about this. It would be rash for me to generalize from this case and draw any conclusions about your other beliefs. But when you disagree with me, I do think you are wrong. If you are not dogmatic, you recognize your own fallibility. You are open to changing your mind if new information comes along. There are circumstances in which it might be rude to tell others that you think they are wrong. And possibly the mere fact that others disagree provides you with some reason to reconsider your views.[14]

4) (CT) does not imply that things cannot change. Consider the proposition that George Washington *is* the president of the United States. That proposition is false. But, it seems, it used to be true. What does (CT) say about this?

There are a few ways to think about this, and a full examination of them would get into technicalities that are not important for present purposes. One good approach says that a sentence such as "George Washington is the president of the United States" expresses a different proposition at different times. The proposition it expressed back in 1789 is true. The proposition it expresses in 2003—the proposition that George Washington is president of the United States in 2003—is false. We can say that the sentence can be used to express a series of propositions about specific times. You can think of a proposition saying that a certain thing has a certain property at one time as a predecessor of a proposition saying that that same thing that same property at a slightly later time. So, when things change, for example, when we get a new president, one dated proposition is true and its successor proposition is false. There is no problem for (CT) here, provided we are careful about the propositions in question.

5) Something similar applies to considerations about location. Suppose someone in Maine is talking on the telephone to someone in Florida. The person in Maine says:

9. It is snowing.

The person in Florida says:

    10. It is not snowing.

These speakers do not disagree about anything. But what, then, should we say about the truth value of the proposition that it is snowing? Is it true or is it false?

    Once again, there are a variety of ways to think about this. For present purposes, a good approach will be to say that by a sentence like (9) the person expresses a proposition that might more clearly be displayed by the sentence

    9a. It is snowing here (in Maine).

Similarly, the person in Florida who says (10) says something that is most clearly displayed in

    10a. It is not snowing here (in Florida).

We may assume both of these propositions are true. Their truth is objective, in that it depends upon the weather conditions in the two places.

6)   There are puzzles about sentences such as

    11. Yogurt tastes good.

Exactly what (CT) says about them depends largely on what these sentences mean. One possibility is that each speaker uses (11) to say, "I like the taste of yogurt." If that is the case, then different people use (11) to express different propositions, each proposition being about what that speaker likes. If a person who does like the taste of yogurt says (11), then the proposition the person expresses is true. If the person does not like yogurt, then the person expresses a proposition that is not true.

    It is not obvious that (11) says something about individual preferences. Maybe it means something like "Most people like the taste of yogurt." If that is what it means, then it does not express different propositions when said by different people. It expresses one proposition about majority tastes, and that proposition is true if most people like yogurt and not true if they do not.

    According to another interpretation, (11) says that yogurt satisfies some standard of taste that is independent of people's likes and dislikes. This assumes some sort of "objectivity" about taste. On this view, (11) could be true even if hardly anyone actually likes the taste of yogurt. You might find this view strange; it is hard to understand what objective good taste amounts to.

    What is crucial for present purposes is to notice that whichever interpretation of (11) is right, there is no trouble for (CT). The proposition expressed by (11) will vary from one speaker to another if the first option is right, but not in the other cases. In all cases, however, the truth value that the proposition(s) (11) expresses depends upon the relevant facts. In this case, the relevant facts are either the likes and dislikes of the speaker, the likes and dislikes of the majority of people, or the objective facts about good taste.

There is no need for us to settle disputes about the right interpretation of sentences such as (11). That complicated matter can be left to those who study aesthetics. The crucial point for present purposes is that whichever interpretation is correct, there is no good objection here to (CT).

7)   (CT) does not imply that we cannot know what is "really" true. Some people react to (CT) by saying something like this:

> According to (CT), truth is "absolute" and what's true depends upon how things are in the objective world. Because this world is external to us, we can never really know what's true. At most, we can know what is "subjectively" true. This subjective truth depends upon our own views about the world. Absolute truth must always be beyond our grasp.

We will discuss skepticism at length in Chapters 6 and 7. Much of epistemology is an effort to respond to it. For now it is enough to note two points. First, from the mere fact that what is true is dependent upon an objective world that exists independent of us, it does not follow that we cannot know what that world is like. Thus, if there is any strong argument for skepticism, it relies on a premise beyond anything stated in the preceding paragraph. We will consider how such an argument might be formulated later.

Second, throughout the next several chapters we will assume, as *The Standard View* does, that we do know things. This is not a matter of prejudging the issues associated with skepticism. Rather, we are examining what the nature and consequences of *The Standard View* are. *The Skeptical View* will get a fair hearing in Chapters 6 and 7.

8)   There is one very puzzling issue associated with the correspondence theory of truth. Consider a sentence such as

12.   Michael is tall.

Suppose that someone asserts (12) in a normal conversational context such as the following: You are about to pick up Michael at the airport. You know that he is an adult male, but you do not know what he looks like. You are given a description, of which (12) is a part. Under these circumstances, if Michael is actually 6'4", then (12) expresses a truth. If Michael is 4'10", then (12) says something false. If Michael is about 5'10", then it is difficult to say whether (12) expresses a truth or a falsehood. That height seems to be a borderline case of being tall (for an adult male).

According to one widely held view about these matters, the word "tall" just does not have a precise meaning. The problem we have in the final situation, when Michael is 5'10", is *not* that we do not know enough about the situation. We can know everything there is to know about Michael's height, average heights for adult men, and anything else that is relevant. On this view, (12) just is a borderline case. There simply are not exact boundaries to the heights to which the word "tall" applies. In other words, "tall" is a *vague* word.

Many other words are vague, including, "healthy", "wealthy", and "wise". Vagueness causes numerous problems in understanding exactly how language works. Fortunately, we can largely ignore those issues while pursuing the epistemological questions that are our focus. However, issues concerning vagueness will arise from time to time, so it is important to have a grasp of the idea.

Furthermore, the existence of vague sentences *may* have some bearing on the adequacy of (CT). Recall the distinction between sentences and the propositions they express. As just noted, vagueness is a feature of sentences. Sentence (12), it seems, is vague. But now consider the proposition (12) expresses on a particular occasion, such as the one just described. If that proposition is vague, or indefinite in truth value, then (CT) needs revision. (CT) says that every proposition is either true or false, depending upon whether it corresponds to the way the world is. But if there are vague propositions, then there are propositions that partially correspond to the way the world is. One might say that there is a third truth value—indeterminate—in addition to the original two—true and false. One might even say that there is a whole range of truth values, that truth comes in degrees. These are complex matters that cannot easily be resolved. We will not attempt to resolve them here. It is enough to realize that (CT) may require modification in order to deal with vagueness.

C. Justification

The third, and final element of the *TAK* is justification. Justification (or rationality or reasonableness) will be the focus of a large part of this book. This section will introduce some preliminary ideas.

Justification is something that comes in degrees—you can have more or less of it. Consider again Example 2.4, in which you pessimistically believed that it would rain on the day of your picnic on the basis of a forecast saying that the odds of its raining were slightly greater than half. Here you have some justification for thinking that it will rain. It is not as if you simply made it up, with no reason at all. But your reasons were far from good enough to give you knowledge. So what clause (iii) of the *TAK* requires is very strong justification. In the circumstances described, you do not have it for the belief that it will rain. If the day of the picnic comes and you look out the window and see rain, then you do have strong enough justification for the belief that it will rain. Under those circumstances you would satisfy clause (iii) of the *TAK*. So clause (iii) should be read to require strong justification, or adequate justification. This may be a bit imprecise, but it will do for now.

You can be justified in believing something without actually believing it. Clause (iii) of the TAK does not imply (i). To see how this works, consider the following example:

Example 2.5: Mr. Insecure's Exam

Mr. Insecure has just taken an exam. The teacher quickly looked over his answers and said that they look good and that the grades will be available the next day. Mr. Insecure has studied hard, taken and done well on the practice exams, found the questions on the actual exam similar to the ones he had studied, and so on. He has excellent reasons to think that he passed the exam. But Mr. Insecure is insecure. He never believes that he has done well and does not believe that he has done well on this exam.

Even though Mr. Insecure does not believe that he has passed the exam, he is justified in believing that he passed the exam. So condition (iii) of the *TAK* is satisfied, but condition (i) is not. To be justified in believing a proposition is, roughly, to have what is required to be highly reasonable in believing it, whether one actually believes it or not.

What is justified for one person may not be justified for another. You have many justified beliefs about your private life. Your friends and acquaintances may have little or no justification for beliefs about those matters. And what is justified for an individual changes over time. A modification of Example 2.4 illustrates this. A week before the picnic, you may not have had justification for believing the proposition that it would rain on Saturday. But by Saturday morning, you might acquire ample justification for that proposition.

It is important not to confuse being justified in believing something from being able to *show* that one is justified in believing that proposition. In many cases we can explain why a belief is justified; we can formulate our reasons. However, there are exceptions to this. For example, a child might have many justified beliefs but be unable to articulate a justification for them.

IV. REAL KNOWLEDGE AND APPARENT KNOWLEDGE

One additional point about *The Standard View* deserves special attention. The things that people regard as knowledge differ in a variety of ways. To take some simple examples, perhaps people in ancient times would have said that among the things they know is the fact that the earth is flat. Perhaps they would have said that they knew the earth to be at the center of the universe (with everything in orbit around it). There may have been widespread agreement in ancient times that they did have knowledge in these cases.

We can grant for the sake of argument that the ancients *thought* they knew that the earth was at the center of the universe. (If you do not like this particular example, substitute another one that illustrates the same idea.) We can even grant that they were quite well justified in believing that they had knowledge of this fact. We might say that they had *apparent knowledge*. Nevertheless, they lacked *real knowledge*. Even though the propositions in question might have quite reasonably appeared in the list of things known in the first chapter of a distant ancestor of this book, the propositions were false. The earth is not, and never was, flat. It is not, and never was, at the center of the universe. They thought, perhaps even with justification, that they had knowledge, but they were mistaken.[15]

Another point deserves mention here. It may be that the claims of those who are most outspoken, most charismatic, or most powerful will often be widely regarded as items of knowledge. This can be distressing to those out of power, especially when they have better justification for competing views. However, questions about what determines what gets counted as knowledge, and how the powerful manage to impose their views on others, are not the focus of this book. Our topic is real knowledge, not apparent knowledge.[16]

V. CONCLUSION

(Q1) from Chapter 1 asked what it took to have knowledge. This chapter has introduced an answer to that question based on *The Traditional Analysis of Knowledge,* according to which knowledge is justified true belief. This analysis has a long history. It seems to fit very well with *The Standard View.* The examples of knowledge endorsed by *The Standard View* seem to be cases of justified true belief. And cases in which we lack knowledge seem to be cases in which we lack at least one of these three factors.

There is, however, a significant objection to the *TAK.* We turn next to it.

ENDNOTES

1. The following examples show general patterns of various kinds of statements, with an example showing how each pattern could be filled out. The patterns make use of variables that can be replaced by specific terms. Following standard practices, "S" is used as a variable to be replaced by a name or description of a person, "x" is used as a variable to be replaced by a name or description of any object (including people), "p" is to be replaced by a full sentence expressing a fact or purported fact (a proposition), and "A" by a description of an action.
2. For discussion of just what is meant by the word "proposition," see Section III, Part A1 of this chapter.
3. It is important to understand the difference between (2) and

    2a. The librarian knows either that there is a book by Salinger in the library or that there is not a book by Salinger in the library.

    (2a) is true; (2a) reports knowledge of a disjunction (an "or" statement) and everyone can have this knowledge. But the librarian must possess special knowledge if (2) is true. She must know which of the disjuncts (the parts of the "or" statement) is true.
4. "~p" means "not-p", or the negation of p. The negation of "There is a book by Salinger in the library" is "It is not the case that there is a book by Salinger in the library."
5. The methodology used here will be important in what follows. One important test of a proposed definition is that there are no counterexamples to it.
6. This definition may need some refinement, but it does capture at least the basic idea under discussion.
7. From *Meno,* translated by G. M. A. Grube. Reprinted in *Plato: Complete Works,* edited by John M. Cooper (Indianapolis, IN: Hackett Publishing Co., 1997), p. 895.
8. A similar idea is presented in another dialogue, *Theatetus,* translated by M. J. Levett, revised by Myles Burnyeat. Reprinted in *Plato: Complete Works.* See p. 223.
9. Roderick Chisholm, *Theory of Knowledge* (Englewood Cliffs, NJ: Prentice Hall, 1966), p. 23.

10. There is an alternative way to think about these matters. Instead of saying that there are three options, you can say that you can believe a proposition to a greater or lesser degree. You can think of these degrees of belief as arranged along a scale. When you accept a proposition with absolute conviction, you believe it to the fullest degree. When you completely and totally reject a proposition, you have the lowest possible degree of belief in it. And in the usual cases, your degree of belief falls somewhere in between. Suspension of judgment is right in the middle.

11. If you have never even considered a proposition, then you neither believe it nor disbelieve it, but you do not suspend judgment either. Perhaps suspending judgment is best characterized as considering a proposition but neither believing it nor disbelieving it.

12. There are hard questions about exactly what kinds of objects propositions are. We can safely ignore those questions here.

13. The term "iff" abbreviates "if and only if." Sentences of the form "p iff q" are true just in case the truth values of p and q agree, that is, just in case both are true or both are false.

14. This topic will be discussed in detail in Chapter 9.

15. At this point you might observe that we might be in a situation like the ancients, in which our claims to knowledge are mistaken. We will take up this issue when we consider *The Skeptical View.*

16. It is possible that some of the attractiveness of *The Relativistic View,* mentioned in Chapter 1, results from confusing apparent knowledge and real knowledge.

CHAPTER THREE

Modifying *The Traditional Analysis of Knowledge*

I. AN OBJECTION TO THE TRADITIONAL ANALYSIS

Recall that *The Traditional Analysis of Knowledge,* the *TAK,* says that knowledge is justified true belief.

This analysis is correct just in case in all possible examples, if a person knows some proposition, then the person has a justified true belief in that proposition, and if a person has a justified true belief, then the person has knowledge. Unfortunately for the *TAK,* there are compelling counterexamples of the second sort—cases of justified true belief that clearly are not cases of knowledge.

The first philosopher to argue explicitly against the *TAK* in the manner to be discussed here was Edmund Gettier. His brief essay, "Is Justified True Belief Knowledge?," may be the most widely discussed and often cited epistemology paper in many years.[1] Gettier presented two examples, each showing that one could have a justified true belief that is not knowledge. Other philosophers have described additional cases establishing the same point.

A. The Counterexamples

In this section we will examine three examples all designed to illustrate a problem in the TAK. The point behind all the objections is the same, but the different examples help to make the issue clearer. The first example is a modified version of one Gettier originally presented.

Example 3.1: The Ten Coins Case

Smith is justified in believing:

1. Jones is the man who will get the job and Jones has ten coins in his pocket.

The reason Smith is justified in believing (1) is that he has just seen Jones empty his pockets, carefully count his coins, and then return them to his pocket. Smith also knows that Jones is extremely well qualified for the job and he has heard the boss tell the secretary that Jones has been selected. On the basis of (1), Smith correctly deduces and believes another proposition:

2. The man who will get the job has ten coins in his pocket.

Smith is justified in believing (2) on the basis of this inference. In spite of Smith's evidence, (1) is not true after all. The boss misspoke when he said that Jones was going to get the job. In fact, the job is going to the company vice president's nephew, Robinson. Coincidentally, Robinson also happens to have ten coins in his pocket.

In this example (2) is true even though (1) is false. Smith was justified in believing (1), correctly deduced (2) from (1), and believed it as a result. So, Smith was also justified in believing (2). And (2) is true. So Smith's belief in (2) is justified and true. But clearly Smith does not know (2). It is just a coincidence that he is right about (2).

Example 3.2:   The Nogot/Havit Case[2]

Smith knows that Nogot, who works in his office, is driving a Ford, has Ford ownership papers, is generally honest, etc. On this basis he believes:

3. Nogot, who works in Smith's office, owns a Ford.

Smith hears on the radio that a local Ford dealership is having a contest. Anyone who works in the same office as a Ford owner is eligible to enter a lottery, the winner receiving a Ford. Smith decides to apply, thinking he eligible. After all, he thinks that (3) is true, so he concludes that:

4. There is someone who works in (my) Smith's office who owns a Ford. (There is at least one Ford owner in Smith's office.)

It turns out that Nogot is a Ford faker and (3) is false. However, (4) is true because some other person unknown to Smith, Havit, works in his office and owns a Ford.

So Smith has a justified true belief in (4), but he does not know (4). It is just a lucky coincidence, resulting from Havit's having it, that makes him right about (4).

Example 3.3:   The Sheep in the Field[3]

Having won a Ford in a contest, Smith goes for a drive in the country. He looks off into a nearby field and sees what looks exactly like a sheep. So he justifiably believes:

5. That animal in the field is a sheep.

Smith's son is in the back seat reading a book and not looking at the scenery. The son asks if there are any sheep in the field they are passing. Smith says "Yes," adding:

6. There is a sheep in the field.

Smith is justified by what he sees in thinking that (5) is true. (6) follows from (5), so he is justified in believing (6) as well.

As it turns out, (5) is false. What Smith sees is a sheep dog (or a sheep statue, or some other perfect sheep look-alike). But (6), as it happens, is true anyway. Out in the field, but out of view, there is a sheep.

So, Smith has a justified belief in (6), and it is true. But he does not know it. It is only by luck that he is right about (6).

It should be noted that the details of the examples can be modified to strengthen Smith's support for his belief in the false proposition in each case. For example, you can add whatever you like to his support for the belief that Nogot owns a Ford. Nogot can show him his keys with a Ford insignia and wear a Ford tee shirt, etc. No matter how much you add to the case, it will remain possible that Nogot is faking his Ford ownership. And given that this is possible, it remains possible to construct a case in which it is coincidentally true that someone in the office owns a Ford. Similar remarks apply to the other examples. Merely requiring stronger reasons for a belief to be justified would not avoid the objections.

B. The Structure of the Counterexamples

Examples 3.1–3.3 share a common structure. In each case, Smith has some basic evidence that strongly supports some proposition. It is the sort of evidence that *The Standard View* counts as good enough for knowledge. He believes that proposition and then draws a further conclusion from it. In each example, the odd-numbered sentence describes the first proposition Smith believes:

1. Jones is the man who will get the job and Jones has ten coins in his pocket.
3. Nogot, who works in Smith's office, owns a Ford.
5. That animal in the field is a sheep.

The even-numbered sentences describe the conclusions Smith draws from the first step:

2. The man who will get the job has ten coins in his pocket.
4. Someone who works in Smith's office owns a Ford. (There is at least one Ford owner in Smith's office.)
6. There is a sheep in the field.

The odd-numbered proposition is false in each case. Still, given the evidence, it is extremely reasonable for Smith to believe it. It is a justified belief. And the final conclusion follows logically from the previous step. The final conclusion is, in each case, true. In effect, the final conclusion is true "by coincidence." It just so happens that the person who got the job has ten coins, that there is a Ford owner in the office, and that there is a sheep in the field. So Smith has very good reasons to believe the first step and follows perfectly good logical principles in deriving the second step. Thus, he has a justified true belief in each of the final conclusions. But in each case the truth of that conclusion is unconnected to the original evidence. Smith does not have knowledge, even though he has justified true beliefs.

Stating the structure of the examples helps to bring out two important principles that they rely on. One principle allows that the person can be justified in believing the odd-numbered propositions even though they are false. We can state this as *The Justified Falsehood Principle*, or *(JF)*:

> JF.   It is possible for a person to be justified in believing a false proposition.

The second important principle is the one that says that the second proposition is justified because it is deduced from the first. This is *The Justified Deduction Principle*, or *(JD)*:

> JD.   If S is justified in believing p, and p entails q, and S deduces q from p and accepts q as a result of this deduction, then S is justified in believing q.

If the three examples just described are possible and these two principles are true, then the *TAK* is mistaken. The examples may be odd, but they are clearly possible. Things like this can, and do, happen. The two principles do seem correct. Thus, it looks as if we have a strong case against the *TAK*. As we shall see, however, some people have tried to defend the *TAK* by rejecting the principles.

To state a Gettier-style example, then, first one has to find a case of a justified false belief. If (JF) is correct, there are such cases. One then identifies some truth that logically follows from that falsehood. There will always be such truths. The example proceeds by having the believer deduce this truth from the justified false belief. If (JD) is correct, the resulting belief will be a justified true belief that is not knowledge.

It appears, therefore, that Gettier-style examples show that the *TAK* is incorrect.

II. DEFENDING THE TRADITIONAL ANALYSIS

You may have some misgivings about Gettier-style examples. Usually, doubts are based on the idea that the person in the example is not justified in believing the final proposition and thus does not really have a justified true belief.[4] And this idea relies on rejecting one or the other of the two principles just stated.[5] In this section we will examine the plausibility of these responses to the examples.

A. Rejecting (JF)

One way to defend the *TAK* is to reject (JF). You might think that if a proposition is false, then a person who believes it must not have good enough reasons for that belief. If correct, this provides a defense of the *TAK* in the following way. It implies that in each of our examples Smith is not justified in believing the false proposition. If Smith is not justified in believing the false proposition (the odd-numbered one), then he is not justified in believing what he deduces from it. Thus, his belief in the even-numbered proposition is not justified either. As a result, Gettier-style examples are not cases of justified true beliefs (because they are not cases of justified beliefs), and thus they do not refute the *TAK*.

Consider how this response applies the Nogot/Havit case. The critic contends that, in spite of the evidence, Smith is not justified in believing proposition (3), that Nogot owns a Ford. The reason for this is that (3) is false, and thus Smith's evidence must not have been good enough. More generally, the critic says, a person can never be justified in believing a false proposition. (JF) is mistaken.

Because Smith's reasons for believing (3) can be extremely strong, this is an implausible response. Moreover, given one very sensible assumption, rejecting (JF) implies that hardly anyone is ever justified in believing anything! To see why, consider any example in which a person has what *The Standard View* regards as a justified belief. Assume that there is nothing odd about the case, and that things are exactly as the person believes them to be. Call this *"The Typical Case."* Now, it is always possible to construct an example that is a variation on *The Typical Case.* In this variant, the person has that very same evidence, but the proposition in question is nevertheless false. Call this variant *"The Unusual Case."* To fill in the details of *The Unusual Case,* it will be necessary to add in unusual efforts at deception and the like. Although such things are unusual, they are possible. The key thing to note is that in *The Typical Case* and in *The Unusual Case,* the believer has exactly the same reasons for believing exactly the same thing. So the belief is either justified in both cases or else not justified in both cases. If (JF) is false, then the belief is not justified in *The Unusual Case* (because it is false). But then it is not justified in *The Typical Case* either, since the reasons are the same. This can be done for virtually any allegedly justified belief, so if (JF) is false, virtually no beliefs are justified.

The reasoning just displayed depends upon *The Same Evidence Principle,* or (*SE*):

> SE. If in two possible examples there is no difference at all in the evidence a person has concerning some proposition, then either the person is justified in believing the proposition in both cases or the person is not justified in believing the proposition in both cases.

(SE) is an extremely plausible principle. If (SE) is true and (JF) is false, then virtually nothing is justified. And that violates our basic assumption (for now, at least) that we do know things. So this first defense of the *TAK* is no good.[6]

Some readers may still think that rejecting (JF) is correct. Recall, however, that the point of the current chapter is to see what the consequences of *The Standard*

View are. *The Standard View* holds that we do know a lot, and rejecting (JF) implies that hardly anything is justified and thus hardly anything is known. So rejecting (JF) requires rejecting *The Standard View*. In other words, (JF) is a consequence of *The Standard View*. Thus, rejecting it is out of place at this stage of our inquiry. We will return to this topic when we examine *The Skeptical View*.

B. Rejecting (JD)

Recall that the Gettier examples depended on (JD) as well as (JF). (JD) says that justification can be transferred through deduction. A second possible basis for defending the traditional analysis from these counterexamples is to reject (JD). The idea is that when you reason properly from justified truths, the result is justified, but when you reason properly from justified falsehoods, the result is not justified. In other words, if you start with a justified true belief and properly draw a conclusion from it, then the resulting belief is justified. However, if you start with a justified false belief—remember, we are accepting (JF)—and correctly draw a conclusion from it, then the resulting belief is not justified. Thus, in this view, in each of the Gettier cases the person is justified in believing the first step—the odd-numbered proposition—but not justified in believing the consequence drawn from it. Advocates of this view therefore reject (JD).

This view also requires rejecting (SE). Imagine an example like any one of the Gettier-style cases but in which there is no trickery going on and the first step is actually true. Drawing the final conclusion is, under those circumstances, justified. But, according to the present proposal, it is not justified in the Gettier cases. Yet the person has exactly the same reasons in each case. This is implausible.

Consider carefully what someone who rejects (JD) would be saying about Smith in each of the Gettier cases. The critic would say of Smith, "Yes, Smith is justified in believing that Nogot, who works in his office, owns a Ford. And it is true that he can deduce from this that someone who works in his office owns a Ford. But, nevertheless, he is not justified in believing that conclusion." This seems absurd. We might sensibly wonder what attitude Smith would be justified in taking toward the proposition that someone in his office owns a Ford. Would it be reasonable for him to believe that Nogot owns one but to deny or suspend judgment about whether someone owns one? Clearly not. But that is what the rejection of (JD) seems to recommend. Rejecting (JD) just is not a good way to defend the *TAK* from Gettier's examples.

These attempts to defend the *TAK* from Gettier-style examples fail. We turn next to responses according to which knowledge requires something in addition to justified true belief.

III. MODIFYING THE TRADITIONAL ANALYSIS

A plausible idea is that you cannot have knowledge if your belief depends on a false proposition. In this section we will consider a few efforts to spell out this idea more clearly.

A. The No False Grounds Theory

One way in which the justification of a belief might depend upon a falsehood is if there is a false proposition among the grounds or reasons for the belief. Michael Clark has proposed a solution to the Gettier problem making use of this idea.[7] Clark suggests the following *No False Grounds* account of knowledge. It adds a fourth condition to the three in the *TAK:*

> NFG.   S knows p = df. (i) S believes p; (ii) p is true; (iii) S is justified in believing p; (iv) All of S's grounds for believing p are true.

The idea here differs from, and is better than, the proposal discussed in Section II, according to which beliefs that have false grounds are not even justified. Here the idea is that having all true grounds is an additional condition for knowledge, but not a condition for justification. Thus, defenders of (NFG) agree that the victims of the Gettier examples are justified in their beliefs. This was what the previously discussed critics denied. Instead, this response says that knowledge cannot depend on any false grounds. In each of the preceding examples, Smith does have a false ground for his final belief. So (NFG) seems to avoid Gettier-style counterexamples.

(NFG) will work provided that (a) in all Gettier cases the believer has a false ground, and (b) there are no cases of knowledge in which the believer does have a false ground. There are reasons to doubt each of these.

Consider (a) first. There are Gettier-style cases in which the person does not explicitly go through a false step in his or her reasoning. As we will see, these *may* be Gettier cases in which the believer does not have a false ground. We can use a revised version of the Nogot/Havit case to illustrate the point.

Example 3.4:   The Alternate Route[8]

Smith notices that Nogot is driving a Ford, has a Ford ownership certificate, and so on. But instead of drawing a conclusion about Nogot, Smith draws the following conclusion:

> 7.   There is someone who works in Smith's office who drives a Ford, has Ford ownership papers, etc.

On the basis of (7), Smith draws the same final conclusion as before:

> 4.   There is someone who works in Smith's office who owns a Ford.

The difference between the two examples is that in the original version Smith explicitly reasoned through a false step to get to his true conclusion, and in the new version he takes an alternate route to get to that same conclusion.

In the original version of the example, Smith's thinking went:

> N.   Nogot, who works in Smith's office, drives a Ford, has Ford ownership papers, etc.

3. Nogot, who works in Smith's office, owns a Ford.
4. There is someone who works in Smith's office who owns a Ford.

(N) is true, (3) is false, and (4) is true. So this route to (4) goes through a falsehood. But in the second case Smith replaces (3) with (7). Smith's thinking now goes:

N. Nogot, who works in Smith's office, drives a Ford, has Ford ownership papers, etc.
7. There is someone who works in Smith's office who drives a Ford, has Ford ownership papers, etc.
4. There is someone who works in Smith's office who owns a Ford.

(N) and (4) are still true, but now the middle step, (7), is also true. So in this version of the example, Smith does not reason through a false proposition. Yet Smith still does not know (4). It is still a Gettier case. Thus, not all Gettier examples rely on a person deriving a truth from a falsehood.

It is true that in Example 3.4 there is still a falsehood "in the vicinity." Proposition (3), Nogot owns a Ford, is false, and this seems to matter. You might even think that (3) is part of Smith's grounds, even though he does not explicitly think about it. Thus, we are faced with a question. In Example 3.4 is (3) part of Smith's grounds for (4) or not?

We can think of what is included in the grounds for a belief in a broader or a narrower way. The narrower account is follows:

G1. The grounds for a belief include just those other beliefs that are explicit steps in the chain of inferences leading to the belief.

If clause (iv) of (NFG) makes use of this account of grounds, then Example 3.4 refutes the theory. It is a Gettier case in which explicit steps of reasoning include no falsehood. This suggests that Clark would be better off appealing to a broader account of the grounds of belief, an account according to which the grounds include more than the explicit steps of reasoning. For example, he might propose:

G2. The grounds for a belief include all beliefs that play any role in the formation of the belief, including "background assumptions" and presuppositions.

If Clark uses (G2) in explaining clause (iv) of his account of knowledge, then Example 3.4 does not refute it. This is because there is a false background assumption in the example, namely (3). So, by appealing to (G2), Clark could plausibly argue that condition (iv) of (NFG) is not satisfied in Example 3.4, and thus his theory has just the right result here: it says that Smith does not know that someone in his office owns a Ford.

The problem with this reply is that the theory now faces a different objection. As was noted earlier in this section, (NFG) works only if there are no cases of knowledge in which there are falsehoods among the person's grounds. However, it is clear that there can be knowledge even when some of one's grounds are false. This is true on either the more-inclusive or the less-inclusive account of grounds, but is especially obvious when the grounds include background beliefs and presuppositions. The following example illustrates the point:

> *Example 3.5:   The Extra Reasons Case*
>
> Smith has two independent sets of reasons for thinking that someone in his office owns a Ford. One set has to do with Nogot. Nogot says he owns a Ford, and so on. As usual, Nogot is merely pretending. But Smith also has equally strong reasons having to do with Havit. And Havit is not pretending. Havit does own a Ford, and Smith knows that he owns a Ford.

In this example, Smith does know that someone in his office owns a Ford. This is because his reasons having to do with Havit are good enough to give him knowledge. Yet one of his reasons, the one having to do with Nogot, is false. This shows that you can still have knowledge even if there is some falsehood somewhere in the picture. This objection is decisive. It shows that Clark's condition is too strong.[9]

Thus, Clark's way of fixing up the *TAK* does not work. If he uses (G1), then Example 3.4 refutes it. If he uses (G2), then Example 3.5 refutes it. The mere fact that there is a falsehood among one's reasons for a belief does not show that one lacks knowledge.

B. The No Defeaters Theory

There is another way philosophers have tried to explain what it is for the justification of a belief to depend upon a false proposition. A notable feature of the Gettier cases may be that there is a true proposition such that if the believer knew about it, then he would not believe (or would not be justified in believing) the proposition in question. In effect, then, the believer's justification depends upon the denial of this truth.[10]

We can apply this thought to our examples. In Example 3.1, if Smith realized that Jones will not get the job (which is true), then he would not believe that the man who will get the job has ten coins in his pocket (or he would no longer have any good reason to believe this). In Examples 3.2 and 3.4, if Smith realized that Nogot does not own a Ford, then, given the rest of the example, he would no longer have any good reason to believe that someone in the office owns a Ford. In Example 3.3, if Smith realized that the thing he was looking at is not a sheep, then he would no longer be justified in believing that there is a sheep in the field. (In contrast, in Example 3.5 he would continue to believe that someone in the office owns a Ford even if he learned that Nogot does not own one.)

Thus, in each Gettier example (Examples 3.1–3.4), there is a false proposition that Smith actually believes. If he did not believe it, and instead justifiably believed its negation (which is true), then he would stop believing, or stop having justification for, the Gettier proposition. That true proposition is said to *defeat* Smith's justification. And the idea is that one has knowledge when there are no truths that defeat one's justification. Thus, the proposal is to add to the *TAK* the requirement that there be no defeater:

> ND. S knows p = df. (i) S believes p; (ii) p is true; (iii) S is justified in believing p; (iv) There is no true proposition t such that, if S were justified in believing t, then S would not be justified in believing p. (No truth defeats S's justification for p.)

(ND) seems to deal correctly with all the examples considered so far.

Unfortunately, there are problems for the no defeaters theory. Here are two.

Example 3.6:   The Radio Case

Smith is sitting in his study with his radio off and Smith knows that it is off. At the time, Classic Hits 101 is playing the great Neil Diamond's great song "Girl, You'll Be a Woman Soon." If Smith had the radio on and tuned to that station, Smith would hear the song and know that it is on.

It may not be immediately obvious why this poses a problem, but it does. In Example 3.6 Smith knows:

8. The radio is off.

Conditions (i)–(iii) of the *TAK* are satisfied. But is (iv) satisfied? That is, is there any true proposition such that if Smith were justified in believing it, then he would not be justified in believing (8)? One true proposition in this story is

9. Classic Hits 101 is now playing "Girl, You'll Be a Woman Soon."

Suppose Smith were justified in believing (9). In any typical case there are many ways in which he might be justified in believing (9). The most likely way is that he would have the radio on. Of course, it might be that he could learn about (9) by having someone call him on the telephone and tell him, or by getting an e-mail message alerting him to the news. But suppose that in our example these other ways are not available. In our example, if Smith were justified in believing (9), then he would have his radio on and he would hear the song. But if that were the case, then Smith would not be justified in believing that the radio is off. So condition (iv) is not satisfied. There is a true proposition, (9), such that if Smith were to be justified in believing it, then Smith would not be justified in believing (8). In a sense (or perhaps in several senses), Smith is lucky not to know (9). For one thing, it enables him to know (8). For another, Smith does not have to hear the song. ̶w̶o̶r̶d̶

This example may be confusing. That is largely because sentences that say that if one thing were true, then another thing would be true are confusing. These sentences are called *subjunctive conditionals*. Applied to this case, the conditional concerns what would be the case if Smith were justified in believing (9). The best way to determine this is to consider how Smith would come to be justified in believing (9). In the circumstances described, the way is that Smith would have the radio on, tuned in to Classic Hits 101, and he would hear the song on the radio. But if that were the case, then Smith would know that the radio is on. So if that were the case, Smith would not be justified in believing that the radio is off. And this is what makes trouble for (ND). It says that Smith does not know (8) if there is some other truth such that if he were justified in believing it he would not be justified in believing (8). But (9) is just such a truth.

Once you see how Example 3.6 works, it is easy to generate additional examples along the same lines. The underlying point is very simple, though surprising. It is that one can know some facts and there can be other facts such that if one knew these other facts, then one would not know the original facts. This is because, if one were in a position to know the latter facts, then one would not be in a position to know the former facts. And, in some cases, if one knew the latter facts, then the former facts would not even be true. The current version of the no defeaters theory says that when there are such facts, one lacks knowledge. Because there typically will be such facts, the theory implies that we know very little.

There is another way that ignorance of some truths can help us to know things. (ND) has a problem with these cases as well. Here is one such example.

Example 3.7:   The Grabit Case[11]

Black sees her student Tom Grabit stick a tape in his coat pocket and sneak out of the library. She knows that Tom took the tape. Now, imagine that Tom's crime is reported to Tom's mother in her room at the psychiatric hospital. And she replies that Tom didn't do it, that it was his twin brother Tim. And imagine further that he has no twin, that this is just another one of her delusions. Black is ignorant of all this.

Why is this a problem? Consider this truth:

10.   Tom's mother said that Tom's twin Tim took the tape.

Notice that (10) itself is true, even though what Tom's mother said is false. If Black were justified in believing just this truth—but not the rest of the story about her—that would defeat Black's justification. It is a misleading defeater.

Again, this may seem confusing. But the idea is relatively simple. If we can know ordinary things, then there can be other truths such that if we learned them, they would undermine our justification for the thing we know. But some of these defeaters are misleading. That is, we actually know things, but we would not know them if we learned about these defeaters. We are lucky not to know about the defeaters. Mrs. Grabit's testimony is like this. Notice that in the Tom Grabit case, unlike the real Gettier cases, things are exactly as Black thinks they are. Black is fortunate to be ignorant of the demented mother's ramblings. Black would have lost her justification for her belief about Tom if she knew about them.

So this version of the no defeaters theory will not work. There are lots of possible variations on (ND), and perhaps some versions avoid the examples considered here. The other variations add more complexity to the analysis, and there are even more odd counterexamples proposed against them, but we will not pursue them here.[12]

D. A Modest Proposal

It is safe to say that there is no agreed-upon solution to the problem Gettier raised for the *TAK*. The defenses of the *TAK* discussed in Section II are inadequate and the modifications considered in this section face serious problems. The Gettier problem remains unresolved.

It remains true, however, that in all the Gettier cases there is a false proposition involved that makes it the case that the person lacks knowledge. Somehow, the justification depends on this falsehood, even if we have not spelled out in detail just how it depends on that falsehood. We can make use of this point in taking at least a modest step toward a solution to the problem.

The key thing in all the Gettier-style cases is that, in some sense, the central belief "essentially depends upon a falsehood." The idea of essential dependence is reasonably clear. For example, in *The Sheep in the Field Case*, Smith's belief that there is a sheep in the field depends essentially on the proposition that what he sees is a sheep. In the *Extra Reasons Case*, Smith has two independent lines of thought that lead to the same conclusion. One line of thought, concerning Nogot, does depend on a false proposition. The other line of thought, involving Havit, does not depend on anything false. In this case, Smith's belief that someone owns a Ford does not *essentially* depend upon the falsehood. This is because there is a justificatory line that ignores the falsehood. That is why there can be knowledge in such a situation, even though the reasoning does involve a false proposition. It does not *essentially* depend upon that falsehood.

The *Alternate Route Case* and other cases in which the belief does not directly rely on the falsehood also help to bring out the idea of essentially depending upon a falsehood. In these cases, Smith does not explicitly reason through a false proposition. However, there is implicit dependence upon a false proposition. Typically, the things one depends upon include things that, if pressed, one would say are relevant.

The idea of essential dependence is admittedly not completely clear. However, it gives us a useful working definition of knowledge with which we can proceed. The definition, then, is

EDF. S knows p = df.
(i) p is true.
(ii) S believes p.
(iii) S is justified in believing p.
(iv) S's justification for p does not essentially depend on any falsehood.

By adding clause (iv), (EDF) makes an important modification to the *TAK*. Nevertheless, it retains the heart of the traditional view, because it retains the idea that knowledge requires justified true belief. It simply adds an extra condition. A key question concerning (EDF), as well as the traditional view upon which it is based, has to do with the concept of justification. We will turn to that in detail in Chapter 4. Following that we will examine the views of some philosophers who think that no relatively minor modification of the *TAK* will yield a correct analysis of knowledge. They think that an entirely different account is preferable. We will examine their views in Chapter 5.

IV. CONCLUSION

The traditional answer to (Q1), which asked what the conditions for knowledge are, was that knowledge is justified true belief. The *TAK* is an elegant and appealing analysis of knowledge, but Gettier's examples show that it is less than fully satisfactory. The moral is that knowledge requires justified true belief and something else as well—there is a fourth condition on knowledge. Saying just what that fourth condition is turns out to be remarkably difficult. The no false grounds theory and the no defeaters theory do not succeed. What seems to be crucial is that the justification not *essentially depend* upon anything false. Although this idea has not been spelled out in complete detail, it does give us a useful account of knowledge. Thus, our answer to (Q1) is that knowledge requires justified true belief that does not essentially depend upon a falsehood.

ENDNOTES

1. *Analysis* 23 (1963): 121–3.
2. This example is based on one presented by Keith Lehrer in "The Fourth Condition for Knowledge: A Defense," *The Review of Metaphysics* 24 (1970): 122–8. See p. 125.
3. An example such as this one was presented by Roderick Chisholm in *Theory of Knowledge,* 2nd ed. (Englewood Cliffs, NJ: Prentice Hall, 1977), p. 105.
4. It is possible to argue that Smith does have knowledge of the even-numbered proposition in each of the examples. But that is an approach almost no philosophers have taken. Careful reflection on the cases yields an almost unanimous verdict on them. You just cannot get knowledge when your belief is coincidentally true, as is the case in all these examples.

5. It is possible to argue that in our examples Smith's reasons just are not very good reasons. But as noted at the end of Section IA, one can make Smith's reasons as strong as one likes. No response along these lines seems promising.

6. In Chapter 5 we will examine some theories that reject (SE). However, even according to these theories, (JF) is true and the *TAK* is refuted by Gettier-style examples.

7. "Knowledge and Grounds: A Comment on Mr. Gettier's Paper," *Analysis* XXIV (1963): 46–48.

8. An example such as this one was presented in Richard Feldman, "An Alleged Defect in Gettier Counterexamples," *Australasian Journal of Philosophy* 52 (1974): 68–69.

9. Note that this objection works whether you use (G1) or (G2).

10. For a defense of a view along these lines, see Peter Klein, "Knowledge, Causality, and Defeasibility," *Journal of Philosophy* 73 (1976): 792–812.

11. A slightly modified version of this example first appeared in Keith Lehrer, "Knowledge, Truth and Evidence," *Analysis* XXV (1965): 168–175.

12. For discussion of these alternatives, see Robert Shope, *The Analysis of Knowing* (Princeton, N.J.: Princeton University Press, 1983), Chapter 2.

CHAPTER FOUR

Evidentialist Theories of Knowledge and Justification

If something like the modified version of the *Traditional Analysis of Knowledge* proposed in Chapter 3 is correct, then justification is a crucial necessary condition for knowledge. Furthermore, justification is an interesting and puzzling concept in its own right. It will be the focus of this chapter and the one that follows. The present chapter will cover a traditional, and still widely accepted, account of justification. The next chapter will introduce some rather different, and more recent, accounts of justification (and of knowledge).

To help focus clearly on the central questions, it will be best to use an example in which two people believe the same thing, but one is justified in that belief and the other is not.

Example 4.1:   Thievery

Someone has broken into Art's house and stolen a valuable painting. Officer Careful investigates the case and comes up with conclusive evidence that Filcher committed the crime. Careful finds the painting in Filcher's possession, finds Filcher's fingerprints at the scene of the crime, and so on. Careful comes to believe:

1.   Filcher stole the painting.

Meanwhile, Hasty also hears about the theft. Hasty happens to live next door to Filcher and has had some unpleasant dealings with him. Hasty dislikes Filcher intensely and blames him for many bad things that happen. Hasty has some vague idea that Filcher works in the art business but has no specific knowledge about what he does. With nothing more to go on, Hasty also believes (1).

The Standard View holds that in Example 4.1 Careful is fully justified in believing (1) but Hasty is not. If you need to add more to the story to convince yourself of those evaluations, you can make those additions. However, the example should be fairly persuasive as it is.

The goal of the present chapter is to spell out in a systematic and useful way what distinguishes Careful's belief from Hasty's and, more generally, to identify the general features that distinguish justified beliefs from unjustified beliefs. There are lots of differences between Careful's belief and Hasty's belief that are irrelevant to this project. For example, Hasty's belief is about his neighbor, but Careful's belief is not about his (Careful's) neighbor. That is true, but it is not what makes one justified and the other not. Neighborly beliefs can be justified, and it is not even remotely plausible that this accounts for the difference in justification. In general, nothing about the subject matter of the belief alone is likely to be of value in answering the question, because people can have justified beliefs, as well as unjustified beliefs, about nearly any topic. What, then, is the difference?[1]

In thinking about this question it will be useful to keep in mind the following idea. Whether a belief is justified or unjustified, its epistemic status is an evaluative fact about the belief. Reflection on this suggests that epistemic status must depend on other, nonepistemic facts. It might be easier to understand the idea by first considering an analogy. Suppose a professor returns a set of graded papers to the students in her class. She says of one paper that it is excellent and gives it a very high grade. She says another one is a poor paper and she gives it a low grade. The teacher thus ascribes certain *evaluative properties* to these papers. These are properties concerning how good the papers are. (Although it is not crucial for the discussion that follows, assume that there is an objective truth about the quality of each paper.) The quality of the paper is dependent upon other features of the paper. For example, having misspelled words detracts from the quality of the paper, as does having ungrammatical sentences. Perhaps being clearly written adds to its quality. There are various other factors that enter into the evaluation. These factors involve the *descriptive properties* of the papers. The key idea to understand is that if there is an evaluative difference in the papers, then there must be a descriptive difference. In other words, if there is no descriptive difference, then there is no evaluative difference either. The following principle captures the idea:

> Necessarily, if two papers have all the same descriptive properties, then they have the same evaluative properties.

This is sometimes described as a *supervenience* thesis—the evaluative properties of the papers supervene on, or depend upon, their descriptive properties.

The plausibility of the supervenience thesis about the two papers can be appreciated by considering the plight of a student who gets a low grade. Suppose such a student asked the teacher what made his paper inferior to the paper of a classmate who got a higher grade. There would surely be something wrong with a teacher who replied to this student, "There is no descriptive difference between the two papers. They are exactly alike in all descriptive ways. It's just that, unfortunately, your paper is not as good as that one." This student can properly complain that if the paper is not as good, there must be something about the two papers that brings about this evaluative difference.

Something similar is true in epistemology. Being justified or unjustified is an evaluative epistemic property of a belief. Facts about the causes of a belief, whether it is true, whether other people also believe the same thing are nonevaluative facts about the belief. In addition, facts about what experiences a person is having, what other things the person believes, and so on are all nonepistemic facts. The evaluative epistemic facts depend upon these other facts. Thus, if one belief is justified and another is not, there must be some nonevaluative difference between the two beliefs that accounts for this evaluative difference. This idea can be summed up in the following epistemic supervenience principle:

> Necessarily, if two beliefs have the same nonepistemic properties, then they have the same epistemic properties. (If two beliefs are exactly alike nonepistemically, then either both are justified or both are not justified, or they are justified to the same degree.)

Defenders of all the theories of justification that we will consider in this chapter and the next agree with this thesis. The difference between the various theories concerns which properties determine epistemic status, or which descriptive facts make an epistemic difference.

I. EVIDENTIALISM

Our question about Example 4.1 concerned what made Careful justified in believing (1) but Hasty unjustified in believing that proposition. It may seem that the answer to our question is rather simple: Careful has good reasons, or evidence, for believing (1) whereas Hasty does not. It is the possession of evidence that is the mark of a justified belief. We will call this *the evidentialist theory of justification,* or *evidentialism.*

While evidentialism may be correct, as stated so far it is not a well-developed theory. Philosophers who agree that justification is a matter of having good reasons differ markedly over just what having good reasons amounts to. There is, then, more to be done to develop a satisfactory account of justification. The questions will become clearer as we examine the idea more carefully.

A. Epistemic Evaluations

In a famous essay, "The Ethics of Belief," published in 1877, William K. Clifford describes the following example:

Example 4.2:   The Negligent Shipowner

A negligent shipowner decides, without doing any careful checking, that his ship is seaworthy. The ship sets sail, and then sinks. Many lives are lost, largely because this shipowner believed that his ship was seaworthy without bothering to get it checked out.[2]

Clifford draws a harsh conclusion about this shipowner. And building upon this example, and some others, he formulates a general conclusion well worth examination. That conclusion is Clifford's thesis, (C):

C. It is wrong always, everywhere, and for anyone, to believe anything upon insufficient evidence.[3]

There are obvious questions to ask about this, most notably, "What counts as insufficient evidence?" We can bypass that question for now, assuming only the following: If a person has more and better evidence for the conclusion that proposition p is false than for the conclusion that proposition p is true, then that person has insufficient evidence for believing that p is true. Maybe Clifford thinks that to have sufficient evidence requires even more, something like very strong evidence. But we can bring out an issue concerning (C) by using this weaker condition. In discussing and defending (C), Clifford writes:

It is not only the leader of men, statesman, philosopher, or poet, that owes this bounden duty to mankind. Every rustic who delivers in the village alehouse his slow, infrequent sentences, may help to kill or keep alive the fatal superstitions which clog his race. Every hard-worked wife of an artisan may transmit to her children beliefs which shall knit society together, or rend it in pieces. No simplicity of mind, no obscurity of station, can escape the universal duty of questioning all that we believe.[4]

His idea is that by believing on insufficient evidence one helps to keep alive "fatal superstitions" and that failing to follow one's evidence will tear society apart ("rend it in pieces"). Although Clifford's claims may seem a bit extreme, perhaps there is some merit to his thesis.

Some critics may object to Clifford's thesis on the grounds that modest amounts of evidence, especially in cases in which a decision must be made quickly, can make belief acceptable. Here is an example designed to illustrate the point.

Example 4.3:   Chest Pains

You are about to go away on vacation. Shortly before you are scheduled to leave, you feel some slight chest pains. You know that such pains are typically associated with indigestion, but they can be signs of heart problems. Worried that there might be a serious problem, you call your doctor.

This is a sensible action. Yet the evidence you have is fairly weak. You do not have sufficient evidence to believe that you have a serious medical problem. Hence, it might be concluded Clifford's thesis is wrong. Sometimes, a little evidence is good enough.

Clifford has a good reply to this objection. (C) is not a thesis about when it is wrong to *act*. It is a thesis about when it is wrong to have a *belief*. So if this example makes any trouble for (C), the example must be one in which having a belief is not wrong, even though one does not have sufficient evidence for it. If the situation is as just described, it would be wrong to believe that you have heart trouble (if the symptoms described are the only reasons you have for thinking this). You are pointlessly going well beyond your evidence if you believe that. But you do have good enough evidence to believe a different proposition, namely that there is a possibility that you have heart problems. Furthermore, this belief provides good reason to take precautionary action. There is nothing wrong with this belief or with acting on its basis. So distinguishing a belief from a related action, and distinguishing the proposition that there is a chance you have a heart problem from the proposition that you do have a heart problem, provides all that is needed to escape this objection.

There are, however, some other objections to Clifford's thesis that are more effective.

Example 4.4:   The Optimistic Batter

A major league baseball player is coming to bat in a crucial situation. This player is a good hitter: He gets a hit about one-third of the times he comes to bat. Still, more often than not, he fails to get a hit. Like many other major league players, he is supremely confident: Each time he comes to bat he believes that he will get a hit. This sort of confidence, we may assume, is helpful. Players do better when they are confident (believe that they will succeed), and they do worse when they lack confidence.

The details of Example 4.4 suggest that it is not wrong for the batter to believe that he will get a hit. In fact, it seems far better for him to believe this. Yet he does not have "sufficient evidence" for the proposition that he will get a hit.

Example 4.5:   Recovery

A person has a serious illness from which few people recover. But this person is not willing to give in to her illness. She is sure that she will be one of the lucky ones. And confidence helps: Those who are optimistic tend to do a little better, even though, unfortunately, most of them do not recover either.

Clifford's thesis says that it is wrong for this patient to believe that she will recover. And that judgment seems to be entirely too harsh. Imagine criticizing the hopeful patient, claiming that it is wrong to be optimistic. If optimism helps, it is hard to find fault with her for being optimistic.

These examples seem to show that there are cases in which it is not wrong to believe something, even though one does not have good evidence for it. Still, Clifford may be right to think that each case of believing on insufficient evidence has one bad feature: It does run the risk of encouraging bad habits of thought. However, (C) depends upon the idea that this factor always outweighs other considerations. The two examples just given are designed to show otherwise. Sometimes the good of believing on insufficient evidence outweighs the potential harm.

You may find that you are of two minds about these cases. On the one hand, past performance suggests that the batter in Example 4.4 will not get a hit. This seems to indicate that there *is* something wrong with the belief that he will get a hit this time. On the other hand, the fact that believing that he will get a hit tends to improve his performance suggests that it is not wrong for him to believe that he will get a hit. After all, this belief aids his performance, just as concentrating, holding the bat properly, and, perhaps, scratching and spitting do. Similar considerations apply to Example 4.5. The statistics about recovery from the disease suggest that there is something wrong with the belief that the patient will recover. The belief "flies in the face of the facts." Yet this is her best chance to recover. How can we condemn a person for trying?

One good way to resolve these apparent conflicts is to say that there are two (or more) different notions of wrongness under consideration here. One notion concerns morality (or prudence or self-interest). The other is more intellectual or epistemological. A plausible thing to say is that in these examples the beliefs are morally right but epistemically wrong. We need not get into any detailed discussion of morality here. It will be enough to say that, typically, behavior is immoral when it has bad effects on others (or oneself) and there is no offsetting benefit. Believing on insufficient evidence *can* have the bad effects Clifford notes. However, in Examples 4.4 and 4.5 there are clear offsetting gains. Clifford's thesis is completely general. He says "everywhere and always" it is wrong to believe on insufficient evidence. If Clifford's thesis is about morality, as it seems to be, then it is incorrect. It just is not immoral to have the optimistic and beneficial beliefs in these circumstances. Thus, it is likely that Clifford went too far in asserting (C) in full generality. Sometimes it is not morally wrong to believe on insufficient evidence.

However, thinking about these examples and Clifford's thesis may help us focus on the more central epistemological issues. Suppose a person interested only in getting at the truth were in the position of the people in our examples or were forming a belief about those people based on exactly the evidence they have. Such a person would set aside self-interested concerns such as winning the game or recovering from the disease. (You might think about a person who is going to place bets on the outcomes and is interested only in winning the bets.) That person would be interested only in what in fact is true. What would that person believe in that situation? It is clear that such a disinterested believer would not believe that the batter will get a hit or that the patient will recover. You might put this point by saying that in these situations, with the evidence as described, there would be something wrong with believing these things. But this is not a moral matter. It is a matter of rationality or reasonableness. In other words, it is epistemically wrong to believe these things in the situations described.

The key idea to get from this is that we can evaluate beliefs in two ways. We can evaluate them morally[5]—are they beneficial? Do they cause any significant harm? In the two examples, the beliefs are beneficial (when held by the batter or the patient). They therefore get a favorable moral evaluation. We can also evaluate beliefs epistemically. In the view about epistemology under discussion here, this is determined by whether they go against the evidence. If Clifford had said that it is *epistemically* wrong to believe on insufficient evidence, he would have asserted a view that many philosophers take to be correct. But his claim about morality is mistaken.

Clifford's discussion helps us focus on the notion of something being epistemically wrong. It is this evaluation that the justification condition of the *TAK* is about. An epistemically justified belief is a belief that is favorably evaluated from an epistemological point of view, no matter what its moral or prudential status.

B. Formulating Evidentialism

The central idea of evidentialism can be stated in the following evidentialist principle about justification:

> EJ. Believing p is justified for S at t iff S's evidence at t supports p.

A version of (EJ) that covers other attitudes is possible as well. It says that the justified attitude—belief, disbelief, or suspension of judgment—is the one that fits the evidence. A fully fleshed-out evidentialist theory will say something about what a person's evidence at any given time consists of and what it is for that evidence to support a particular belief.

In general, evidentialists will say that the evidence a person has at a given time consists of all the information the person has to go on at that time. This will include the memories the person has and the other justified beliefs he or she has. When evidentialists speak of someone "having evidence," they do not mean the same thing someone discussing a legal matter might mean by that phrase. Suppose a certain document is a crucial item in a case. You have that thing among your possessions, but you do not know about it. In the legal sense of "having evidence," you may have the relevant evidence. But in the sense intended here, it, and facts about it, are not part of your evidence. The evidence you have consists of the information you have available, in some hard-to-specify sense, for your use. The key idea, then, is that the evidence a person has consists of the data the person has to go on in forming beliefs, not of the items the person physically possesses.

For it to be true that a person's evidence supports a proposition, it must be that the person's total evidence, on balance, supports that proposition. It is possible to have some evidence that supports a proposition and some evidence that supports the denial of that proposition. If these two bodies of evidence are equally weighty, and the person has no other relevant evidence, then the person's total evidence is neutral and suspending judgment about the proposition is the justified attitude. If one portion of the evidence is stronger than the other, then the corresponding attitude is the justified one. In all cases, it is the total evidence that determines which attitude is the justified one. Call this the *total evidence* condition.

There is a distinction, not so far mentioned, that is important to evidential-ism. An analogy from ethics will make the distinction clear. A person can do the ethically right thing for the wrong reasons. For example, suppose a wealthy person is asked to give some money to a charity and agrees to transfer the funds electronically. The charity gives her the account number so that she can make the transfer. Armed with this information, the person decides to take money from the charity rather than to give money to the charity. However, by mistake she pushes the wrong button and does transfer money to the charity. She does the right thing, but she does it by mistake. Her action is right, but it is not "well intentioned" or "well motivated." She is to be condemned for her character and motivations, even though she did the right thing.

There is an epistemological analogue of this example. Suppose that you have good reasons to believe something and you do believe it. However, you believe it not on the basis of those good reasons but because of an astrological prediction or as a result of some logical blunder. You believe the right thing for the wrong reasons. In such cases, believing that proposition really does fit your evidence, and so according to (EJ) believing it is the justified attitude. But it is an epistemically "bad" belief. You are not doing so well, epistemically speak-ing, in holding that belief.

These examples show that there are two related ideas of justification that we should distinguish. One is properly expressed in (EJ). It is the epistemic analogue of the action that is in fact good, i.e., the best one to do, given the sit-uation. There are several different ways we will express this idea:

> S is justified in believing p.
>
> Believing p is justified for S.
>
> S has a justification for believing p.

None of these imply that S actually does believe p. They just imply that S has what is needed to make believing p epistemically appropriate.

The second sort of justification is the epistemological analogue of the idea of doing the right thing for the right reasons. This is the idea of a "well-formed" or a "well-founded" belief. We will typically express this idea by saying such things as

> S's belief in p is justified
>
> S's belief in p is well founded.
>
> S justifiably believes p.

Sentences of these forms do imply that S believes p and that S does so for the right reasons. Here is a more precise account of this concept:

> BJ.   S's belief that p at time t is justified (well founded) iff (i) believing p is justified for S at t; (ii) S believes p on the basis of evidence that supports p.[6]

Clause (ii) of (BJ) is intended to capture the idea of believing on the basis of the right reasons. Call this the *basing* condition. A generalized version of (BJ), applying to disbelief and suspension of judgment, could also be developed.

Evidentialism affirms of both (EJ) and (BJ). It holds that the justified attitude toward a proposition for a person at any time is the attitude that fits the total evidence the person has at that time. And an actual belief (or other attitude) is a justified (well-founded) one provided it fits the person's evidence and the belief is held on the basis of evidence that really does support it.

C. Two Objections to Evidentialism

C1. Objection 1: Epistemic Irresponsibility

Example 4.6:   Movie Times

A professor and his wife are going to the movies to see *Star Wars, Episode 68*. The professor has in his hand today's newspaper, which contains the listing of movies at the theater and their times. He remembers that yesterday's paper said that *Star Wars, Episode 68* was showing at 8:00. Knowing that movies usually show at the same time each day, he believes that it is showing today at 8:00 as well. He does not look in today's paper. When they get to the theater, they discover that the movie started at 7:30. When they complain at the box office about the change, they are told that the correct time was listed in the newspaper today. The professor's wife says that he should have looked in today's paper and he was not justified in thinking it started at 8:00.

This example is designed to be a counterexample to both (EJ) and (BJ). We will restrict our discussion to (BJ), but the points made could easily be revised to apply to (EJ). Because the professor has been derelict about looking at today's paper, he has missed some evidence about when the movie starts. As a result, it is true that

2. Believing that the movie starts at 8:00 fits the evidence the professor actually had (as he was driving to the theater), and he bases his belief on this evidence.

Given (2), (BJ) has the result that his belief is justified (well founded). However, the critics of evidentialism (and the professor's wife) say that

3. The professor's belief that the movie starts at 8:00 is not justified (because he should have looked in the paper and thereby gotten more evidence, which would not have supported that belief.)

So (BJ) is wrong, because it implies that this belief is justified.

This example depends upon a principle according to which justification depends in part upon the evidence that one should have had. Call this the *Get the Evidence Principle (GEP):*

GEP.   If S's actual evidence supports p, but S should have had additional evidence, and this additional evidence would not support p, then S's belief in p is not justified.

(GEP) may seem sensible, and it is easy to see why critics of evidentialism might be persuaded by the examples, such as Example 4.6, that appeal to it. Applied to this example, (GEP) implies that the professor's belief is not justified because he had readily available evidence, he should have looked at this evidence, and this additional evidence does not support his belief about the time of the movie.[7]

However, evidentialists have a good response to this objection. We should distinguish epistemic justification from other matters. The question relevant to evidentialism, and to theories of epistemic justification generally, is "What should S believe now, given the situation he's actually in?" Apply this question to Example 4.6. As the professor is driving to the theater, it would be quite irrational for him to do anything other than believe that the movie starts at 8:00. After all, he knows that it was at 8:00 yesterday and that theaters usually show the movies at the same time each night. He has no reason at all to think that it is at any time other than 8:00. It would be quite unreasonable for him to believe that it starts at 7:30. So given the situation he is actually in, this is the justified attitude. Evidentialism has exactly the right result in this case.

It is important to distinguish some related questions. The one just discussed has to do with what it is reasonable to believe given the situation one is actually in. Other questions have to do with whether one should get more evidence (or get into a different situation). Suppose it is true that the professor should have looked at today's newspaper. He messed up and did not do that. Still, the question remains, given that he has been negligent and not done what he should, what is it most reasonable for him to believe? The answer is that it is most reasonable for him to believe that the movie starts at 8:00. More generally, it is most reasonable to believe what is supported by the evidence one does have. Because one does not know what the evidence one does not have will support, it would be unreasonable to be guided by that evidence. So (GEP) is mistaken. Even when one should get more evidence, the thing to do at any given time is to be guided by the evidence one does have.

In the example, perhaps it would have been a good idea to look at the listings in today's newspaper. However, before drawing that conclusion it is worth noting that it is almost always possible to be even more careful and to look for more evidence. The professor had good reason to think that the movie started at 8:00 and to believe that the newspaper would say that it did. With hindsight, it is easy to criticize him. But if he should have checked today's newspaper, then perhaps he also should have checked the movie listings online, or he should have called the theater to confirm what the newspaper said. Maybe he should have called a second time to get someone to confirm what was said on the recording heard during the first call. Further checking is almost always possible. Depending upon the seriousness of the situation, the likelihood that new information will be helpful, and other factors, it is sometimes in your interest to do some further checking. However, it is surely not always sensible to keep on checking. But all of this is independent of the reasonableness of believing what he did given the situation he actually was in.

C2. Objection 2: Loyalty

Example 4.7:   The Accusation

A good friend is accused of a crime, and you are aware of some incriminating evidence. You also know this friend well and have evidence that committing such a crime would be out of character. Your friend is terribly distressed by the charges brought against her, and she calls you for support. Out of loyalty to your friend, and given the mixed quality of your evidence, you believe that your friend is not guilty.

This is a praiseworthy reaction. It displays loyalty toward a friend in need. One might be tempted to say that believing that your friend is not guilty is justified, even though your evidence does not support your belief. It is, perhaps, plausible to say that matters of loyalty and friendship take precedence here, and that it is better for you to go against your evidence in this case. This may seem to be a problem for evidentialism, because evidentialism says that evidence alone determines what is justified. It entirely discounts considerations of loyalty, friendship, and the like. That, you might think, is a mistake.

The evidentialist response turns on a point discussed earlier in this chapter. Epistemology generally, and evidentialism in particular, are about the nature of rational belief. They do not address questions about morality. The rational attitude in this case is, as evidentialism asserts, to suspend judgment, or perhaps believe that your friend is guilty. This may be a case in which a morally good person will set rationality aside. But that is another matter. That fact casts no doubt on evidentialism's verdict about what the epistemically rational attitude is in this example.[8]

Evidentialism is thus able to withstand these initial objections. Hard questions remain. Recall the list of things that *The Standard View* says that we know. There are hard questions about exactly what our evidence for these things is and how that evidence manages to provide support for our beliefs. We turn next to some views about how these matters work out. These are not alternatives to evidentialism. They are, instead, some ways in which the details of evidentialism might be spelled out. We will use one of the most famous arguments in the history of philosophy as a way to begin discussion of these matters: *The Infinite Regress Argument*.

II. THE INFINITE REGRESS ARGUMENT

Statements of *The Infinite Regress Argument* go way back—some say to Sextus Empiricus (third century A.D.), others say to Aristotle (fourth century B.C.). The argument begins with the observation that what makes a belief justified, at least in the typical case, are other beliefs or reasons. This just seems to be a statement of evidentialism itself. But if you think about this for a moment, you will notice that a problem arises. If one belief is based on some reasons, but those reasons do not have a basis themselves, then it looks as if what depends on those reasons is no better justified than a belief for which one has no reasons at all. For example, if, in Example 4.1, Hasty concocted out of thin air a whole story about why Filcher stole the painting, he might be able to cite this story as his "reason" for believing (1). But if he has no good reason to believe the supporting story, then, in the end, he has no good reason to believe (1). In short, it seems that you need reasons for your reasons if your belief is to be justified. And this looks like trouble. There is a regress threatening: You need reasons for your reasons, and you need reasons for those reasons, and so. But it does not seem as if any of us could ever have this endless supply of reasons.

The problem just posed has had a central role in epistemology, both because it has been historically influential and because it is useful to organize theories on the basis of how they respond to it. Some terminology will help in the discussion that follows. It seems that as a matter of logic, there are two possibilities about justified beliefs: Either every justified belief is justified because it is supported by some other beliefs or else there are some justified beliefs that do not depend on other beliefs. Beliefs of the latter sort are said to be *justified basic beliefs*. Other terms for the same category are *immediately justified beliefs* and *noninferentially justified beliefs*. We can state this as a formal definition:

JB.   B is a justified basic belief = df. B is justified, but is not justified on the basis of any other beliefs.

Nonbasic justified beliefs (*mediately justified beliefs, inferentially justified beliefs*), then, are beliefs that are justified on the basis of other beliefs.

Another useful idea is that of a *chain of reasons* or an *evidential chain*. This is a structured sequence of beliefs, each of which is justified by its predecessors. It is important to notice that an evidential chain need not have just one proposition at each link or level. For example, in tracing out the evidential chain associated with Careful's belief in (1), we might have the facts about the fingerprints and the possession of the painting as the reasons for (1). There will be further reasons for each of these, perhaps involving the results of the fingerprint tests and the like.

There seem to be a limited number of ways evidential chains can be structured. One possibility is that they are infinitely long—for each step there is a prior reason. Another possibility is that they go in loops or circles—if you trace the reasons for a belief back far enough, you eventually come back to that very belief. Another possibility is that evidential chains really do have beginnings. At the beginning of any evidential chain are justified basic beliefs. A final possibility is that evidential chains trace back to beliefs that are not justified at all.

This is a rather puzzling set of options. None of them seems entirely satisfactory. How could we have an infinite series of justified beliefs? How could a belief be justified if it traces back to itself? That seems like blatantly objectionable circular reasoning. How could a belief be justified without the support of other beliefs—how could there be justified basic beliefs? How could beliefs be justified if they trace back to beliefs that are not themselves justified? Every account of evidential chains seems unpromising.

We can formulate these considerations into a precise argument. The main value of formulating this argument is that it makes explicit a variety of ideas and assumptions involved in the considerations just put forward. Furthermore, theories about justification can usefully be grouped according to how they respond to this argument.

> *Argument 4.1:   The Infinite Regress Argument*
>
> 1-1. Either there are justified basic beliefs or each justified belief has an evidential chain that either
>   (a)   terminates in an unjustified belief
>   (b)   is an infinite regress of beliefs
>   (c)   is circular
> 1-2. But beliefs based on unjustified beliefs are not themselves justified, so no justified belief could have an evidential chain that terminates in an unjustified belief (that is, not (a)).
> 1-3. No person could have an infinite series of beliefs, so no justified belief could have an evidential chain that is an infinite regress of beliefs (that is, not (b)).
> 1-4. No belief could be justified by itself, so no justified belief could have an evidential chain that is circular (that is, not (c)).
>
> ---
>
> 1-5. There are justified basic beliefs (1-1)–(1-5).

The argument is valid. That is, if the premises in the argument are correct, then the conclusion must be correct as well. If the argument goes wrong at all, it must have a false premise. Thus, either we must accept the conclusion that there are justified basic beliefs or else reject one of the premises. Theories in epistemology can be classified in part by what they say about this argument:

Foundationalism: The argument is sound. There are justified basic beliefs, and they are the foundation upon which all our other justified beliefs rest.

Coherentism: The argument goes wrong at premise (1-4). The justification for one proposition can be another, which is itself justified by still others. More generally, a person's belief is justified when it fits together with the person's other beliefs in a coherent way. A belief is thus justified by a whole system, of which it is a part. Hence, a belief is partially justified by itself, and (1-4) is false.

Skepticism: Because neither foundationalism nor coherentism is at all plausible, and there is no other place at which the argument goes wrong, it must go wrong right at the start when it assumes that there are justified beliefs. There cannot be any justified beliefs.

Other responses to the argument are possible. Some philosophers have said that evidential chains terminate in beliefs that are not justified, so they reject (1-2). Others say that infinite chains of reasons are possible. So they reject (1-3). We will not consider such views here.

For a long time, foundationalism was the prevailing view, and the main issue was whether foundationalists had any decent way to defend their view from skepticism. A large part of this involved clarifying just what foundationalism amounted to—explaining just what a basic belief would be like. In recent years, many philosophers have rejected foundationalism and some have accepted coherentism. Foundationalism and coherentism are the focus of the rest of this chapter.

III. CARTESIAN FOUNDATIONALISM

Foundationalism involves two fundamental claims:

> F1.   There are justified basic beliefs.
> F2.   All justified nonbasic beliefs are justified in virtue of their relation to justified basic beliefs.

These assertions prompt the following questions for foundationalists:

> QF1.   What are the kinds of things our justified basic beliefs are about? Which beliefs are justified and basic?
> QF2.   How are these basic beliefs justified? If they are not justified by other beliefs, how do they get justified?
> QF3.   What sort of connection must a nonbasic belief have to basic beliefs in order to be justified?

Different versions of foundationalism can be identified by their answers to these questions.

A.   The Main Idea of Cartesian Foundationalism

René Descartes was an extremely influential seventeenth-century philosopher. He is widely known as a defender of a particular version of foundationalism. It is, however, difficult to extract from his writings the version of foundationalism frequently attributed to him.[9] We will call the view to be discussed *Cartesian foundationalism,* and in some places introduce aspects of the view by saying, "The Cartesian view is that . . ." even though it is unlikely that Descartes actually would agree to all aspects of the view to be described.

The Cartesian foundationalist answer to (QF1) singles out as basic beliefs our beliefs about our own states of mind. Propositions describing what one seems to see, what one thinks, how one feels, etc. are basic. Descartes seems to have thought that basic beliefs were beliefs that were in some sense indubitable or free from all possibility of error. He noted that your own belief that you exist could not be mistaken, and this seemed to put it in the class of basic beliefs. The rest of what we know, according to Cartesian foundationalism, is what we can deduce from our basic beliefs. So if we have knowledge of the world around us, it is because we can deduce the things we know from these basic beliefs.

B. A Detailed Formulation of Cartesian Foundationalism

It is important to understand properly the beliefs Descartes counts as basic. Consider a sentence such as:

4.   René seems to see a tree.

There might not actually be things of the sort René seems to see. (4) just describes how things look to him. Things can look this way when he really sees a tree. But they can also look this way in other circumstances, such as when he is dreaming or suffering from an illusion. (4) simply describes his internal state of mind. Descartes thinks of feeling pain in an analogous way. One can "feel pain" even if there is nothing going on in the part of the body that seems to be hurting.

In general, then, Descartes's answer to (QF1) says that basic beliefs include beliefs about states of mind—beliefs about how things look or sound to you, what you seem to remember, etc. These beliefs are *appearance beliefs* and the inner states they describe are *appearances*. It is important to realize that appearance beliefs are not limited to beliefs about how things look. They include beliefs about how they sound, taste, feel, and smell. In addition, beliefs about what you seem to remember and perhaps beliefs about what you yourself believe are included. In general, appearance beliefs are beliefs about the current contents of your own mind.

By themselves appearance beliefs do not imply anything about what is in the world outside one's own mind. In other words, they do not by themselves imply anything about the *external world*. In principle, you could have the same inner state in a dream, hallucination, or normal perception. As philosophers use the phrase *external world*, then, it refers to everything outside of one's own mind. So your own experiences and your beliefs about them are inside your mind. Everything else is, from your perspective, part of the external world. Thus, things in the minds of your friends and neighbors are, from your perspective, part of the external world.

There is a distinction here worth noting. You could take "It seems to me that p" to mean "I believe that p." Similarly, you might take (4) to mean that René believes that he sees a tree. This is not what we mean. Rather, we mean that his state of mind is one of seeming to see a tree. The image before his mind is "tree-like." As we understand (4), Descartes would believe (4), and it would be true, if he had a tree-like image before his mind that he knew had been induced artificially in some sort of psychological experiment. He could say in such a case, "I seem to see a tree, but I do not believe that I really see a tree."

One interpretation of the Cartesian foundationalist answer to (QF2) relies on the idea that the basic beliefs are beliefs in propositions that one *cannot doubt*. They are said to be *indubitable*. In other words, the basic beliefs are appearance beliefs that cannot be doubted, or disbelieved. Perhaps when a tree-like image is before your mind, you cannot help but believe that you seem to see a tree. If this is the idea behind the answer to (QF2), then the general answer seems to be that basic beliefs are justified because they are beliefs in propositions that, in the circumstances, we are incapable of doubting. But this is not a good answer to (QF2). The inability to doubt a proposition does not make believing it epistemically justified. It may instead be the result of a psychological limitation. Suppose a person is so psychologically dependent upon his mother's love that he cannot doubt that his mother loves him. That does not make the belief epistemically justified. The person may have plenty of good reasons to believe otherwise but lack the capacity to believe what his reasons support. So inability to doubt does not make something justified, and thus cannot explain why it is a justified basic belief.

There is another theme in Descartes's writings. He suggests that beliefs about our own internal states are beliefs that could not be mistaken. The idea is that if he believes a thing like (4), then he could not be mistaken about that. He might be mistaken about whether there really is a tree there, but not about whether it looks as if there is a tree there. More generally, the idea is that basic beliefs are justified because they are beliefs in propositions about which we cannot be mistaken. In other words, we are *infallible* about them. So we will take the Cartesian foundationalist answer to (QF2) to be that basic beliefs are justified because we cannot be mistaken.

Consider next what is commonly taken to be Descartes's answer to (QF3). He apparently thought that everything else that is justified must be *deduced* from the justified basic beliefs. Thus, he held that to get justified beliefs about the external world you must combine basic beliefs in ways that guarantee the truth of those beliefs about the world. Because statements about how things look or seem have no such guarantee, this is a difficult task. Descartes's own approach went as follows.[10] He claimed that certain elementary beliefs about logical and conceptual matters were also basic. Perhaps his idea was that elementary propositions about these matters are ones that we can just see to be true, simply by reflecting on them. Examples might be the proposition that everything is identical to itself or the proposition that if the conjunction *P and Q* is true, then *P* is true. Without examining this issue in detail here, it will suffice to identify this class of basic beliefs as *elementary truths of logic* and attribute to Descartes the view that our beliefs in these propositions are also justified basic beliefs.

Descartes's way of arguing that some external world beliefs are justified, given his answers to (QF1), (QF2), and (QF3), was to argue that the elementary truths of logic included propositions on the basis of which he was able to prove conclusively that God exists and that God would not or could not be a deceiver. But if our appearance beliefs were misleading, then God would be a deceiver. Using this conclusion combined with his appearance beliefs, he derived a large number of external world beliefs. In this way, he concludes that we do have knowledge of lots of facts in the world.

Cartesian foundationalism, then, is the view characterized by the following three claims, which comprise answers to the three questions for foundationalists:

CF1.   Beliefs about one's own inner states of mind (appearance beliefs) and beliefs about elementary truths of logic are justified basic beliefs.

CF2.   Justified basic beliefs are justified because we cannot be mistaken about them. We are "infallible" about such matters.

CF3.   The rest of our justified beliefs (e.g., our beliefs about the external world) are justified because they can be deduced from our basic beliefs.

C. Three Objections to Cartesian Foundationalism

C1. We Are Not Infallible About Our Own Mental States   The combination of (CF1) and (CF2) can be refuted if it can be shown that we are not infallible about our own mental states. The following example shows that there is good reason to think that we can be mistaken, even about these matters.

Example 4.8:   The Frying Pan

You are walking toward a counter that has an electric frying pan on it. You have just been told to be careful of the pan because it is very hot. As you approach the counter, you trip and put your hand out to stop your fall. Your hand unfortunately comes down right on the pan. You immediately pull it away, thinking:

5.   I am now having a sensation of extreme heat.

In fact, as you soon realize, the pan is actually not on. You did not feel heat at all.[11]

It is alleged that in this sort of example you believe (5), that (5) is a proposition about your own current mental states, and that (5) is false. If all of this is right, then we are not infallible about our own mental states.

To assess this example, it is important to be careful about exactly what (5) means. The word *sensation* is ambiguous. It can be used in ways that imply that there really is an external thing that is being sensed. It can also be used to refer to a purely internal state. According to the first usage, (5) is true only if there is actual contact with a very hot thing. So understood, (5) does not express the sort of belief that Cartesian foundationalists claim to be basic. It is not about one's mental state. Instead, it is about the causes outside of the mind of the current experience. On this interpretation, (5) says that an extremely hot thing is causing the current feeling of heat.

The second interpretation of (5) makes it about your internal state alone. It just says that you are having the hot feeling, that you feel heat. It says nothing about any external source of this feeling. This is the sort of belief that the Cartesians had in mind as basic. Unfortunately for Cartesian foundationalism, the objection seems to work when (5) is interpreted in this second way. Objectors can plausibly argue that you not only have the mistaken belief that is roughly equivalent to "I've touched something very hot." You also have a mistaken belief about the character of your experience itself. You mistakenly think that you are having the hot feeling. If the example is possible when understood in this second way, then we really can be mistaken about our experiences. This is trouble for Cartesian foundationalism. And it does seem possible. What prevents people from making mistakes about their experiences?

There are things defenders of Cartesian foundationalism might say in response to this example.[12] For example, the objection requires that it is possible for expectations to affect our beliefs about our sensations. That does indeed seem possible. However, it may be that expectations also affect our sensations themselves. That is, perhaps if this sort of thing were to happen, the person actually would have a sensation of heat for a moment. If that is what happens, then the belief is not false after all. Thus, what proponents of the example rely on is that expectation and anticipation affect what you *believe* about a sensation but do not affect the sensation itself. If it did alter the sensation, then you do not have a mistaken belief about your inner state after all.

Still, to defend Cartesian foundationalism one must argue that expectations must always affect both sensation and belief or neither. It is hard to see why this is true. Furthermore, a Cartesian foundationalist who used this reply would have a very puzzling account of what goes on in the example. There comes the moment of realization in the example, the point at which you realize that the pan is not hot. But if you really are having a sensation of heat when you think you are, what exactly is it that makes your sensation (and your belief) change? Why do you decide you were wrong? After all, the reply says that things *did* seem as you thought they did. The critic of Cartesianism, in contrast, has a plausible account of the moment of realization. After a while, you realize that you do not feel the way you thought you did. Your beliefs change, but your sensation does not. You made a mistake about your sensation.

Another example points toward that same conclusion. In one such example, a person is told that itches are mild cases of pain.[13] The person feels an itch, believes that he is feeling an itch, and infers that he is therefore feeling pain. However, this conclusion is mistaken. Itches are not pains, and he is not having a sensation of pain. Once again, we are not infallible about these matters.

These examples refute any version of foundationalism that implies that *all* beliefs about one's own sensations are true. Perhaps Cartesian foundationalism does imply this. But a modified form of the theory, to be discussed later in this chapter can avoid this result.

There is an additional reason not to accept (CF2). It is very hard to see why the fact (if it is a fact) that you cannot be mistaken about something is a justifying fact. Suppose that some proposition could not be false. It is a law of logic, or perhaps a law of nature, that it is true. If you believe that proposition, then your belief could not be mistaken. But your belief could be a mere lucky guess or the result of a series of errors that happened to lead to a true belief. If you *knew* that you could not be mistaken, that would provide you with a reason. But if you do not know about that, it is unclear why that fact makes your belief justified. So (CF2) implies that if a belief is one that cannot be mistaken, then it is justified. And that seems, on reflection, to be wrong.

Our fallibility about our own mental states is not the only problem for Cartesian foundationalism. We turn now to a second problem.

C2. Beliefs About Inner States Are Uncommon Cartesian foundationalism says that all justification stems from justified basic beliefs, which are beliefs about our own inner states. But in ordinary circumstances, we do not form beliefs about our inner states. When you look around the room, you do not typically believe things such as "I seem to see something chair-shaped over there" and then infer "There is a chair over there." You just believe "There's a chair over there." Consider also the example with which we started the chapter. In that example Careful believed that Filcher stole a painting. Foundationalism would seem to have it that this belief is well founded only if Careful bases his belief ultimately on beliefs about his own current states of mind. It is just barely possible to imagine Careful doing this. He might form beliefs about the sounds and images before his mind, infer from them some things about the existence and nature of a crime, and then, ultimately, infer that Filcher stole the painting. But this would be a complex and tedious chain of reasoning. Hardly anyone ever does anything like that.

Cartesian foundationalism thus seems subject to the following objection:

Argument 4.2:   The Beliefs About Inner States Are Rare Argument

2-1.   People rarely base their beliefs about the external world on beliefs about their own inner states.

2-2.   If Cartesian foundationalism is true, then external world beliefs are well founded only if they are based on beliefs about one's own inner states.

2-3.   If Cartesian foundationalism is true, then people rarely have well-founded beliefs about the external world. (2-1), (2-2)

2-4.   It is not true that people only rarely have well-founded beliefs about the external world. (*The Standard View*)

2-5.   Cartesian foundationalism is not true. (2-3), (2-4)

This is a troubling argument for Cartesian foundationalists. Premise (2-1) seems to be an accurate description of the way we form beliefs. Premise (2-2) is clearly a consequence of Cartesian foundationalism. Premise (2-4) is clearly a consequence of *The Standard View,* which we are assuming to be true for now. The conclusion follows from these premises. Cartesian foundationalists can defend their view only if they can find a way to reject one of these premises, and (2-1) seems to be the best candidate. Other versions of foundationalism can avoid the objection by proposing a new answer to (QF1). Before turning to those theories, it will helpful to consider whether there is any plausible reason to reject (2-1) of this argument.

What is clearly true, and what is offered in support of premise (2-1), is the observation that as we go through the day we do not consciously entertain propositions about the contents of our minds. We do not consciously form thoughts such as "I am now seeming to see something chair-like" or "I am now seeming to hear something that sounds like a bell." However, there are reasons to think that at any given time we have many more beliefs than those that we are consciously entertaining at that time. At least three categories of such beliefs suggest themselves. The first category consists in beliefs that are stored in memory. You presumably had a moment ago beliefs about your own name, who the president is, and so on. You were not thinking about those matters at the time. So stored beliefs are one class of beliefs that exist without being consciously considered.

A second possible category of nonconscious beliefs is beliefs that help to explain behavior. Suppose that you walk into a room and notice that the light is not on. You want to read, so you walk over to a nearby light switch and flip it. If asked to explain your behavior, you might say that you wanted to turn on the light and you believed that the switch operated the light. This explanation seems just fine, even if you did not say to yourself anything like "This switch operates this light." This belief need not have been consciously formulated. Nevertheless, you did have that belief and it played a role in your behavior.

A final possible category of nonconscious beliefs consists in beliefs that are entirely obvious once considered, even though you have not thought about them previously. Suppose someone tells you that George Washington never visited Disneyland. You might never have thought about that before. But it hardly comes as news to you. Given everything else you know, it is obvious. Perhaps this suggests that you already believed it, though not in a conscious way.

All these examples are controversial, and they raise difficult questions about what it is to believe something. What remains to be seen is whether they can help defenders of Cartesian foundationalism. One defender of this aspect of Cartesian foundationalism, Timothy McGrew, has proposed that beliefs about our own conscious states constitute another category of nonconscious beliefs. McGrew says that "awareness of visual, tactile, and auditory stimuli is often subconscious but not therefore irrelevant to the justification of empirical beliefs."[14] His idea seems to be that we have a subconscious awareness of the characteristics of our experiences, that we therefore have subconscious beliefs about these characteristics, and that these are the basic beliefs that justify our external world beliefs. If he is right about the existence of these beliefs, then premise (2-1) of *The Beliefs About Inner States Are Rare Argument* is false.

McGrew's position has some merit. There are, however, reasons to question it. For one thing, "awareness of the stimuli" differs from having beliefs about the stimuli. To say that we are aware of certain stimuli is to say that we have a conscious experience of those stimuli. Thus, if you walk into a room and see a chair, then you have a perceptual experience with certain characteristics. You are aware of certain stimuli. But it does not follow from this that you form a belief to the effect that you are experiencing those stimuli. Such a belief would seem to involve a kind of monitoring of one's experiences that we do not ordinarily do.

Furthermore, in the examples of nonconscious beliefs mentioned earlier, it is at least typically the case that the believer will acknowledge the beliefs if asked about them. But appearance beliefs are not quite like this. It is often difficult to get people to think about such matters. Many are disinclined to say that they have such beliefs other than in unusual circumstances in which they are made to focus on the possibility of hallucinations, perceptual illusions, and the like. This casts some doubt on the idea that people are nevertheless routinely forming beliefs about these matters.

Finally, McGrew's account makes justification depend upon the details of our psychological systems in a peculiar way. An example will bring this out. Suppose that two people walk into a room in which a chair is clearly visible. They both look toward the chair and they form the belief that a chair is present. Finally, suppose that one of them does form the subconscious belief that he seems to see a chair, while the other bypasses this step and goes directly from the experience to the belief that there is a chair there. McGrew's proposal apparently has the result that the former is justified in believing that a chair is there, but the latter is not. It is difficult to believe that this subconscious psychological difference can make a difference in justification.

These considerations do not definitely refute McGrew's suggestion. The issues depend in part upon difficult questions about the nature of belief and the ways we process information. Still, they are significant enough to make it reasonable to look for a better version of foundationalism.

C3. Deduction Is Too Restrictive The final objection to Cartesian foundationalism is the most decisive one. It concerns (CF3), the requirement that justified nonbasic beliefs be deducible from basic beliefs. Suppose for the sake of argument that there are satisfactory answers to the objections so far considered and that (CF1) and (CF2) are correct. Thus, we are assuming for the sake of argument that, for example, when you walk into a room you have a large number of justified beliefs about how things look and seem to you. We can add that you have large stock of justified beliefs about your apparent memories and about other aspects of your current mental states. If your beliefs about the external world are justified, given (CF3), you must be able to *deduce* from this collection of basic beliefs things such as that there is a chair in the room, that the lights are on, and so on. Applying the same considerations to Example 4.1, if Careful is to be justified in believing that Filcher stole the painting, then this conclusion must be deducible from the combination of Careful's basic appearance beliefs. However, this requirement is simply not satisfied.

To say that the external world propositions can be deduced from the appearance propositions is to say that it is not even possible for the appearance propositions to be true while the external world propositions are false. Unfortunately, it is possible. It is possible to have a dream or hallucination in which you have experiences just like those you have when you enter the room. Careful could have the experiences he has had as a result of some elaborate scheme in which Filcher is framed for the crime. In general, no set of experiences logically guarantees any particular external world propositions. The deduction condition in (CF3) is too stringent.

D. Conclusions on Cartesian Foundationalism

It is clear that Cartesian foundationalism is not a satisfactory theory, given the truth of *The Standard View*. There are the following problems:

1. Beliefs about one's own mental states are not immune from error. So if beliefs about these matters are basic, whatever it is that makes them justified has to be something other than this property. We need a different explanation of what makes basic beliefs justified. So (CF2) must be revised.
2. Not *all* beliefs about one's own mental states are basic justified beliefs. Beliefs about one's own mental states can be derived from other beliefs, and thus can be nonbasic. Beliefs about these matters can be unjustified.
3. The things that Cartesian foundationalists count as basic are things that in ordinary circumstances we do not believe at all. It seems that the starting point for our beliefs is ordinary observations of the world, not introspections. So (CF1) needs to be revised. (Of course, this point is controversial.)
4. Much of what we know (according to *The Standard View*) cannot be deduced from what is basic. This is clearly true if our basic beliefs are beliefs about our own internal states. But even if we take spontaneous judgments about the external world to be basic, much of what we know goes beyond what can be deduced from that.

Before examining a version of foundationalism that attempts to make the changes these points suggest, it will be helpful to consider the other approach to justification that has been influential in the history of philosophy, coherentism.

IV. COHERENTISM

A. The Main Idea of Coherentism

The central idea of coherentist theories of justification is that every justified belief is justified by virtue of its relations to other beliefs. In other words, no beliefs are foundational or basic. So coherentists reject premise (1-4) of *The Infinite Regress Argument*, the step of the regress argument that rejects circular evidential chains. This is not because they think that you can justify one belief by another, that second by a third, and then justify the third by appeal to the first. Rather, their idea is that justification is a more systematic and holistic matter, that each belief is justified by the way it fits into one's overall system of beliefs.

Thus, coherentists endorse the following two central ideas:

> C1. Only beliefs can justify other beliefs. Nothing other than a belief can contribute to justification.
>
> C2. Every justified belief depends in part on other beliefs for its justification. (There are no justified basic beliefs.)[15]

Coherentists think that a belief is justified when it coheres with, or fits together well with, one's other beliefs. This idea has considerable intuitive force, as is brought out by the following examples.

Example 4.9: Growing Hair

Harry has a generally hard-headed attitude concerning the effectiveness of medications. He always wants to see the evidence before he believes they will work. He rejects outlandish claims based on individual testimonials. He is sensibly dubious about the alleged miracle cures touted in advertisements. But Harry is starting to lose his hair and he is quite upset about this. One day he hears somebody say that Miraclegro cures baldness, and he believes it.

It should strike you that Harry's belief that

> 6. Miraclegro cures baldness

is not justified. And what is particularly notable is that the belief is quite incongruous for Harry. You might say that he should know better than to believe such a thing. Indeed, he *does* know better, in that his own principles tell him not to believe (6) in these circumstances. Coherentists would agree. They would say that this belief is incoherent for him—it does not fit with his other beliefs. Harry accepts something along the lines of

> P. A medical treatment is effective only if there is good clinical evidence showing that it is effective, and there is no good clinical evidence that Miraclegro is effective.

Yet, Harry believes (6) in the absence of the needed evidence. We can see a kind of incoherence in his system. The belief about Miraclegro is the one that stands out as the "bad" belief in his system.

Example 4.9 illustrates one way a belief can fail to cohere with one's other beliefs. It is an individual belief that violates the believer's own general principles. Another example illustrates another way a belief can fail to cohere.

Example 4.10:   Falling Tree Limbs

Storm's family owns two cars—one rather new and one an old junker. Each night the cars are parked in the driveway. One night there is a major ice storm and large quantities of ice are forming on the tree limbs, causing branches to break from the trees and fall. There is a tree overhanging the driveway. Storm hears the sound of a branch crashing into a car right out in the driveway. Storm thinks that the branch must have hit the old junker.

Example 4.10 is similar to Example 4.9 in that some wishful thinking is involved. However, in Example 4.10 Storm may not be violating any general principle he accepts. Unless he has other beliefs about the specific locations of the car and the sound of the branch, his belief about the car is simply thrown into the system without anything supporting it. We might say that in Example 4.10 Storm's belief *lacks positive coherence:* There is no positive support for it within the system. In contrast, in Example 4.9 Harry's belief had *negative coherence:* It was in conflict with the rest of the system. For a belief to be justified, according to coherentism, it must not be like either of these. However, these considerations do not amount to a precise account of what coherence is. Nothing said so far constitutes any clear explanation of what sort of conflict with other beliefs rules out coherence nor what sort of internal support is needed for coherence. Furthermore, as will become clearer in the next section, there is an important question about exactly what it is that a belief must cohere with in order to be justified according to coherentist standards.

An initial formulation of coherentism, then, is as follows:

CT.   S is justified in believing p iff p coheres with S's system of beliefs.

To develop a reasonably precise coherentist theory, coherentists must address two questions:

QC1.   What counts as S's system of beliefs?
QC2.   What is it for a belief to cohere with a system of beliefs?

To see the force of the questions, suppose that coherentists made two assumptions:

A1.   S's system of beliefs = everything S believes.
A2.   A proposition coheres with a system of beliefs provided it logically follows from the conjunction of everything in the system.

Applying (A1) and (A2) to (CT) yields the following coherentist theory:

CT1.   S is justified in believing p iff p logically follows from the conjunction of everything S believes.

A moment's reflection reveals that (CT1) has the absurd consequence that everything anyone believes is justified. The argument for this is simple. Suppose S believes p. The conjunction of everything S believes will then be a long conjunction, one conjunct of which is p itself. A simple law of logic is that a conjunction implies each of its conjuncts. Thus, if S believes p, q, r, s, and so on, then the conjunction of everything S believes will be the long proposition "p and q and r and s . . ." Trivially, this conjunction implies p. According to (CT1), it follows that S's belief that p is justified, no matter what p is and no matter how well it fits the rest of what S believes. According to this theory, then, Harry's belief in Example 4.9 and Storm's belief in Example 4.10 are justified. This is just what coherentism was supposed to avoid. Coherentists need something better than (CT1).

In attempting to develop a better version of coherentism, it is important to keep the following point in mind. Assume, just for the sake of argument, that we have a reasonably clear understanding of the idea of a coherent system of beliefs. Using this idea, we can formulate the following proposal:

> CT2. S is justified in believing p iff S's system of beliefs is coherent and includes a belief in p.

The idea behind (CT2) is that justified beliefs are beliefs that are components of coherent systems and unjustified beliefs are components of systems that are not coherent. Given a reasonably clear idea of what coherence is, (CT2) would be a reasonably clear proposal.

However, (CT2) is not the least bit plausible. There may be something desirable about having coherent systems of belief. However, few of us manage to achieve this. We all make some mistakes, we succumb to wishful thinking, we fail to realize the consequences of our beliefs. There are, in all realistic cases, some beliefs that render our systems at least to some degree incoherent. According to (CT2), if that's the case, then none of us is ever justified in believing anything. Consider your belief that you exist. Even if you are making some big mistakes on other matters, this is something that you are justified in believing. According to (CT2), that belief is justified only if you do believe that you exist and your system of beliefs is coherent. As noted, if you resemble a normal human being with respect to your beliefs, then your belief system is not coherent. Hence, by (CT2), your belief that you exist is not justified.

The problem with (CT2) can be stated in a more general way. It says that all beliefs in a coherent system are justified and all beliefs in a noncoherent system are not justified. Any individual's belief system is either coherent or not coherent. So the theory implies that for each individual, either all of his or her beliefs are justified or else all of them are not justified. Because, in fact, any real person falls short of a coherent system, the theory implies that no real person has any justified beliefs. However, the truth about each of us is not so extreme. We each have some justified beliefs and some unjustified beliefs. (CT2) cannot account for this simple fact. A successful version of coherentism must be more selective than (CT2) is.

It would not help matters to say that the degree to which a belief is justified depends upon the level of coherence of the believer's overall system. Suppose your belief system is, on the whole, moderately coherent. The present proposal would yield the result that all of your beliefs are moderately well justified. This fails to distinguish properly between your well-justified beliefs and your wild speculations.

It is clear, then, that coherentists need new and better answers to (QC1) and (QC2). Somehow, coherentism has to be formulated in way that enables it to identify some beliefs as justified and some as unjustified.

B. A Version of Coherentism

Coherence, whatever exactly it is, is a property that a system of beliefs may have to a greater or lesser degree. One system of beliefs may be more coherent than another. Philosophers have proposed various things that add to, or detract from, coherence.[16] It is easiest to grasp these ideas by considering systems of belief that are largely alike, with only a few differences introduced to highlight factors that affect coherence. For example, suppose two people each believe a large number of propositions—p, q, r, and so on. Let us assume that there are no logical conflicts among the propositions these people believe. That is, it is at least possible that all their beliefs are true. And then suppose that one of the people forms the belief that p is false, and the person simply adds this belief to his system. Now there is a contradiction in the belief system. It includes beliefs in both p and ~p. It cannot be that both of these are true. Now the system contains an inconsistency. And that makes it less coherent. Inconsistencies need not be as obvious as the one just described. A person might believe several propositions and fail to realize that they imply the denial of another proposition that the person believes. This belief system is also inconsistent, although the inconsistency is not so blatant. In any case, inconsistency detracts from coherence.

One thing that adds to the coherence of a system is the fact that it contains beliefs that constitute explanations for other beliefs in the system. Suppose that gardener #1 believes that all of the plants in his garden are wilted and that it has not rained in a long time. Suppose gardener #2 believes these things and also believes that plants wilt when they do not get any water for a long time. (Perhaps gardener #2 also believes that rain provides plants with water.) Gardener #2 has a richer, more fully developed belief system. The richness comes in part from the way it links together beliefs that are isolated from one another in gardener #1's belief system. Having these kinds of connections is often thought to add to the coherence of a belief system.

Perhaps having individual beliefs that conflict with one's general principles also detracts from the coherence value of one's system of beliefs.

We will say that factors such as these determine the *coherence value* of a system of beliefs. This does not constitute a complete account of coherence values, but it does provide some explanation of the idea. Coherentists can make use of the coherence values of systems of beliefs to formulate a version of coherentism that gets around the initial difficulties covered in the previous section.[17] We can formulate the theory this way:

> CT3. S is justified in believing p iff the coherence value of S's system of beliefs would be greater if it included a belief in p than it would be if it did not include that belief.

The intended implications of (CT3) can best be seen by considering two situations, one in which a person already does believe a proposition and one in which a person does not believe it. If the person does believe the proposition, then the coherence value of the system as it actually is can be compared to its coherence value with that belief removed from the system. If removing the belief detracts from the coherence value of the system, then believing that proposition is justified. If the person does not already believe the proposition, then the coherence value of the actual system can be compared to the value of the system that would be formed if that belief were added. (CT3) says that when the version of the system with the belief has a higher value than the version without it, then the belief is justified. In accord with (CT3), we will say that a belief coheres with a system of beliefs when it enhances the coherence value of that system. Thus, (CT3) preserves the idea that a belief is justified when it coheres with one's system of beliefs.

(CT3) may deal reasonably well with Examples 4.9 and 4.10. In Example 4.9, Harry had a general belief about effective treatments and a specific belief about Miraclegro that did not fit together well. Intuitively, the belief about Miraclegro was the bad guy. It is plausible to hold that Harry's belief system would be more coherent if that belief were dropped. So (CT3) has the correct result that it is not justified. In Example 4.10, Storm has a belief that is unconnected with his other beliefs. So perhaps his system would gain coherence by dropping it. Again, (CT3) seems to have the right results for this case.

There are, however, vexing details that need to be worked out for (CT3). Consider again Harry from Example 4.9. Harry has an unjustified belief in (6), the proposition that Miraclegro cures baldness. Intuitively, we judge that his system of beliefs would be more coherent if this belief were dropped. (CT3) assesses justification by looking at what happens to the coherence value of the system if this belief alone were to be dropped. The problem with this is that Harry may well believe a number of other propositions that are connected to (6) in crucial ways. For example, if he just bought some Miraclegro, then he may believe

> 7. I just bought some stuff that cures baldness.

If we assess the justification of (6) by looking to see what happens to the system if it alone is dropped, then we are to assess the coherence value of Harry's system if he stops believing (6) but continues to believe (7). He may also believe many other propositions closely connected to (6). For example, he may believe

> 8. Miraclegro cures baldness but spray paint does not.

His system may lose coherence if he continues to believe things like (7) and (8) but drops (6). Due to its connections to other beliefs, then, dropping (6) alone may detract from coherence, even though believing (6) is not justified. Hence, it is not clear that (CT3) does deal properly with this example. The fact that any belief, even one that is not justified, can still have logical connections to many other beliefs poses a hard problem for coherentists. It is not clear how to revise coherentism to avoid this problem.

There is another puzzle that advocates of (CT3) must face. Consider Harry's justified belief in (P), the proposition saying that treatments do not work without clinical evidence of their effectiveness and there is no evidence of the effectiveness of Miraclegro (for baldness). Coherentists say that Harry's system would be more coherent if he dropped (6) from his system. Ignore the problem just discussed and suppose that this is true. However, it is also true that he could gain some coherence by dropping (P) from his system. This is because (P) also contributes to the incoherence his system displays. Hence, (CT3) implies that his belief in the principle is not justified either. Generally, when one's current system is incoherent because two beliefs conflict, there is an increase in coherence from dropping either one. The theory seems to imply that neither belief is justified. Yet that need not be the case, as Example 4.9 illustrated. A better version of coherentism will somehow allow for the possibility that one of the conflicting beliefs, or one group of conflicting groups of beliefs, is justified. Perhaps coherentists can come up with some way to cope with this problem.

The two problems just discussed surely do not show that coherentism is mistaken. They show only that there are difficult problems for coherentists to solve. Perhaps they can solve them by specifying in a better way the system of beliefs with which a belief must cohere in order to be justified. For example, in some of the examples a key feature is that a belief is held more out of wishful thinking than out of an effort to get at the truth. Coherentists could define justification in terms of coherence with this truth-directed subsystem.[18] Possibly some such account will avoid the problems considered so far.

There are some other objections to coherentism that are intended to go to the heart of the theory. Some critics contend that the central coherentist idea is wrong. They argue that justification is not entirely a matter of how one's beliefs fit together. We will turn next to two objections that attempt to capitalize on this point.

C. Objections to Coherentism

C1. The Alternative Systems Objection
Here is a statement of a commonly expressed objection to coherentism:

> According to a coherence theory of empirical justification . . . the system of beliefs which constitutes empirical knowledge is epistemically justified *solely* by virtue of its internal coherence. But such an appeal to coherence will never even begin to pick out one uniquely justified system of beliefs, since on any plausible conception of coherence, there will always be many, probably infinitely many, different and incompatible systems of belief which are equally coherent.[19]

Here is one way to spell out this objection.[20] Consider the proposition that Abraham Lincoln was assassinated. If, as the objectors contend, there are many different, and incompatible, coherent systems of beliefs, there will be some systems that include this belief and others that include its negation. If that belief is part of your actual system, you can imagine a system that replaces everything supporting it or following from it with different propositions. By carefully constructing the new system, you could get one just as coherent as your current system, but including the proposition that Lincoln was not assassinated. Thus, if there are all these different coherent systems, then you can make any belief you want justified simply by picking and choosing the rest of your beliefs appropriately. That cannot be right. Here is a more formal statement of the argument:

Argument 4.3:   The Alternative Systems Argument

3-1. If (CT) is true, then a belief is justified iff it coheres with the believer's system of beliefs.

3-2. A person can make any selected belief cohere with his system of beliefs by properly adjusting the rest of the system to make it fit with that one.

3-3. If (CT) is true, then a person can make any selected belief justified by properly adjusting the rest of his beliefs. (3-1), (3-2)

3-4. But it is not the case that one can make any selected belief justified by properly adjusting the rest of one's beliefs.

3-5. (CT) is not true. (3-3), (3-4)

There is strong reason to doubt that this is a good objection to coherentism.[21] One problem with it is that (3-2) is false. People simply do not have that much control over their beliefs. But this is not the major problem with the argument.

Consider again the belief about Lincoln with which this subsection began. Coherentists are not committed to the absurd conclusion that you already are justified in believing both that Lincoln was assassinated and that he was not. Nor are they committed to the idea that you have the power to adjust your beliefs to build up a coherent system around either of these options. Coherentists are not stuck with the implausible claim that we can form our beliefs at will. They are committed to the idea that someone could have the belief that Lincoln was assassinated, and that this belief could cohere with his belief system, and that therefore this belief could be justified. They are also committed to the conclusion that a person could have the belief that Lincoln was not assassinated, that this belief could also cohere with a different system he could have had, and that therefore this belief also could be justified. Far from being false, however, this conclusion seems exactly right. Conflicting beliefs, in alternative systems, can be justified. People who have had different experiences and learned different things might justifiably believe very different things. There may be some people who have been taught nonstandard things and who, as a result, have a justified belief that Lincoln was not assassinated. There is no good objection to coherentism here.

The Alternative Systems Argument is supposed to be a working out of the idea that coherentism is somehow stuck with the result that alternative systems of belief can be justified, with no coherentist grounds for choosing between them. It may be, however, that this commitment is not implausible. Surely people in radically different circumstances can have fully coherent, and well-justified, systems of beliefs that differ greatly from one another. For example, a person living in the Middle Ages might have a fully coherent, and completely justified, set of beliefs that differs radically from the fully coherent, and completely justified, set of beliefs of a modern counterpart. The idea behind this objection to coherentism is mistaken.[22]

C2. The Isolation Objection As we have seen, the key idea of coherentism is that whether one belief is justified depends only upon the believer's other beliefs. If only beliefs do the justifying, then experiences seem not to matter. And that is not right. Reconsider Example 4.1, in which Hasty believes that Filcher is guilty simply out of a general dislike for him. If only Hasty's other beliefs matter, then, according to coherentism, this belief will be justified if he believes not only that Filcher is guilty but also a larger story about him. Similarly, in Example 4.10, Storm hears tree limbs falling on a car. Suppose his wishful thinking causes him to add beliefs to the effect that the crunching sound was one that only the junk car would make, that the junk car was directly under a branch, etc. Unless there is some input to the system that justifies these other beliefs, he is not justified in this belief. Merely fabricating a larger tall tale does not add to justification. He must somehow account for the "data of experience." Coherentism seems to omit this.

Other examples make the point sharper, although they have an air of unreality about them. These are cases in which a person's beliefs are detached from reality, in that they are not connected to his experiences in the world. Consider the following example:

Example 4.11:   The Strange Case of Magic Feldman

Professor Feldman is a rather short philosophy professor with a keen interest in basketball. Magic Johnson (MJ) was an outstanding professional basketball player. While playing a game, we may suppose, MJ had a fully coherent system of beliefs. Magic Feldman (MF) is a possible, though unusual, character, who is a combination of the professor and the basketball player. MF has a remarkable imagination, so remarkable that while actually teaching a philosophy class, he thinks he is playing basketball. Indeed, he has *exactly* the beliefs MJ has. Because MJ's belief system was coherent, MF's belief system is also coherent.

According to coherentism, MF's beliefs are justified, because they form a coherent system. However, his beliefs are radically detached from reality. It's not just that they are false. Worse, they do not even take into account the nature of his own experiences. His experiences—what he sees and feels—are the experiences of a teacher. His beliefs are those of a person in an entirely different situation. Far from being justified, they are an absurd fantasy.

The argument based on this example can be spelled out as follows:

Argument 4.4:   The Isolation Argument

4-1.   If (CT) is true, then in all possible cases a belief is justified iff it coheres with the believer's system of beliefs. [Definition of coherentism]

4-2.   MF's system of beliefs = MJ's system of beliefs. [Assumption about example]

4-3.   MJ's belief that he is playing basketball coheres with his system of beliefs. [Assumption about example]

4-4.   MF's belief that he is playing basketball coheres with his system of beliefs. (4-2), (4-3)

4-5.   If (CT) is true, then MF's belief that he is playing basketball is justified. (4-1), (4-4)

4-6.   But MF's belief is not justified. [Assumption about example]

4-7.   (CT) is not true. (4-5), (4-6)

There is another way to make the same point. If only other beliefs can justify a belief, then, since MF and MJ have the same beliefs, MJ does not have anything to justify his beliefs that MF lacks. So MJ cannot be better justified than MF. But he is. The reason for this is that part of what determines what is justified is the character of one's experiences.

Coherentists may reply that MF is not possible. It must be conceded that the example is quite unusual. Still, it suffices to make an important point about coherentism: It omits from its account of justification something that seems absolutely central: one's experiences. Furthermore, critics need not resort to bizarre examples like MF to make the point.

Example 4.12:   The Psychology Experiment

Lefty and Righty are in a psychology experiment. They are extremely similar people, with all the same relevant background beliefs. The experiment is one in which they see an image on a monitor and they form beliefs about what they see. They are told that they will see two lines on the monitor and they are to form a belief about which one is longer. They are both led to believe that the one on the right will be longer. The lines then appear on the monitors and they both believe that the one on the right is longer. However, expectations are playing a role. In fact, for one of them, Lefty, the one on the left is longer, and it looks that way. Lefty simply ignores the character of his experience and forms his belief entirely on the basis of what he was led to believe.

The critic contends that how the line looks makes some difference to what is justified for Lefty. Lefty thinks the line on the right is longer, but he has not paid attention to how the line actually looks, even though that information is right there before his mind. Coherentism implies that he is justified in believing that the line on the right is longer, because that belief is supported by his prior beliefs and he has no other beliefs that defeat it. Yet Lefty does have experiential evidence—the way the lines look—that counts against this belief. Coherentism improperly leaves this out of the picture. It says that only what Lefty believes matters. It gives an incorrect account of this more realistic example.

Some defenders of coherentism might reply that one's beliefs *must* conform to one's experiences. If so, then Examples 4.11 and 4.12 are not even possible. However, if that is the case, then it turns out that a core element of foundationalism is right after all—these beliefs about experiences seem to be in some sense "infallible" or "incorrigible"—we have to be right about them. So if you reject this argument against coherentism on these grounds, you seem to be appealing to a foundationalist idea.

This suggests that it would be a good idea to reconsider foundationalism in an effort to come up with a version that avoids the difficulties of Cartesian foundationalism.

D. Conclusions on Coherentism

1. The main idea of coherentism can be given in two characteristic coherentist claims:

   C1. Only beliefs can justify other beliefs. Nothing other than a belief can contribute to justification.

   C2. Every justified belief depends in part upon other beliefs for its justification. (There are no justified basic beliefs.)

2. We have not yet found a suitable way to formulate the coherentist theory. Among the problems for coherentists are these: (a) Distinguishing sensibly among actual beliefs to characterize some as justified and some as unjustified; (b) saying what coherence actually is.

3. Many critics think that (C1) has been refuted by *The Isolation Argument*. This argument shows that experiences matter for justification.

V. MODEST FOUNDATIONALISM

A. The Main Idea

Recall that foundationalists must answer these questions:

   QF1. What are the kinds of things our justified basic beliefs are about? Which beliefs are justified and basic?

   QF2. How are these basic beliefs justified? If they are not justified by other beliefs, how do they get justified?

   QF3. What sort of connection must a nonbasic belief have to basic beliefs in order to be justified?

In recent years, philosophers have developed versions of foundationalism that avoid the problems encountered by Cartesian foundationalism.[23] These contemporary versions of foundationalism, often called *modest foundationalism,* typically hold that basic beliefs are ordinary perceptual beliefs about the external world, that these beliefs can be justified without being immune from error, and that nonbasic beliefs can be justified if they are well supported by basic beliefs without being deducible from them. The conditions placed on justified beliefs are thus less demanding, or more modest, than those endorsed by Cartesian foundationalism.

The modest foundationalist idea is as follows: As people navigate their way around the world, they are routinely bombarded with sensory stimuli. They regularly form beliefs, not about the internal effects of those stimuli, but about the world outside them. They believe such things as that the lights are on, there's a book on the table, and so on. Modest foundationalists regard these as justified basic beliefs. They do not say that we cannot be mistaken about these matters. Nevertheless, they hold that beliefs such as these are often very well justified. Finally, they say that these justified basic beliefs can provide justifying reasons for additional beliefs about the world even if the further beliefs are not deducible from the basic ones.

This all seems entirely plausible, but hard questions arise when we attempt to spell out the details. We turn next to that.

B. Versions of Modest Foundationalism

Modest foundationalists think that our basic beliefs are typically beliefs about the world around us, beliefs about the things that we see or otherwise sense. We typically form these beliefs automatically, without any conscious reasoning or deliberation. When you walk into a room you might immediately come to believe that the lights are on, that there is a blue chair in front of a brown table, and so on. Modest foundationalists think that beliefs such as these are basic and that they are often justified. This does not imply that you can never be wrong about such matters or that all beliefs like these are justified.[24] The details of modest foundationalist views about these matters will emerge from discussion of their answers to (QF1) and (QF2). Before examining that part of their theory, consider how they will answer (QF3). In other words, how, according to modest foundationalism, are the rest of our beliefs justified? What can replace the deduction condition in Cartesian foundationalism?

Consider again Example 4.1. Careful had strong reasons to think that Filcher stole the painting. Those reasons are summed up in proposition (9):

> 9. The painting was in Filcher's possession, Filcher's fingerprints were at the scene of the theft, . . .

While (9) may not contain only propositions that are basic, according to the present view, it is not too hard to see how a belief in (9) might be based on things that are basic. Perhaps the observations that constitute Careful's basic beliefs in this case are propositions about the things he has observed: that there were fingerprints of such and such a kind, that someone said that he had seen Filcher in the area of the crime, and so on. The picture, then, is this:

> *Basic Beliefs:*   Careful's observational beliefs, e.g., there is a painting of such and such a description in Filcher's home, there were fingerprints of a certain sort in Filcher's home, etc.

He infers (9) from this, and from (9) he infers:

> 1.   Filcher stole the painting.

The links between the propositions here are less than deductive. They include seemingly good inferences of the kind people make all the time. Sometimes inferences like these are said to be *inductive inferences.*[25] Included in this is the sort of inference you make when you observe that a wide range of things of a certain type have all had a certain property and you conclude that the next thing of that type will have that property. This is known as *enumerative induction.*

Another nondeductive inference is *inference to the best explanation.* It is plausible to regard Careful's inference from (9) to (1) as being of this sort. Given the facts he has assembled, it is possible that someone else stole the painting. However, any alternative requires a rather bizarre and unlikely set of coincidences or contrivances. The best account of the facts is that Filcher did it. Modest foundationalists hold that when a particular proposition enters into the best explanation of one's justified basic beliefs, believing that proposition is justified.

Thus, the modest foundationalist answer to (QF3) can be summed up in the following principle:

> MF3.   Nonbasic beliefs are justified when they are supported by strong inductive inferences—including enumerative induction and inference to the best explanation—from justified basic beliefs.

Two clarifications of (MF3) are important. Recall the total evidence condition and the basing condition mentioned in Section I. The former said that a belief is justified only if it is supported by one's total evidence. Just having evidence that supports a proposition is not enough for justification, because that evidence might be undermined by other evidence. The second condition amounted to the idea that a justified belief must be based on supporting evidence. If one has some good reasons to believe something, but believes that thing as a result of wishful thinking or bad reasoning, then the resulting belief is not well founded. Modest foundationalists want to include both of these ideas in their theory. So a better statement of their view about nonbasic beliefs would be this:

> MF3a.   Nonbasic beliefs are justified (well founded) when (a) they are supported by strong inductive inferences—including enumera-

tive induction and inference to the best explanation—from
justified basic beliefs and (b) they are not defeated by other
evidence.[26]

This completes our account of the modest foundationalist answer to (QF3).
It is not unreasonable to have questions about the adequacy of this answer.
Some of these questions will be taken up later in this chapter and in the chap-
ters that follow.

Consider next what modest foundationalists say about basic beliefs. One feature of the beliefs that modest foundationalists count as basic is that they are
spontaneously, or noninferentially, formed. To get the idea here, contrast two
cases in which you form a judgment about the kind of tree in front of you. In
one case, imagine that you are quite familiar with trees and when you look at this
tree, you immediately and without reflection believe that it is a pine tree. There
is no inference made in this case. In the other case, you are far from an expert.
It takes thought and reflection to figure out what kind of tree you are seeing. You
notice that the tree has long thin clusters of needles, you recall that pines charac-
teristically are like that, and you conclude that the tree is a pine. In each case, you
get from the look of the tree to the belief that it is a pine. However, in the second case you go through a conscious inferential step concerning the shape of
the leaves. You do not do this in the first case. In the first case, then, you have
the spontaneous, noninferential belief that the tree is a pine. In the second case,
you do not have this spontaneous belief, although you do have the spontaneous
belief that the tree has long, pointy, needle-like leaves. Generalizing from these
examples, modest foundationalists can say that whenever a person forms a belief,
it traces back to some spontaneously formed belief or other. But there is no uniform content to these beliefs. They can be beliefs about classifications of objects, they can be beliefs about the sensory qualities (colors, shapes, etc.) of
objects, and they can be about one's sensory experiences themselves. These
same propositions can be believed as a result of inferences as well.

Modest foundationalists can make use of the idea of spontaneously formed
beliefs in constructing their theory. They can say:

MF1.   Basic beliefs are spontaneously formed beliefs. Beliefs about the
       external world, including beliefs about the kinds of objects expe-
       rienced or their sensory qualities, are often justified and basic. Be-
       liefs about mental states can also be justified and basic.
MF2.   Being spontaneously formed makes a belief justified.

Unfortunately, this simple version of modest foundationalism is highly implausible. Surely not all spontaneously formed beliefs are justified. When you
walk into a room, see a table, and spontaneously form the belief that there is a
table there, your belief is not justified simply because it is spontaneously formed.
What's crucial is that the belief is, in some sense, a proper response to the perceptual stimulus. Some spontaneous beliefs are not like that. Suppose you
are hoping that a friend will stop by your house to visit, though you have no

particularly good reason to think she will. You hear a car driving down your street and spontaneously form the belief that your friend has arrived. In this case, you have a spontaneously formed belief, but it is not a well-justified belief. Things could be even worse. You could have strong evidence against your spontaneously formed belief—perhaps you have reason to think that your friend is out of town. In that case, your spontaneously formed belief is not justified at all. Additional examples establishing this point are easy to come by.

These considerations show that modest foundationalists must replace (MF2) with a better principle. Here is one way the theory might be revised. Instead of saying that all spontaneously formed beliefs are justified, they might say that they are justified provided one does not have evidence against them. As some would put it, they are "innocent until proven guilty."

> MF2a.   All spontaneously formed beliefs are justified unless they are defeated by other evidence the believer has.

The idea here is that if a person forms a belief spontaneously, not on the basis of any inference, then that belief is justified provided the person does not have reasons that undermine that belief.

(MF2a) does not take into account a fact suggested by some of the examples we have considered. When spontaneous beliefs are justified, they are connected to experience in an important, though difficult to describe, way. When you walk into a room, see a table, and form the belief that there is a table there, what makes your belief justified is not simply the fact this belief is spontaneously formed or even the fact that it is spontaneously formed combined with the fact that you do not have evidence against there being a table there. (Suppose you have no other evidence one way or the other about whether there is a table there.) What seems central is that your belief is a proper response to the perceptual stimulus you have. It is a suitable thing to believe given that experience. To believe something that does not fit that experience at all, such as that there is an elephant in the room, would not be a proper response to that experience. To believe something that goes beyond what is revealed in the experience, such as that there is a table that is exactly 12 years old, would not be a proper response to that experience.

A more refined version of modest foundationalism makes use of this idea of a proper response to experiences. To respond properly to an experience is to believe what that experience, by itself, indicates to be present. The victim of a perfect hallucination, then, responds properly to experience by believing what seems to be true, even though it is not true. But when people read too much into their experiences, or misinterpret them, then they are not responding properly. Thus, modest foundationalists can say:

> MF2b.   A spontaneously formed belief is justified provided it is a proper response to experiences and is not defeated by other evidence the believer has.

Other examples clarify the idea. Compare a novice bird-watcher and an expert walking together in the woods, seeking out the rare pink-spotted flycatcher. A bird flies by and each person spontaneously forms the belief that there is a pink-spotted flycatcher there. The expert knows this to be true, but the novice is jumping to a conclusion out of excitement. The expert has a well-founded belief, but the novice does not. In the same situation, both the novice and the expert may have well-founded beliefs about the color, shape, and size of the bird they see. This suggests that there is some relevant difference between properties such as being gray with pink spots and about 4 inches long and properties such as being a pink-spotted flycatcher. One might say that the former properties are "closer to experience" than the latter. Anyone with proper vision can discern the former properties in experience. This is not true of the latter.

This suggests two factors about when beliefs are properly based on experience. First, when the contents of the belief are closer to the direct contents of experience, they are more apt to be properly based on experience. Second, modest foundationalists can say that training and experience affect what counts as a proper response to experience. The expert's training makes her response proper. For beliefs that are more distant from experience, such training is necessary for the belief to be properly based on experience. Thus, modest foundationalism is captured by the following principles:

> MF1.   Basic beliefs are spontaneously formed beliefs. Typically, beliefs about the external world, including beliefs about the kinds of objects experienced or their sensory qualities, are justified and basic. Beliefs about mental states can also be justified and basic.
>
> MF2b.   A spontaneously formed belief is justified provided it is a proper response to experiences and it is not defeated by other evidence the believer has.
>
> MF3.   Nonbasic beliefs are justified when they are supported by strong inductive inferences—including enumerative induction and inference to the best explanation—from justified basic beliefs.

C. Objections to Modest Foundationalism

Modest foundationalism is an attractive theory. The central problem facing it concerns the idea of a belief being properly based on experience.

C1. Objection 1: Nothing is Basic In a widely discussed book, Laurence BonJour raises a general objection to the very idea that there are justified basic beliefs. Here is one way he formulates his argument:

> . . . the fundamental role which the requirement of epistemic justification serves in the overall rationale of the concept of knowledge is that of a *means* to truth; . . . Thus if basic beliefs are to provide a secure foundation for empirical knowledge, . . . then that feature, whatever it may be, by virtue of which a particular belief qualifies as basic must also constitute a good reason for thinking that the belief is true . . . .

If we let Φ represent the feature or characteristic, whatever it may be that distinguishes basic empirical beliefs from other empirical beliefs, then in an acceptable foundationalist account a particular empirical belief B could qualify as basic only if the premises of the following justificatory argument were adequately justified:

(1)   B has feature Φ.
(2)   Beliefs having feature Φ are highly likely to be true.

Therefore, B is highly likely to be true.

. . . But if all this is correct, we get the disturbing result that B is not basic after all, since its justification depends on that of at least one other empirical belief [namely, (2)].[27]

BonJour's idea is simple and important. Justification is supposed to be indicative of truth. If some feature makes a belief justified, then the believer must be justified in believing that this feature is a truth indicator. If the person lacks justification for this, then the belief is not justified. But if the person has that justification, then it is part of an argument for the belief, and thus the belief is not basic after all. So no belief could be basic and justified. Foundationalism cannot be right.

Call the sort of argument that BonJour thinks one must have for an allegedly basic belief a "Truth Indicative Feature" (TIF) argument for that belief. A TIF argument is an argument showing that the belief results from some factor that is indicative of its truth. For example, suppose Tom believes something about car repair on the basis of the fact that Ray said it. His belief in this proposition is justified, according to BonJour's thinking, only if he has a TIF argument for it. Such an argument might say that his belief is based on the fact that Ray told him, and Ray is usually right about such matters. Similarly, if someone has a belief based on perception or introspection, then that belief is justified only if the person is justified in believing that perception, or introspection, usually gets things right.

BonJour's general argument against foundationalism can be spelled out this way:

Argument 4.5:   BonJour's TIF Argument

    5-1.   For any proposition p that S believes, either S has a TIF argument for it or S doesn't.

    5-2.   If S has a TIF argument for it, then S's belief in p is supported by that argument and is not a justified basic belief.

    5-3.   If S does not have a TIF argument for it, then S's belief in p is not justified and thus is not a justified basic belief.

    5-4.   S's belief in p is not a justified basic belief. (5-1), (5-2), (5-3)

If (5-4) is true, then there are no justified basic beliefs and no version of foundationalism could be right.

BonJour's argument is intriguing and complicated. Understanding the modest foundationalist response to the argument is central to understanding modest foundationalism itself. Their central idea is that it is *not* the general reliability of introspection or perception that makes some justified basic beliefs justified. Rather, they contend, there is some more direct relation between experience and belief that is crucial here. Their idea is that, at least in the typical case, when you have a clear view of a bright red object, then your experience itself justifies the belief that you are seeing something red. That belief is the proper response to that experience. Beliefs about the reliability of your perceptual system simply are not necessary for justification. Of course, most of us do have beliefs about the reliability of our perceptual systems, but the modest foundationalist point is that these beliefs are not needed for justification. Similarly, if you feel warm, your reason for thinking that you feel warm is just your sensation (experience) of warmth. You do not have to know that experiences are good reasons for beliefs or know that your belief that you feel warm is justified. You can, nevertheless, know (and be justified in believing) that you feel warm. The modest foundationalist idea, then, is that experiences themselves can be evidence. You may be enough of an epistemologist to be able to formulate some sort of TIF argument for a belief that is supported by this experiential evidence, but this TIF argument is extra justification. You do not need it for your belief to be justified.

These considerations show that both (5-2) and (5-3) of BonJour's argument are mistaken. Because an experience can directly justify a belief, without the believer having a TIF argument for it, (5-3) is false. And even if the person does have the TIF argument for it, the belief may also be justified directly by experience and still be a justified basic belief. The TIF argument is, in effect, superfluous. Hence, (5-2) is false.

C2. Objection 2: Proper Responses to Experiences? The second objection to modest foundationalism is more a request for clarification than an attempted refutation. Modest foundationalists can say, perhaps with some plausibility, that certain beliefs are properly based on experience and others are not. But it would be good to have a more systematic and general understanding of just why things work out the way modest foundationalists say they do. Why, exactly, is the belief that there is a table in the room properly based on experience, but the belief that the there is an 84-year-old table in the room not properly based on experience? Consider also a person who sees a clearly displayed triangular-shaped object. The person is justified in believing that there is a triangular-shaped object there, and a belief in that proposition would be properly based on experience. Contrast this with a person who sees a clearly displayed 44-sided object directly in front of him. The proposition that there is a 44-sided object would not be justified for him, and a belief in that proposition would not be properly based in experience. But what is the difference between these cases?[28] What determines which beliefs are properly based in experience and which are not?

These are good questions about modest foundationalism. It strikes many philosophers that there must be some good answer to them, because it is plainly clear that the table and triangle beliefs are justified by experience, while the 84-year-old table belief and the 44-sided object belief are not justified by experience. Yet it is difficult to see exactly how to formulate a general reply. We will see in Chapter 5 that there are some answers that might be given to these questions by philosophers who depart from the evidentialist theory in an important way. And we will see in Chapter 7 that skeptics raise a more general question about modest foundationalist claims concerning what is properly based on experiences. We will reconsider the plausibility of modest foundationalist views in that chapter.

D. Conclusions About Modest Foundationalism

Modest foundationalism is an attractive theory. The central conclusions about it are as follows:

1. By allowing for nondeductive connections between basic justified beliefs and nonbasic justified beliefs, modest foundationalists are able to avoid the result Cartesian foundationalism seems stuck with, that hardly any beliefs about the external world are justified.
2. By allowing that we need not be infallible about the subject matter of basic beliefs, modest foundationalists are able to avoid the result that there are too few basic justified beliefs.
3. By allowing that basic beliefs can be beliefs about the external world, rather than restricting them to beliefs about one's own inner states, modest foundationalists have a better chance than Cartesian foundationalists of finding a broad-enough foundation for our knowledge of the world.
4. By requiring that basic beliefs be properly connected to experiences, modest foundationalists avoid *The Isolation Objection* that undermines coherentism.
5. A more fully developed account of the conditions under which a belief is properly based on experience is desirable.

ENDNOTES

1. In asking this question, we turn our attention to question (Q2) from Chapter 1.
2. W. K. Clifford, "The Ethics of Belief," originally printed in *Contemporary Review* (1877), reprinted in Clifford's *Lectures and Essays* (London: MacMillan, 1879).
3. "The Ethics of Belief," p. 183.
4. "The Ethics of Belief," p. 180.
5. A common thesis is that only voluntary behavior is the proper subject of moral evaluation. It is unclear whether belief is often, or even ever, a voluntary activity. So there is some doubt about whether belief is often, or even ever, a proper subject for moral evaluation. If it is not, then there is a further objection to Clifford's thesis. Roughly, the claim is that believing on insufficient evidence is not morally wrong because believing is not a voluntary action.

6. There are details about this that need to be worked out. Presumably, a person does not believe anything on the basis of all his other beliefs. So the idea in clause (ii) is that the person bases his belief on a part of the evidence that really does support the belief. Clause (i) requires that the total evidence condition is satisfied. For further discussion of this, and of evidentialism generally, see Earl Conee and Richard Feldman, *Evidentialism* (Oxford University Press, forthcoming).

7. One might think that his belief is not justified even if the evidence he didn't consider does support his belief. More generally, one might think that the phrase "and this evidence would not support p" can be dropped from (GEP). The discussion that follows would apply equally well to this modified version of (GEP).

8. In answering this objection to evidentialism we have also addressed question (Q3) from Chapter 1.

9. Probably the most widely read work by Descartes is his *Meditations*. It is reprinted in *The Philosophical Works of Descartes*, translated by Elizabeth S. Haldane and G. R. T. Ross (Cambridge, UK: Cambridge University Press, 1973).

10. See Descartes, "Meditation VI" in *The Philosophical Works of Descartes*, pp. 185–199.

11. Keith Lehrer presents a similar example in *Knowledge* (Oxford: Oxford University Press, 1974), p. 96. It is discussed by Louis Pojman in *The Theory of Knowledge: Classical and Contemporary Readings* 2nd ed. (Belmont, CA: Wadsworth, 1999), p. 187.

12. For discussion, see Timothy McGrew, "A Defense of Classical Foundationalism," in Louis P. Pojman, ed., *The Theory of Knowledge: Classical and Contemporary Readings*, 2nd ed., pp. 224–35.

13. See Lehrer, *Knowledge*, pp. 97–99.

14. Timothy McGrew, "A Defense of Classical Foundationalism," The quotation is from p. 230.

15. We will examine an argument in support of this claim in Section V of this chapter.

16. For discussion, see Keith Lehrer, *Knowledge*, Chapters 7–9 and Laurence BonJour, *The Structure of Empirical Knowledge*, (Cambridge, MA: Harvard University Press, 1985) Chapters 5–8.

17. A theory along these lines is suggested by Jonathan Dancy in *An Introduction to Contemporary Epistemology* (Oxford: Blackwell, 1985).

18. See Keith Lehrer, "Reply to My Critics," in John Bender, ed., *The Current State of the Coherence Theory* (Dordrecht: Kluwer, 1989).

19. Laurence BonJour, *The Structure of Empirical Knowledge*, p. 107.

20. For another recent statement of the objection, see Louis Pojman, *What Can We Know?* 2nd ed. (Belmont, CA: Wadsworth, 2001), p. 118.

21. Earl Conee makes similar points about this objection in "Isolation and Beyond," *Philosophical Topics* 23(1995): 129–46.

22. For discussion of related issues, concerning the possibility of reasonable people having different beliefs, see Chapter 9.

23. See Robert Audi, *The Structure of Justification* (Cambridge, UK: Cambridge University Press, 1993); Susan Haack, *Evidence and Inquiry: Towards Reconstruction in Epistemology* (Oxford: Blackwell, 1993); and James Pryor, "The Skeptic and the Dogmatist," *Nous* 34 (2000): 517–549. Haack classifies her theory as *foundherentism*—a combination of foundationalism and coherentism. However, it seems to fit the modest foundationalist view described here.

24. A basic belief need not be justified. If one forms a belief directly and not on the basis of other beliefs, then it is basic. For example, if a belief just comes to you on a whim, it is a basic belief but not justified. Some philosopher use the word "*basic*" to refer only to justified beliefs that are not dependent upon other beliefs for their justification. However, we then would have had no simple term to refer to beliefs that are not justified and which are not based on other beliefs.

25. It is possible to raise skeptical questions about induction. Such questions will be discussed in Chapter 7.

26. It is important to realize that for clause (a) to be satisfied it is not enough that one merely have some supporting evidence. It is required that the supporting evidence be very strong—strong enough to provide knowledge-level justification.

27. Laurence BonJour, *The Structure of Empirical Knowledge* (Cambridge, MA: Harvard University Press, 1985), pp. 30–31. A similar line of thought is presented in BonJour's widely reprinted essay, "Can Empirical Knowledge Have a Foundation?" *American Philosophical Quarterly* 15 (1978): 1–13.

28. Ernest Sosa asks a question such as this in Chapter 6 of *Virtue Epistemology* in *Blackwell Great Debates: Epistemology: Internalism Versus Externalism* (forthcoming).

CHAPTER FIVE

Nonevidentialist Theories of Knowledge and Justification

The theories discussed in Chapter 4 gave accounts of justification elaborating on the evidentialist idea that justification is a matter of fitting one's beliefs to one's evidence. Although no decisive objection to evidentialism emerged from our discussion, many contemporary epistemologists reject that view. No one denies that evidence often matters to justification and no sensible epistemologists urge people to disregard their evidence when forming beliefs. Rather, they think that making one's belief fit one's evidence is only part of the story. The larger story, they think, brings in considerations about the processes that initiate and sustain beliefs. Four theories of this sort will be examined in this chapter.[1]

I. THE CAUSAL THEORY

A. The Main Idea

The first proposed replacement for the *TAK* is *the causal theory of knowledge.* Alvin Goldman was an early proponent of this view.[2] To appreciate the idea, first think about any device that receives and processes information about its environment. Familiar devices such as thermometers and barometers are examples. The temperature surrounding the thermometer and the pressure in the air around the barometer cause the measuring devices to be in particular states or conditions. We sometimes speak, metaphorically, of the thermometer "knowing" what the temperature is. In some ways we are like elaborate thermometers. When we are in the presence of a red object with our eyes open and sufficient light available, we see a red object and believe that there is something red there. There is a causal process, initiating with light reflecting off the red object into our eyes, going through our perceptual system, and culminating in the belief that there is a red object present. The causal theorist's main idea is that when a fact in the world leads to a belief in that fact, it is a case of knowledge. When a person has a belief that is not causally connected with the associated fact, there is no knowledge.

This central idea needs elaboration and clarification, but it does seem to have some initial plausibility. We can initially formulate the idea this way:

C. S knows p iff S's belief in p is caused by the fact p.

The causal theory retains the *TAK*'s implication that knowledge requires true belief. Suppose you believe p, but this belief is false. If p is not true, then there is no fact p, and hence it cannot be that the fact p caused your belief in p. And if you do not believe p, then, of course, it is not the case that the fact p causes your belief in p. So, the truth and belief conditions are retained by this theory. But the justification condition is replaced by the causal connection requirement.

Goldman concludes the essay in which he defended this theory by saying that it "flies in the face of a well-established tradition in epistemology, the view that epistemological questions are questions of logic or justification, not causal or genetic questions."[3] His idea, then, is that whether you have knowledge depends not on what your reasons are but rather on what the cause of your belief is. A key aspect of the theory, then, is that it eliminates the *TAK*'s justification condition and the fourth condition designed to deal with Gettier's examples and replaces them with a causal connection condition. As we examine this theory, we will look to see if this replacement is a good idea.

To see the merits of the causal theory, notice how well it deals with common examples. Consider first some cases in which a person has a true belief that is not knowledge. Suppose that you have to be out of town on the day of a scheduled picnic. At the time of the picnic, without having heard any reports about the weather back home, you form the belief that it is raining at home. You have this belief only as a result of your nasty disposition: you do not want the others to have a good time that you must miss. And suppose that you happen to be right. In this case, you have a true belief that it is raining in your hometown, but you lack knowledge. And, just as the causal theory would have it, there is no causal connection between the fact that it is raining and your belief. So the theory gets this case exactly right. If, on the other hand, you believed that it was raining because your friends called you and told you that it was raining, and they had seen the rain, then there would be a causal connection going from the rain, through your friends, and on to you. So you would have knowledge. Thus, the theory gets this case right as well. And, of course, if you had seen the rain yourself, there would have been a causal connection and you would have had knowledge. These simple cases seem to work out very well.

Even some more complicated cases go well for the causal theory. Consider Gettier cases such as Example 3.3, in which Smith believes that there is a sheep in the field. Smith's belief is true, but the presence of the sheep did not causally contribute to that belief. The belief traces back to the dog (or the statue, or, . . .). So, the causal theory seems to get this right as well.

B. Developing the Causal Theory: Goldman's Theory

To appreciate the merits and the problems of the causal theory, it is best to examine a specific version of it. Here is what Goldman proposed:[4]

> C*. S knows p if and only if the fact p is causally connected in an appropriate way with S's believing p.

There are silly, but convincing, examples that make it clear why Goldman includes the requirement that the belief and the fact be connected in an "appropriate way." This can best be seen by considering the following example involving an inappropriate connection.

Example 5.1: The Blow to the Head

Gerald has fallen down the steps and hit his head. The blow to his head scrambles his brain in such a way that he forms a variety of wild beliefs. Among other things, he believes that eating lettuce causes obesity, that the Chicago Cubs will win the World Series, and that he has just fallen down the steps. In fact, he has no recollection of the sensation of having fallen. This belief, like each of the other two just mentioned, is simply a direct result of the blow to the head.

In this example, Gerald believes

1. I, Gerald, have just fallen down the steps.

Gerald believes (1), and there is a causal connection between the fact that (1) and Gerald's belief that (1). Still, clearly, Gerald does not know (1) if he comes to the belief in this way. In something like what happens in Gettier cases, he has fortuitously (in some sense) come upon a true belief. Goldman says that although there is a causal connection between the fact and the belief in this example, the connection in this sort of case is not an appropriate connection. This example illustrates why (C*) is better than (C).

Goldman gives the following examples of appropriate causal connections between facts and beliefs: perception, memory, and proper reconstructions of causal chains.[5] The first two of these are relatively easy to understand: If seeing a tree causes you to believe that there is a tree in front of you, there is an appropriate connection and you have knowledge. If a memory causes you to retain that belief, you still have knowledge. Some cases are more complex, and they involve mental reconstructions of causal chains.

Example 5.2:   The Missing Tree

Smith returns home and sees a lot of sawdust and wood chips on the ground where there used to be a large tree. He recalls that the tree was diseased and that he received a notice stating that the city tree service was going to cut it down. So he infers, and thereby comes to know, that the tree was cut down.

In this case, Smith did not perceive the tree being cut down and he does not remember that it was cut down. But he does know that it was cut down. Goldman's theory accounts for this fact by allowing for appropriate connections between a fact and a belief when the belief results from a proper reconstruction of the causal chain leading from the fact to the belief. Smith is able to reconstruct in a sensible way the causal chain involved and thus has knowledge. In this case, there is a causal chain leading from the cutting down of the tree, to the presence of wood chips and sawdust, to the belief that the tree was cut down. Because he can reconstruct the causal chain from the tree being cut down to his belief, Goldman counts this as a proper reconstruction of a causal chain and thus it makes for an appropriate causal connection. His theory implies, correctly, that there is knowledge in this case.

Some other properly reconstructed causal chains differ slightly from this one. Suppose Black sees a fire in the fireplace and believes that there is smoke coming out of the chimney. The smoke coming out of the chimney does not cause her belief that there is smoke coming out of the chimney. Rather, the fire causes both the smoke to come out the chimney and her belief that it is. In this case, then, there is something, namely the fire, that leads to both a certain fact—the smoke coming out—and her belief in that fact. In other words, there is a common cause of the fact and her belief in the fact. Goldman says that when a person reconstructs a causal chain like this correctly, the fact and the belief are causally connected in an appropriate way and the causal condition in his analysis is satisfied. Thus, the theory implies, correctly again, that she does know that there is smoke coming out of the chimney.

Goldman's idea is clever and innovative. It deals with many common examples effectively. It may also deal with many Gettier-style examples in a good way. Typically, in those examples, there is no causal connection, or no appropriate one, between the fact that p and the belief in p.

However, the causal theory is not without serious problems. We turn next to them.

C. Puzzles and Problems for the Causal Theory

C1. Knowing Generalizations The causal theory works best when we restrict our attention to knowledge of specific observable facts in the world. But *The Standard View* implies that we know more than that. For example, it allows that we can have knowledge of generalizations such as

2.   All men are mortal.

The problem is that generalizations do not seem to be causes. (2) does not cause your belief in (2), so there is no causal connection, and thus no appropriate causal connection, between this fact and your belief in it. It is belief in specific instances of mortality (and other information) that causes the belief. So, how could you know (2), according to Goldman's causal theory?[6]

C2. Overdetermination Cases

Example 5.3: Poison and Heart Attack

Edgar knows that Allan has taken a fatal dose of a poison that has no antidote. Enough time has passed so that Edgar knows that Allan is dead. But Allan didn't die from the poison; instead, so upset at what he had done, he had a fatal heart attack. Edgar's reconstruction of the causal chain is not correct.

This is a problem for Goldman's theory because Edgar does know that Allan has died but has not reconstructed the causal chain properly. In this case, Edgar knows something—that Allan has taken a fatal dose—that is causally sufficient for Allan to be dead. On this basis Edgar can know that Allan is dead. It is not required that this be the actual cause of Allan's death. You can know that something happened even if you are mistaken about how it came about. You do not have to reconstruct the causal chain properly.[7]

This is a very serious problem for the causal theory. To repair the theory, it would be necessary to say that there is a proper causal chain between an event and a belief in cases in which a person believes that the event has occurred because he justifiably believes that something causally sufficient for it has occurred. But this brings the idea of justification (and evidence) back into the picture in exactly the way Goldman wanted to avoid. The truth is that knowledge just does not require that there be a causal connection between an event and a belief in its occurrence. It requires justified belief.

C3. Perception and Evidence

Example 5.4: The Trudy/Judy case

Trudy and Judy are identical twins. Smith sees one and, for no good reason, forms the belief that he sees Judy. It is true, and it is a case of perception. He reconstructs the causal chain between Judy's presence and the belief properly. He knows about Trudy, but rashly discounts the possibility that she is the one he sees.[8]

This is also a serious problem for the causal theory. Here, there is a causal connection between a fact and the belief in that fact. Nevertheless, there is no knowledge. And the reason is that the reasons for believing that the causal chain is the way it is are not good ones. The mere existence of a causal connection is not good enough.

A causal theorist could develop the theory in a way that deals properly with this case. The idea would be to require that the believer be *warranted* or *justified* in reconstructing the causal chain in the proper way. Smith is not justified in this case, since he has no good reason to think he sees Judy rather than Trudy. But the belief in this case is just a perceptual belief—Smith just sees a person and forms the belief that it is Judy. That is just like a case in which he sees a table and forms the belief that it is a table. If we say that he needs warranted beliefs about the causal history in the Trudy/Judy case, then the same should be required in a case in which he forms a true belief that there is a table there. The result of these considerations is that any good version of the causal theory will not be different from the *TAK* in the way Goldman says it is.

There is a dilemma for causal theorists: either they do require "explicit evidence" about the causes of perceptions or they do not. If they do not, then the Trudy/Judy case is a counterexample because there is a causal connection that the believer has reconstructed correctly (though unjustifiably). If, on the other hand, causal theorists do require explicit evidence about the causes of perception, then the causal theory turns out not to differ significantly from the *TAK*. The central difference is that it adds the causal connection condition, which Example 5.3 shows to be a mistake.

D. Conclusions on the Causal Theory

The idea that knowledge can be analyzed in terms of causal connections rather than justification is an interesting one, but it seems not to work out very well when it is considered in detail. It is true that there is often a causal connection between the facts we know and our beliefs in those facts. But we can have knowledge without there being such a causal connection, as Examples 5.2 and 5.3 show, and we lack knowledge even when there is a causal connection, as Example 5.4 shows.

II. TRUTH TRACKING

A. The General Idea

Recall the idea used to introduce the causal theory: thermometers "know" what the temperature is since they respond to the temperature in a regular way. The causal theory did not make full use of this idea. What is true of the thermometer is not just that its being 50° causes the thermometer to display "50°." When it is that temperature, the thermometer says that it is, and when it is not that temperature, the thermometer says that it is not. Something analogous is true of people who know about the world around them. Consider, for example, a dog owner and her dog, Rex. When Rex is in the room with her, she believes that he is. Rex makes his presence felt, and she is receptive to his ways of doing this. When he is not in the room, she believes that he is not in the room. Her beliefs about this topic "track the truth," in somewhat the way the thermometer tracks the temperature.

One idea, then, is that knowers are "truth trackers." Robert Nozick was a leading proponent of this theory.[9] The idea of truth tracking as an account of knowledge is this: a person who knows a proposition, a knower, is a person who tracks its truth. Just as a thermometer's readout tracks the temperature, a knower's attitudes toward a proposition reflect the truth value of the proposition. This idea is expressed in the following definition:

TT. S knows p iff (i) p is true, (ii) S believes p, (iii) S's attitude toward p tracks the truth value of p: When p is not true, S does not believe p; and when p is true, S does believe p[10].

Like the causal theory, the tracking theory retains from the *TAK* the idea that knowledge requires true belief. But it replaces the justification condition and the Gettier condition with the tracking requirement.

The tracking theory works well for some simple cases. An office worker knows that his computer is now turned on, but if it were off he would believe that it is off. His beliefs about the computer's condition track its actual condition. He does not know whether or not his neighbor is home, though he thinks she is. But that thought is based on vague recollections of general patterns. Even if she were out, he would still think she is at home. His beliefs do not track her location.

Principle (TT) has the right results for many other cases. It seems to have the right results in the cases that caused problems for the causal theory. The theory can even handle some Gettier cases quite effectively as well. For example, in one of the cases Smith did not know that someone in his office owned a Ford. He based his belief on the Nogot evidence but his belief was true because of Havit. However, if his belief were false, perhaps because Havit sold his Ford, Smith would still have had the Nogot evidence and would still have believed that someone in the office owned a Ford. So, if the proposition that someone in the office owned a Ford were false, he would have believed it anyway. He was not a truth tracker for this proposition, and thus, according to (TT), did not have knowledge.

B. Developing the Tracking Theory: Nozick's Theory

Nozick argued that a theory along the lines of (TT) is not quite right as it stands and that it needs some "refinements and epicycles."[11] He is surely right about that. He presents examples such as the following to bring out the reason for this:

Example 5.5: Lucky Knowledge

Black is hard at work in her office. From time to time she looks up from her desk and computer to stretch her neck. On one such occasion she happens to glance out the window toward the street. Just at that moment she sees a mugging on the street. She has a clear view of the event. She is a witness.

In this case, Black knows that a mugging has occurred. Yet the tracking condition is not satisfied. It could easily happen that Black does not glance out the window at the crucial moment. In that case, the mugging still takes place, yet she does not believe it. She is not a truth tracker for the proposition that a mugging is taking place. So Example 5.5 is a counterexample to (TT). Black does have knowledge, but she is not a truth tracker.

Another example illustrates a similar point.

Example 5.6:   The Grandma Case[12]

Old frail Grandma sees grandson Johnny playing happily before her. She knows that Johnny is well and playing happily. But suppose Johnny were sick. The family would tell Grandma that Johnny is well and playing happily, but that he's doing this at a friend's house. They do not want to make Grandma worry. So, if Johnny were sick, she would still believe that he is well.

Grandma does not track the truth. Yet she has knowledge, since she actually does see him.

Nozick has a proposal on how to fix things up.[13] He suggests that what goes wrong in these cases is that there is a switch in the methods by which the person comes to the belief. Simplifying slightly, we can attribute the following view to him:

TT*.   S knows p iff (i) p is true, (ii) S believes p, (iii) S used method M to form the belief in p, and (iv) when S uses method M to form beliefs about p, S's beliefs about p track the truth of p.[14]

The idea is that to know a proposition, you must be a truth tracker for the proposition when you stick to the same method for forming a belief about it. In the *Grandma Case,* she actually uses "looking at him" as her method. As the example is told, if he were not well and she had been told that he was well, she would then be using a different method. The fact that this other method would lead her to a false belief does not matter when (TT*) is applied to the case. To apply (TT*), we must consider what would happen if he were not well and she were to use the method of looking at him to come to her belief. Presumably, under those circumstances, she would see that he is sick and would not believe that he is well. Thus, if she sticks to this method, she gets things right. So, this deals with Example 5.6.

C. Problems for The Tracking Theory

C1. Tracking Is Not Necessary for Knowledge Consider again Example 5.5, the *Lucky Knowledge* case. This is an example in which Black does have knowledge, but she could just as easily have failed to have knowledge because she could easily have glanced out the window at a slightly different time. In this case, condition (iii) of (TT) is not satisfied. Defenders of the theory might think that (iv) of the revised analysis, (TT*), is satisfied. However, this does not seem to be right. If the method in question is "glancing out the window," then the revised

analysis is no better than the original. The key question is whether condition
(iv) is satisfied in this case. That condition, applied to the example, yields:

> When Black uses the method of glancing out the window to form beliefs
> about whether there is a mugging occurring there, her beliefs track the
> truth (that is, if there were a mugging, she typically would believe that
> there is; and if there were no mugging, she typically would not believe
> that there is one.)

If we just add a minor detail to the story, it will be easy to see that this condition need not be true even if Black does actually know that the mugging has happened. Suppose that Black has a view of only part of the street outside her
window. There is a large part she cannot see. In our example, Black's method,
looking out on the street, enabled her to know that there was a mugging. But
it could quite easily have failed. That is, it could have led her to believe that there
was no mugging even if there had been one. It would have done this if the
mugging had been in a slightly different place, just out of her view. So the
method she used—looking out on the street—is not all that reliable for forming a correct belief about whether or not there is a mugging on the street.[15] She
does not track the truth even when she uses that method. So the theory implies that she does not know that there is a mugging going on even when she
sees it clearly. This is a mistaken outcome.

This is a forceful objection to the tracking theory of knowledge. It shows
that one can have knowledge without being a truth tracker, even if one sticks
to the same method for forming a belief about that proposition. Perhaps the
example is not entirely decisive since it is less than clear what counts as using
the same method. Perhaps a defender of the theory could say that when Black
looks out on the street and does not see a mugging, then the method of belief
formation differs from the method used when she does see the mugging. Lacking any clear idea of exactly what counts as using the same method, it is difficult to be sure about this. At the very least, then, this objection reveals that the
theory is unclear in this crucial way.

C2. Absurd Distinctions Another objection is due to Saul Kripke.[16]

Example 5.7:   Fake Barns

Smith is driving down a country road. He sees lots of barns of various colors, looks at one, and believes

   3.   I see a barn.

He also believes, based on what he sees:

   4.   I see a red barn

Both of these are true, just as he believes. However, unknown to Smith,
there have been quite a few barn fires lately, and the locals have erected barn

facades to please the tourists. Hence many of the things he has taken to be barns are not barns. One final detail: none of the fake barns is red because the material the fakes are made from reacts unfavorably to red paint.

Philosophers are divided about whether Smith knows that he is seeing a barn in this situation. Some think that the presence of fakes in the vicinity makes him lack knowledge. Others deny this. But virtually everyone would agree that either he knows both (3) and (4) or he knows neither of them. It is entirely implausible to hold that he knows one but not the other. Yet this is exactly the consequence (TT*) seems to have.

Here is why the tracking theory has such odd implications. To test whether Smith knows these propositions, the theory has us consider whether Smith's method for forming beliefs about them tracks their truth, i.e., reliably gets the right answer. His method for identifying barns seems not to be very reliable. This is because he would believe that there is a barn there even if what he saw were a fake. The presence of the fakes in the vicinity makes this possibility a realistic one, and thereby makes him not a truth tracker for (3). In contrast, his method for deciding about (4) is extremely reliable. Because there are no fake red barns, and he can distinguish red from other colors, when he is seeing a red barn he thinks that he is, and when he is not seeing a red barn, he thinks that he is not seeing one. So Smith tracks the truth of (4) much better than he tracks the truth of (3).

Thus, the theory implies that he knows that he sees a red barn there, but does not know that he sees a barn. This is an unacceptable result. If you think that the presence of fakes in the vicinity ruins his knowledge, then you think that Smith knows neither (3) nor (4). If you think that the presence of fakes in the vicinity does not ruin his knowledge, then you think that he knows both (3) and (4). Either way, this is trouble for the tracking theory.

D. Conclusions on the Tracking Theory

In spite of its initial appeal, then, the tracking theory just does not work. Knowing does not amount to tracking the truth. A large part of the reason for this is that whether you track the truth is independent of the quality of your reasons. In the final objection just considered, the unusual circumstances made you able to track one proposition but not another. However, your reasons for the two propositions were equally good. Once again, it seems that knowledge depends on reasons in a way that the tracking theory fails to acknowledge.

III. RELIABILISM

A. The Main Idea

Reliabilism is in some ways similar to the tracking theory, though there are important differences. Reliabilism is often formulated as a theory of justification, not as a theory of knowledge. Thus, reliabilists can agree that knowledge is justified true belief (plus something to deal with Gettier cases). On these points, they agree with defenders of the evidentialist theories discussed earlier. However, they interpret the justification condition in a way that is quite different from those theorists. Reliabilists deny that justification is largely a matter of having good evidence. Rather, they say, justification depends on the actual accuracy (or reliability) of the processes or methods used to form the beliefs. We will examine this idea in this section.

The most influential proponent of reliabilism is Alvin Goldman. As part of his explanation and defense of his theory, he writes:

> . . . what kinds of causes confer justifiedness? We can gain insight into this problem by reviewing some faulty processes of belief-formation, i.e., processes whose belief-outputs would be classed as unjustified. Here are some examples: confused reasoning, wishful thinking, reliance on emotional attachment, mere hunch or guesswork, and hasty generalization. What do these faulty processes have in common? They share the feature of *unreliability:* they tend to produce *error* a large proportion of the time. By contrast, which species of belief-forming processes are intuitively justification conferring? They include standard perceptual processes, remembering, good reasoning, and introspection. What these processes seem to have in common is *reliability:* the beliefs they produce are generally true. My positive proposal, then, is this. The justificational status of a belief is a function of the reliability of the process or processes that cause it, where (as a first approximation) reliability consists in the tendency of a process to produce beliefs that are true rather than false.[17]

What Goldman says here is persuasive. Confused reasoning, wishful thinking, and guessing do result in unjustified beliefs. And they do seem to share the property of being unreliable, in that they often lead to false beliefs. In contrast, perception, remembering, and good reasoning do result in justified beliefs. And these processes do seem to share the property of being reliable, in that they typically lead to true beliefs. The idea that it is reliability that is central to justification is thus well worth considering.

B. Developing Reliabilism: Goldman's Theory

B1. Recursive Definitions Before stating Goldman's theory, it will be helpful to comment briefly on the way some theories are formulated. People often worry about definitions being circular. Consider the following proposal:

> J.   S is justified in believing p iff S is justified in believing that S's source for p is reliable.

This is unacceptable. It explicitly uses the idea of justification in attempting to explain or define justification. However, some proposals that may seem similarly objectionable are actually importantly different. These are *recursive definitions*. Suppose we say that there are two ways to be a citizen: pass the citizenship test or be the child of a citizen. We could spell this out as a definition, or statement of conditions for, citizenship:

> Z.   S is a citizen iff (1) S has passed the citizenship test, or (2) S is the child of a citizen.

In (Z) the concept of a citizen does seem to be used in spelling out what it is to be a citizen. However, (Z) is not objectionably circular. One reason for this is that it is possible to reformulate (Z) so that it does not have this feature. The way to do this is to replace (2) with "S is a descendent of someone who passed the citizenship test." Another way to think about this is that clause (1) specifies one way into the class of citizens. This is the "base case." Clause (2) specifies a relation to someone who is already in the class of citizens that gets you into that class as well.

Goldman's theory, to be presented next, will provide a recursive account of justification. It will provide a base clause and a relation to beliefs that satisfy that condition that also makes a belief justified. The proposal is not circular.

B2. Details of Goldman's Theory It is easy to come up with an initial formulation of reliabilism, and equally easy to see that this initial formulation must be modified in order to capture the main idea correctly. Consider:

> R.   S justifiably believes p if and only if S's belief in p is caused by a reliable process.

A process is reliable provided it generally leads to true beliefs. There is some indefiniteness about just how reliable a process must be for the condition in (R) to be satisfied, but that is not grounds for criticism. In fact, reliabilists might plausibly say that a belief is justified to the extent that the causal process leading to it is reliable: the more reliable the process, the more justified the belief. For a belief to be justified sufficiently to satisfy the justification condition for knowledge, the process that caused it must be very reliable. This is comparable to evidentialists claiming that one needs very strong evidence. In neither case is any exact boundary specified.

Unfortunately, things are more complicated than (R) suggests. One complication grows out of the fact that some beliefs result from inferences from other beliefs. It is possible that a perfectly good inference leads to a false belief. This can happen when the premises of the inference are false. Consider, then, the process of making a certain sort of inference, for example, inferring Q from the premises P and if P then Q. This is good reasoning. Presumably, beliefs formed using that process can be justified. However, reasoning like that could turn out to lead to lots of false beliefs. This can be the case if people frequently use this pattern of inference starting with premises that are false.

Reasoning in the way just described may not always lead to truths. In fact, it may not even usually lead to truths if it happens to be applied most often to false beliefs. But it is bound to lead to truths whenever the premises from which it starts are true. Goldman says that a process like this is *conditionally reliable: it usually (or always) yields true beliefs when the beliefs it starts with are true.* He calls processes that start with some beliefs and yield new beliefs *belief-dependent belief-forming processes* and processes that do not begin with beliefs *belief-independent belief-forming processes.* Certain basic perceptual processes might be belief-independent. In those cases, a particular experience causes a belief, without other beliefs playing a role. These ideas all enter into the formulation of Goldman's reliabilist theory:

R*.
  i. If S's belief in p at t results from a belief-independent process that is reliable, then S's belief in p at t is justified.
  ii. If S's belief in p at t results from a belief-dependent process that is conditionally reliable, and the beliefs the process operates on are themselves justified, then S's belief in p at t is justified.
  iii. The only way beliefs can be justified is by satisfying the conditions in (i) and (ii).

Reliabilism as formulated in (R*) seems to contrast with evidentialist theories in a few significant ways. While reliabilists and evidentialists can agree over many cases, they differ most clearly when it comes to the beliefs that satisfy clause (i) of (R*). These differences will emerge most clearly when objections to reliabilism are considered. What should be noted for now is that reliabilists seem to have something reasonably clear and sensible to say about why perceptual beliefs are justified. Modest foundationalists were hard-pressed to explain exactly why a person's belief that he sees something red is justified when he forms this belief as a result of seeing something red. Perhaps the answer ultimately arrived at—involving properly basing the belief on experience—is satisfactory, but it is worth comparing this to what reliabilists might say. The reliabilist view is that the belief-forming process involved in forming this belief is a very reliable one. That seems right. People do not frequently make mistakes about the color of medium-sized objects in plain view. The perceptual process at work thus appears to be highly reliable.

Reliabilism also seems to have the right results in cases in which the tracking theory went wrong. The tracking theory required that the method one used to form a belief enabled one to track the truth of that very proposition. In contrast, reliabilism requires that the method generally be a reliable way to form beliefs. Arguably, the methods used in the examples that caused trouble for the tracking theory are generally reliable, and thus the examples do not undermine reliabilism.

C. Objections to Reliabilism

C1. The Brain in a Vat Objection An example that plays a major role in discussions of skepticism poses a problem for reliabilism. An old version of the example concerns an evil demon who controls a person's experiences. A contemporary version of the example concerns a brain in a vat.[18] The brain in the vat is a perfectly normal human brain, except that all the stimuli coming to the brain are the result of computer-generated impulses. The brain thinks that it is living a normal human life. It thinks that it is housed in a body, that it is navigating its way around the world, and so on. All of this is wrong. However, the brain reasons in a perfectly acceptable way from the experiences it has. In fact, we may assume that the brain has experiences exactly like those of a normal person who does have a body and is navigating around the world and so on.

> *Example 5.8: The Brain in the Vat*
>
> Brian is a normal person with accurate and well-justified beliefs about the world around him. Brain is Brian's mental duplicate. Brain has experiences just like Brian's. And Brain's beliefs are analogues of Brian's. When Brian believes that he, Brian, is eating a hot fudge sundae, Brain believes that he, Brain, is eating a hot fudge sundae. When Brian believes that he, Brian, is taking a stroll in the park, Brain believes he, Brain, is taking a stroll in the park. When Brian believes that he, Brian, is seeing a bright red object, Brain believes that he, Brain, is seeing a bright red object. Brian is right about each of these things, as he usually is. Poor Brain is wrong every time.

It is worth noticing the potential skeptical implications of this example. Some philosophers argue that you cannot tell whether you are like Brian or like Brain, and so you cannot know things like the propositions mentioned in the example. We will address this argument when we turn to skepticism in Chapter 6. Given *The Standard View*, however, Brian can know these things. Hence, beliefs such as these are justified. So reliabilism seems to have exactly the right result with respect to Brian. Brian's belief-forming processes are extremely reliable.[19] (R*) implies, correctly, that his beliefs are justified.

The problem concerns Brain. Brain is just as reasonable as Brian. Indeed, he believes comparable things for comparable reasons. Brain's beliefs seem to be equally well justified. However, the processes that Brain uses to form his beliefs routinely lead to false beliefs. It seems to follow that Brain's processes are not reliable. If so, (R*) has the wrong result here. It implies that Brain's beliefs are unjustified, when in fact they are justified. This looks bad for reliabilism.

Notice that the claim about Brain is not that he has knowledge. He does not. Almost all his beliefs are false, and so they are not cases of knowledge.[20] But he is justified in his beliefs, just as justified as Brian. But reliabilism seems to evaluate them very differently. The same sort of thing can happen in less extreme cases. Suppose that a person's color vision processes are messed up, so that she is not reliable in forming beliefs about certain colors. But the topic just is not discussed in her presence, people do not correct her, and she has every reason to think that this process works well in her. Then she is justified in her beliefs, even though the process is not reliable.

These cases suggest that reliability is not necessary for justification. It will not help reliabilists to say that if people justifiably believe that the process they are using is reliable, then their belief is justified. This would introduce an objectionable kind of circularity into the theory.

C2. Accidental or Unknown Reliability In some cases, a person uses a reliable process but has no reason to think that it is reliable. The belief should seem to the person like a mere hunch. Goldman himself mentions two varieties of this sort of case. In one sort, the person has no reason to believe that a certain process is reliable, even though it actually is reliable. In the second sort, the person has reason to believe that the process is unreliable, even though it actually is reliable. Goldman says that the second kind of case is "worse" than the first, and he proposes a modification of his analysis to deal with this. The modification involves a change in clause (i) of his analysis. He proposes:

> i*. If S's belief in p at t results from a reliable cognitive process, and there is no reliable or conditionally reliable process available to S which, had it been used by S in addition to the process actually used, would have resulted in S's not believing p at t, then S's belief in p at t is justified.[21]

The idea behind (i*) is to add a "no defeater" condition on justification. Suppose a person forms a belief as a result of a process the person has reason to think is unreliable. The person then has available an alternative reasoning process, a process making use of this fact. If the person were to make use of this process, she would end up not keeping the original belief. Roughly, she would think: I came to believe p as a result of an unreliable process. She would then stop believing p. This is, apparently, a reliable process.[22] Thus, there is a reliable defeater process for the original belief, and this shows that it is not justified. So that is how Goldman would deal with examples in which a person uses a process that actually is reliable, but the person has reason to think that it is not reliable. Although the point is highly controversial, let us suppose that this works out satisfactorily.

Consider again cases in which a person has no idea one way or the other whether the process is reliable. In that sort of case, the person does not seem to have a defeater process for the belief. He does not have a reliable line of reasoning that would lead him to reject his belief. A widely discussed instance of this sort of example has been proposed by Laurence BonJour.

Example 5.9: Clairvoyance

Norman, under certain conditions which usually obtain, is a completely reliable clairvoyant with respect to certain kinds of subject matter. He possesses no evidence or reasons of any kind for or against the general possibility of such a cognitive power, or for or against the thesis that he possesses it. One day Norman comes to believe that the president is in New York City, though he has no evidence either for or against this belief. In fact the belief is true and results from his clairvoyant power, under circumstances in which it is completely reliable.[23]

BonJour thinks that Norman's belief is not justified even though it results from a process that is reliable and Norman has no available defeater process for it. Some philosophers regard this as a serious objection to reliabilism. Perhaps it is. However, there are some lines of response open to reliabilists. Consider what it is like for the person in BonJour's example. Apparently, the thought that the president is in New York City suddenly comes over him. Given the description of the case, he has no reason to think that such thoughts are generally true. Suppose he thought about why he had this seemingly random thought about the location of the president. He might think: "This is very odd. I have no reason to believe this. It just popped into my head, seemingly out of nowhere." This might lead him to stop having the belief. And *maybe* that sort of reasoning counts as the sort of available defeater process introduced by (i*).

It is unclear, then, whether examples like BonJour's constitute a serious problem for reliabilism. In part, that is because of the lack of clarity in the idea of an available cognitive process. There is another unclarity, however, that is potentially more troubling.

C3. Generality The discussion of the first two objections to (R*) made use of unstated assumptions about the processes involved in the formation of the beliefs in the examples.[24] For example, in the brain in a vat objection, it was assumed that the process Brian used was reliable and the one Brain used was unreliable. And there is something to that assumption. But it is also true that each of them is thinking in the same way; each is forming an analogous belief on the basis of an analogous experience. Maybe, then, they are using the same process. If they are, then, if that process is generally reliable, then (R*) implies that both are justified in their belief, and if it is not reliable, then neither is justified. Why did we think that the processes they used differed in reliability?

In the discussion of BonJour's example, we assumed that the relevant process was "clairvoyance" and that was said to be reliable. But we could also have described the process as "forming a belief in a way one has no reason to trust" and that seems to be unreliable. Why did we think that he used the reliable process rather than this unreliable one?

This may seem to work in favor of (R*), because it suggests that reliabilists can find ways to describe the processes that enable them to avoid the proposed counterexamples. However, the response hides a problem. The problem is that there are many different ways to characterize the process that is used in any case. In what has been presented here, there is no systematic way to figure out which general pattern to consider in evaluating any example. As a result, the theory is simply not spelled out well enough to evaluate. We do not know what implications it has for any example. Moreover, when we think more carefully about the various kinds of processes, problems emerge.

In the passage quoted at the beginning of this section, Goldman mentions as unreliable processes things like

P1. brief and hasty scanning

in contrast to

P2. detailed and leisurely observation.

And he says that

P3. seeing distant objects

is less reliable than

P4. seeing nearby objects.

But this will not do. If these are the processes to consider in evaluating beliefs on reliabilist standards, then the theory has plainly unsatisfactory results. It will imply that all beliefs resulting from one of those processes are equally reliable. That is, if (P1) is unreliable, then all beliefs resulting from it are unjustified. If (P2) is reliable, then all beliefs resulting from it are justified. If (P3) is less reliable than (P4), then all beliefs formed by (P3) are less justified than any beliefs formed by (P4). But none of these results is correct. By process (P1) one might come to know that there is a chair in the room, a tree on the quad, etc. These are all very well justified beliefs. One might use (P2) to come to the conclusion that a particular person is a freshman but not be justified in drawing that conclusion. Other times, detailed and leisurely observation does yield justified beliefs. By (P3) one gets to know that there's a star in a certain place in the sky, and sometimes seeing nearby things does not yield justification, as when novices identify trees. So, sometimes what results from (P4) is better justified than what results from (P3). These classifications do not work. The key fact is that each process type yields beliefs of all different levels of justification.

Here is a more systematic statement of the problem. Reliability, as reliabilists understand it, is a property of processes that happen over and over again. The specific process that causes a particular belief happens just once, but it is a kind of process, or an instance of a type of process. The specific process is said to be a "process token" and the general categories are "process types." Every token is an instance of many types. Suppose you look out the window one night and see a street light. The process that occurs is a case of forming a belief about what you see on the basis of (i) perception, (ii) vision, (iii) vision at night, (iv) vision of a bright object at night, and so on. These types can vary in reliability. For example, (iii) is less reliable than (iv). The reliabilist theory says that a particular belief is justified to the degree that its process is reliable. But there are all these different process types associated with your belief that you see a street light. Which one is the one whose reliability determines how well justified the belief is? Is your belief that you see a street light not so well justified because it is an instance of (iii), or is it better justified because it is an instance of (iv)? If reliabilism is to be a good theory, there must be a systematic way to answer questions like this. It is easy enough for a reliabilist to look at a specific case, such as this one, decide first that the belief is justified, and then say that the process is (iv) so that the theory has the right result. But some more general theory is needed.

Each belief, then, is caused by a single process that falls into many categories or types. If reliabilism is to be a good theory, it must identify in some systematic way one of these types for each belief as the one whose reliability counts in determining whether the belief is justified. Let's call the type for each token whose reliability determines how well justified it is "the relevant type" for that belief. We do not have any account yet of what the types are. Using this idea of relevant types, we can state the base clause of Goldman's reliabilist theory more clearly. It is:

i**.   If S's belief in p at t results from a belief-independent process token whose relevant type is reliable, then S's belief in p at t is justified.

(We could apply this to the revised analysis Goldman gives, but we'll ignore that complication.) And now the problem for reliabilists is to provide an account of relevant types in a way that makes the theory have plausible results.

In attempting to deal with this matter, reliabilists face a serious problem. The theory has the implication that all beliefs that result from the same process type are equally well justified. They are all as well justified as the process is reliable. But any process you can think of, at least any ordinary sort of process that you can think of, will produce some justified and some unjustified beliefs.

To support this claim, consider another example. Suppose a baseball umpire is calling balls and strikes. There are clear-cut calls and tough calls. If the umpire uses the same process in all cases, then all his beliefs about the pitches are equally justified. This seems like a bad result, because sometimes it is clear whether the pitch is a strike and sometimes it is not. For reliabilism to work, there must be some way to distinguish the process used in clear cases from the process used in unclear cases.

Another example may make the problem a little clearer. Suppose a person looks at the leaves of a tree and, on the basis of their shape, correctly believes that the tree is a maple. We might say the process type that occurs there is the "maple leaf shape to maple tree" process, i.e., the process whereby the characteristic maple leaf shape leads to the maple tree belief. This process is very reliable—whenever one thinks a tree is a maple tree on the basis of that shape, one is right. No other leaves look that way. So reliabilism seems to say that the person is justified in believing that the tree is a maple. But is the process used to form the maple belief the same as the process the person uses to form beliefs about oaks and pines, i.e., a tree identifying process? Of course tree identification is just a special case of plant identification, so possibly the process in question is really the more general process of plant identification. There are, then, a great many processes and it is entirely unclear which ones we are to use in assessing a belief for reliability and justification.

As you think about these examples, you should start to see that critics and defenders of reliabilism are just making up, for each case, a description of the process that gets them the result they want. There is no general theory here.

The generality problem is currently an unsolved problem for reliabilists. Some philosophers think that there are good replies, and it is surely not possible to prove otherwise.[25] But lacking a good solution, there is reason to be dubious about the merits of this theory.

D. Conclusion on Reliabilism

Any conclusions drawn about reliabilism are bound to be controversial. Some philosophers believe that objections such as the brain in a vat objection show a fundamental flaw in reliabilism. It is simply not the case, these philosophers contend, that reliability is necessary for justification. Reliabilists are not without possible responses, however. Notice that the objection relies on the assumption that Brain uses an unreliable process in forming his beliefs, because his beliefs are largely false. However, one need not evaluate the reliability of a process in this way. Perhaps the process Brain uses counts as reliable, because it is the same as the process we use, and our process is reliable.[26] Furthermore, any assessment of the implications of reliabilism for specific cases rests on some solution to the generality problem, and this too is a matter of ongoing controversy. It is safe to say, at the very least, that reliabilists have difficult problems to solve.

A final point deserves mention. In Chapter 3 we discussed *The Same Evidence Principle*. Reliabilism seems to be inconsistent with this principle, although puzzles about how processes are identified and reliability is measured make this less than completely clear. It seems clear that a process that is reliable in one situation may be unreliable in another. If that is indeed possible, then reliabilism will imply that two believers who are in the same internal state, that is, two people who believe the same thing for the same reasons, may have beliefs that differ in justification. It is this implication of reliabilism that the brain in a vat example exploits. Some philosophers think that any theory of justification that violates *The Same Evidence Principle* must be wrong. But reliabilists are apt to think that allegiance to this principle is a mistake.

Some reliabilists think that an advantage of their theory emerges in connection with skepticism. We will turn to this topic briefly in Chapter 7.

IV. PROPER FUNCTION

A. The General Idea

We turn next to a final nonevidentialist theory. The general idea of this theory is that a belief is justified when it results from the proper functioning of the believer's cognitive system. To understand the significance of this idea, it will be helpful to first consider something unrelated to cognition and belief formation. For example, consider the heart. It is reasonable to say that there is a way that a human being's heart is "supposed" to function. It should beat at a rate within some range, it should pump blood around the body in a way that meets the body's needs, and so on. There is no need to suppose that the proper function of the heart is the result of someone deciding what it is supposed to do. It is, instead, a biological fact about its role in maintaining life. Of course, some theists will say that the proper function of the heart really is the result of intentional design, but we need not make that assumption here. Whether the proper function of the heart is determined by God or by "Mother Nature" is not crucial for now. What is crucial is that there is such thing as a properly functioning heart.

The same idea of proper function carries over to cognition as well. There is a way human cognitive systems are "supposed" to function. This is not to say that we are supposed to believe specific propositions. It is just to say that we are supposed to go about forming beliefs in certain ways. We are designed to use perception and memory. We are designed to make certain sorts of inferences. Which specific things we believe will depend upon the specifics of our own circumstances. Of course, sometimes our systems will not work quite right, just as one's heart may not always work properly. The proper function theory holds that when one's cognitive system produces a belief, that belief is justified if and only if the system has functioned properly in producing it.

Proper function is plausibly thought to be a complex descriptive property of a system. Hence, if justification can be explained in terms of it, then we will have an account of the descriptive conditions under which a belief has the evaluative property of being justified. Whereas reliabilism held that justification depended upon the reliability of the process that produced the belief, proper function theory holds that it depends upon the system functioning properly.

B. Formulating Proper Function Theory: Plantinga's Theory

A leading defender of the proper function theory is Alvin Plantinga. He has written extensively on the topic and the following discussion will only scratch the surface of his views. Plantinga formulates his theory clearly and concisely in the following passage:

> . . . a belief has warrant for me only if (1) it has been produced in me by cognitive faculties that are working properly (functioning as they ought to, subject to no cognitive dysfunction) in a cognitive environment that is appropriate for my kinds of cognitive faculties, (2) the segment of the design plan governing the production of that belief is aimed at the production of true beliefs, and (3) there is a high statistical probability that a belief produced under those conditions will be true.[27]

Several preliminary comments are in order.

1)   Plantinga talks about "warrant" rather than "justification" in the passage quoted. We will take these terms to be equivalent, although Plantinga may have been interested in analyzing a concept somewhat different from justification.

Perhaps it would be best to say that we are adapting Plantinga's ideas to a theory of justification.

2)   In the passage quoted here Plantinga says that a belief has warrant "only if" the conditions he mentions are satisfied. He does not say that the conditions are sufficient for warrant. But elsewhere he does say that they are sufficient.[28]

3)   Plantinga includes in clause (1) of his account the idea that the system must be in an environment that is "appropriate" or suitable for that system. An example will illustrate why. Suppose a human heart were removed from a person and put in an eagle. Most likely, things would not work out very well. But it is hard to say how a human heart is supposed to work in that setting. It is not designed to be there at all. It would be somewhat odd to say that it malfunctioned. Similarly, according to Plantinga's theory, the human cognitive system is designed to work in certain sorts of environments. It yields justified beliefs when it functions properly in those environments (provided the other conditions are satisfied as well). It does not yield justified beliefs elsewhere. In particular, perhaps, it is not designed to work in brains in vats or in other radically nonstandard environments.

4)   Plantinga adds in his clause (2) the requirement that "the segment of the design plan governing the production of that belief is aimed at the production of true beliefs." This raises difficult issues, some of which will come up briefly in the critical discussion of the theory. The idea behind this requirement is as follows: we can assume that our cognitive system is supposed to function in a way that best enables us to survive or, perhaps, best increases the chances that our genes will be passed on. However exactly we understand this, it seems clear that we are not designed to form only epistemically reasonable beliefs. To mention one example, it may be entirely natural—part of our design plan—to have favorable beliefs about our children. A kind of bias might be built in. But beliefs resulting from that sort of feature are not always epistemically justified. Another example involves optimism. We might be designed to be somewhat overly optimistic in some circumstances. Such beliefs are not the result of malfunction, but they are not epistemically justified. Plantinga's idea is to separate the different parts of our system into those that are aimed at getting us true beliefs about the world around us and the parts that have a different aim. Justification results only from the parts aimed at the truth.[29]

5)   Very roughly, the final condition in Plantinga's account is a kind of general reliability condition. Suppose someone were actually in the situation of designing a cognitive agent. If you like, imagine someone designing a robot and assume that the robot has beliefs about the world it is in. Suppose further that the designer is totally inept and builds into the robot a system that uniformly gets things wrong. The robot then might form beliefs as it was designed to—it is functioning properly—but it is not getting anything right. Intuitively, such a poorly designed robot does not have justified beliefs, even though clauses (1) and (2) of Plantinga's account are satisfied. Clause (3) is supposed to deal with this sort of case.

We can summarize the proper function theory in the following brief formulation:

PF.   S's belief in p is justified iff (i) S's belief in p results from the proper functioning of S's cognitive system in a suitable environment, (ii) the segment of the system that produced the belief is aimed at the truth, and (iii) the overall system usually produces true beliefs when it is in a suitable environment.

Like reliabilism, the proper function theory can plausibly address one of the issues that caused trouble for modest foundationalism. Modest foundationalists were hard-pressed to explain exactly why perceptual beliefs were justified. The theory ended up, in our discussion, making use of the idea that some beliefs are "properly based" on experience. The proper function theory can say instead that we are designed to form these beliefs on the basis of our experiences. That is, when we see something red, we are designed to believe that there is something red before us. Similarly for the other beliefs.

Unlike coherentism, the proper function theory gives experiences a suitable role in the account of justification. As just noted, some beliefs are responses to experiences, and when the responses are as they are designed to be, the beliefs are justified.

Plantinga's theory is original and interesting, but not without problems. The next section examines some of them.

C. Objections to the Proper Function Theory

C1. Accidental Reliability One of the problems for reliabilism, given an intuitive account of relevant types, is the accidental reliability problem. The problem arises because a belief-forming process can be accidentally reliable. The beliefs it produces are not justified, yet reliabilism seems to imply that they are. Plantinga himself offers just this sort of objection to reliabilism. He favors colorful examples, and here is one he presents:

Example 5.10:   Cosmic Rays

[S]uppose I am struck by a burst of cosmic rays, resulting in the following unfortunate malfunction. Whenever I hear the word "prime" in any context, I form a belief, with respect to a randomly chosen natural number less than 100,000, that it is not prime. So you say "Pacific Palisades is prime residential area" or "Prime ribs is my favorite" . . . ; I form a belief, with respect to a randomly selected natural number between 1 and 100,000 that it is not prime. The process or mechanism in question is indeed reliable (given the vast preponderance of non-primes . . .) but my belief—that, say, 41 is not prime—has little or no positive epistemic status. The problem isn't simply that the belief is false; the same goes for my (true) belief that 631 is not prime, if it is formed in this fashion. So reliable belief formation is not sufficient for positive epistemic status.[30]

Consider how Plantinga's theory deals with this example. One might think that the proper function requirement rules out beliefs produced in this way from being warranted. Surely we are not designed to reason that way. But Plantinga's theory is supposed to cover the general idea of justification, and thus it is supposed to apply to other beings in possible examples as well. (The example Plantinga used against reliabilism is, obviously, merely possible as well.) Suppose, then, a less than fully competent designer of cognitive systems, or one suffering from a sort of serious confusion, designs a robot that generally has reasonable and accurate beliefs, but also has built into the system an unusual segment that works exactly like the one Plantinga describes in his example. The robot forms a belief in just the way Plantinga describes. The belief does result from the proper function of the system in its intended environment, it is aimed at the truth, and the system is generally reliable. It looks as if this is just as much a problem for (PF) as it is for reliabilism. Of course, the example involves mixed-up designers of cognitive systems and is therefore somewhat unrealistic. But that does not count against it.

C2. Proper Function and Good Function There is a difference between something functioning as it was designed to function and its functioning well. A poorly designed system might function as designed yet not function very well. This is most clearly seen when considering things that have been designed by conscious agents. Suppose some people have produced an underpowered car. They see that it accelerates very slowly. They might say, on the one hand:

> The car is functioning as it was designed to. There are no malfunctions. It is doing exactly what it is supposed to (given the way it was designed).

But on the other hand, they might also say:

> That car does not work very well. It accelerates too slowly.

In other words, it functions properly (as designed) but not well.

If there is in fact a distinction between proper function and good function, then there is trouble for the proper function theory of epistemic justification. Whether a system forms justified beliefs when it functions properly depends upon whether the system is well designed. If it is a well-designed system, then justified beliefs will result from proper function. But if it is not well designed, then there can be a divergence. It will therefore be useful to consider a system that is not well designed.

Imagine a situation in which you form a certain belief on the basis of some evidence. You draw an inference, perhaps automatically. A critic then points out that your conclusion is not justified because it is not really well supported by your premises. Suppose you replied, "Well, it might be better if we formed beliefs differently. But we don't. That's how we reason. Our system is designed that way. So, my belief is justified." It might be true that you are not malfunctioning when you draw the bad inference, just as the poorly designed car is not malfunctioning when it accelerates slowly. Perhaps that *is* the way we form beliefs. But it does not follow that your belief is a justified one. It does not follow that this is good functioning. To turn this sort of case into an objection to Plantinga's theory we need only add that the specific bad inference is part of a generally reliable system. So let us add that assumption.

The objection to (PF) is that it is an entirely contingent matter whether we have justified beliefs when our system functions properly. If we are entirely well designed, then perhaps we do have justified beliefs whenever we function properly. But functioning as designed is not what makes for justification. Had our system been not so well designed, then functioning as designed would not yield justified beliefs, even if the general reliability condition is satisfied.

This point leads to a related objection. Suppose that there is a flaw in our design, one that leads us to form mistaken beliefs in certain situations. Suppose further that some people are able to overcome those flaws and do better than they are designed to do. For example, there is some reason to think that people are not very well designed to do certain sorts of probabilistic reasoning. We use various shortcuts and simplifications that are convenient but not quite right.[31] But suppose some people manage to do better than the design calls for; they figure out a way to improve upon the built-in tendencies. If proper functioning is functioning as designed, then the person who improves upon the design is not functioning as designed. The theory then has the implausible implication that his beliefs are not justified.

One might be inclined to say that the person who improves upon the design is functioning properly. But to say this one must give the word "proper" an interpretation other than its intended one. One possibility would be to say that a cognitive system is functioning properly when it forms beliefs that are supported by the evidence available to the system. But to say this, of course, is to return to an evidentialist theory. The proper function theory was designed to be a rival to evidentialism, not a terminological variant of it. This, then, seems to be an unpromising approach.

No doubt defenders of the proper function theory could produce responses to these objections that are, at the very least, worthy of consideration. But it is fair to say that significant challenges to the theory have been raised.[32]

D. Conclusions on the Proper Function Theory

Oversimplifying significantly, the proper function theory holds that a belief is justified provided it results from the proper functioning of the cognitive system of the believer, where this is taken to be functioning the way the system was designed to function, the way it is supposed to function. Some of the conclusions drawn about the theory in this section are

1)   The theory seems to have some advantages over evidentialist theories in its account of basic beliefs.[33]

2)   A variation of an example Plantinga uses to criticize reliabilism seems to apply to his own theory.

3)   There is a difference between functioning as designed and functioning well. Proper function theory makes use of the former notion in defining justification. If we focus only on well-designed beings, then functioning as designed and functioning well will coincide. But where a being is not well designed, where its proper function is not so good, the theory has the incorrect implication that it forms justified beliefs when it conforms to this bad design. The general reliability condition that is included in the theory does not solve this problem.

V. CONCLUSIONS

In this chapter we have examined four nonevidentialist accounts of justification and knowledge. Ignoring details, the theories can be summarized as follows:

1.   The causal theory holds that a true belief is a case of knowledge when the fact the belief is about is causally connected to the belief in a suitable way.
2.   The tracking theory holds that a person has knowledge of a particular proposition when the person's beliefs about that proposition track its truth (provided the person uses the same method of belief formation).
3.   Reliabilism holds that a belief is justified provided it results from a belief-forming process that reliably leads to true beliefs.
4.   The proper function theory holds that a belief is justified provided it results from the proper function of the believer's cognitive system.

Each of these theories runs into serious difficulties. There can be knowledge without causal connections and there can be causal connections without knowledge. People can have knowledge without being truth trackers, and they can be truth trackers without having knowledge. Justified beliefs can result from generally unreliable processes, and reliable processes can yield unjustified beliefs (given suitable assumptions about which processes are relevant). And properly functioning cognitive systems can have unjustified beliefs, while systems that are not functioning properly can have justified beliefs.

There are, of course, ways to modify and improve upon the theories considered in this chapter. It is possible that versions of the theories could be developed that escape the problems mentioned. However, it is plausible to think that what goes wrong with these theories is that they understate the role of reasons, justification, and evidence in the account of knowledge. If that is the case, then modest foundationalism emerges as the most plausible of the theories presented here.

Each of the theories discussed in this chapter, as well as modest foundationalism, seems to provide support for *The Standard View*. Causal theorists will say that the beliefs *The Standard View* identifies as knowledge are beliefs that have the right sorts of causal connections to the facts they are about. Tracking theorists could contend that we track the truth of those propositions. Reliabilists will claim that our beliefs in those propositions are caused by reliable processes, and proper function theorists will claim that the beliefs result from the proper function of our cognitive systems. As we saw in Chapter 4, modest foundationalists will say that our basic beliefs are proper responses to our experiences, and the rest of what we know (according to *The Standard View*) follows from those justified basic beliefs by good inferences.

All these views, therefore, seem to lend some support to *The Standard View*. In the chapters to follow we will examine a series of objections to *The Standard View*. These objections will generally be formulated to apply most directly to modest foundationalism. However, in at least some cases, the objections can be reformulated so that they apply given one of these other views. We turn next to these objections.

ENDNOTES

1. Another theory of this sort, the relevant alternatives theory, will be discussed at the end of Chapter 7.
2. Alvin Goldman, "A Causal Theory of Knowing," *Journal of Philosophy* 64 (1967): 357–72. See also David Armstrong, *Belief, Truth and Knowledge* (London: Cambridge University Press, 1973).
3. "A Causal Theory of Knowing," p. 372.
4. "A Causal Theory of Knowing," p. 369.
5. "A Causal Theory of Knowing," pp. 369–70.
6. Goldman was aware of this problem and presented a solution to it in "A Causal Theory of Knowing," pp. 368–69. We will not take up the adequacy of that response here.
7. Bryan Skyrms proposes an example such as this one in "The Explication of 'X knows that p'," *The Journal of Philosophy* 64 (1967): 373–89.
8. Goldman himself presents an example similar to this one in "Discrimination and Perceptual Knowledge," *Journal of Philosophy* 73 (1976): 771–91, Section II.
9. Robert Nozick, *Philosophical Explanation* (Cambridge, MA: Harvard University Press, 1981), Chapter 3.
10. Some details of Nozick's formulations have been modified here in order to avoid unnecessary complications.
11. *Philosophical Explanations*, p. 178
12. Nozick himself presents this example (*Philosophical Explanations*, p. 179). He goes on to modify the theory in a way to be discussed below.
13. It is not clear that this modification deals with a different objection. It may be that you can be a truth tracker without having knowledge. If I arrange things so that your guesses about some topic are always right, your beliefs may track the truth. If you don't have any feedback on this—you don't realize that your guesses are right—then you are truth tracker but lack knowledge.
14. *Philosophical Explanations*, p. 179.
15. It may be true that using this method she will never think that there is a mugging when there actually is not one. She'll only go wrong in the other direction: She might think that there is no mugging when there actually is one. But the tracking theory requires that she get it right both ways.
16. Kripke, unpublished papers.
17. Alvin Goldman, "What is Justified Belief?" in G. S. Pappas, ed., *Justification and Knowledge* (Dordrecht: D. Reidel, 1979), pp. 1–23.

18. Stewart Cohen raises this objection in "Justification and Truth," *Philosophical Studies* 46: 279–95. See especially pp. 281f. See also Richard Foley, "What's Wrong with Reliabilism?" *Monist* 68 (1985): 188–202.
19. An assumption here is that the processes by which Brian forms the simple beliefs about the world around him are belief-independent processes covered by clause (i) of R*.
20. Depending upon the details of the example, it may turn out that some of Brain's external world beliefs are true. For example, Brain may be fed a "tree experience" and he may think that there is a tree nearby. If in fact there is a tree nearby, Brain's belief will be true. Brain is in this example the victim of a Gettier-like case.
21. "What is Justified Belief?" p. 20.
22. There's a hard puzzle here. How do you measure the reliability of a process that results in suspension of judgment?
23. Laurence BonJour, *The Structure of Empirical Knowledge* (Cambridge: Harvard University Press, 1985), p. 41.
24. The issue raised here is discussed in greater detail in Richard Feldman, "Reliability and Justification," *Monist* 68 (1985): 159–74.
25. For a defense of reliabilism from the objection raised here, see William Alston, "How to Think About Reliability," *Philosophical Topics* (Spring 1995): 1–29. And for a reply to Alston, see Earl Conee and Richard Feldman, "The Generality Problem for Reliabilism," *Philosophical Studies* 89 (1998): 1–29.
26. For discussion of this issue, see Ernest Sosa, *Virtue Epistemology*, Chapter 7, in *Blackwell Great Debates: Epistemology: Internalism Versus Externalism* (forthcoming).
27. Alvin Plantinga, *Warrant and Proper Function* (New York: Oxford University Press, 1993), p. 59.
28. *Warrant and Proper Function*, pp. 22–23, 267.
29. It is possible that this leads to a problem for the proper function theory analogous to the generality problem that reliabilism faces. Plantinga argues otherwise. See *Warrant and Proper Function*, pp. 35–36.
30. Alvin Plantinga, *Warrant: The Current Debate* (New York: Oxford University Press, 1993), p. 265.
31. We will consider some related issues in Chapter 8.
32. For further discussion of the theory, see Jon Kvanvig, ed., *Warrant in Contemporary Epistemology: Essays in Honor of Plantinga's Theory of Knowledge* (Lanham, MD: Rowman & Littlefield, 1996).
33. It is worth considering how it compares to modest foundationalism with respect to nonbasic beliefs and the problems of skepticism to be covered in Chapter 7.

CHAPTER SIX

Skepticism (I)

We turn now to the first of the alternatives to *The Standard View* described in Chapter 1: *The Skeptical View*. Going back as least as far as the times of the ancient Greeks, philosophers have devoted a great deal of thought to arguments about *skepticism*, the view that we do not, or cannot, have knowledge. While it is unlikely that most philosophers accept the arguments for general skepticism, many do find the arguments intriguing. Some nonskeptics find them at least troubling, calling into serious question the claims to knowledge found in *The Standard View*. Other nonskeptics are confident that we do know about as much as *The Standard View* says we do but still find the arguments for skepticism challenging. For this second group, it is clear that you know such things as that you are reading a book, that you recently ate dinner, that you saw a movie last night, and that there is a maple tree outside your window. However, when they examine some of the arguments for skepticism, they find that it is no easy task to figure out what is wrong with them. For them, the challenge of skepticism is to identify the flaws in the arguments. In examining these arguments, we will be trying to answer (Q4) from Chapter 1, which asked whether there were any good responses to the arguments of the skeptics.

The issue raised by skepticism is largely about whether the reasons we have for our ordinary beliefs are good enough to yield knowledge. This question may be more compelling for philosophers who accept evidentialist theories of justification than for those who accept nonevidentialist theories. If knowledge and justification require causal connections, or truth tracking, or reliability, or proper function rather than evidence or good reasons, then we can have knowledge and justification even if our reasons for our beliefs are not so good. The arguments for skepticism to be considered here will largely (though perhaps not entirely) be rejected by defenders of these nonevidentialist theories on the grounds that they depend on (what they regard as) mistaken views about what is required for knowledge. Some defenders of nonevidentialist theories may think that it is a virtue of their theory that it thus avoids the problem of skepticism. On the other hand, critics of those theories are apt to think that they are defective because they evade, rather than solve, the problem of skepticism.[1]

In any case, even those who accept nonevidentialist theories may nevertheless have reason to think about the merits of skeptical arguments. After all, the arguments raise difficult questions about the quality of our reasons for our ordinary beliefs. This is in itself of interest, regardless of the implications the answer has concerning knowledge. It would be disturbing to learn that our reasons are not so good, even if good reasons are not needed for knowledge.

I. VARIETIES OF SKEPTICISM

A. Global v. Limited Skepticism

Versions of skepticism differ in the scope or range of things over which they deny knowledge. *Global skepticism* holds that no one knows anything at all. It is universal in scope. In contrast, *limited skepticism* denies knowledge in certain areas or topics. Thus, someone who is a skeptic with regard to knowledge of the future holds that no one ever knows anything about the future. Someone who is a skeptic about religion holds that no one ever knows anything about religious matters.

Virtually everyone is some sort of limited skeptic. That is, each of us thinks that there is some class of propositions such that no one knows the truth about the propositions in that class. Consider, for example, propositions describing, for each large desert on earth, the exact number of grains of sand in it. One of these propositions has the form "the Sahara has exactly n grains of sand," another has the form "the Mojave has exactly x grains of sand," and so on. Almost everyone would agree that no one knows any of these propositions to be true. Thus, almost everyone is a "desert skeptic." There are numerous other classes of propositions that we can agree have no members that we know to be true. Hence, we all agree that some forms of limited skepticism are true.

Other versions of limited skepticism raise more difficult issues. Some philosophers have argued that we do not know any perceptual propositions to be true or that we do not know anything on the basis of memory. These sorts of limited skepticism challenge *The Standard View* in a significant way. We will turn to them shortly.

B. The Strength of Skeptical Claims

Versions of skepticism differ in the strength of the claim they make. We will use skepticism about the future to illustrate the point. Skepticism about the future denies knowledge of the future. In its strongest form, skepticism about the future is the thesis that knowledge of the future is impossible:

SF1.   It is impossible for anyone to know anything about the future.

(SF1) is analogous to claims such as

1. It is impossible for any person to construct a cubical box with 9 sides.
2. It is impossible for any person to be a married bachelor.

The reason (1) is true is that it is impossible for there to be box that is both cubical and has 9 sides. It is not as if a carpenter more clever and resourceful than any actual person could make such a box. Such boxes are themselves not among the things that there could be. Hence, no one can construct one. Similarly, the reason (2) is true is that it is impossible for there to be a married bachelor. It is not as if a person could be a married bachelor simply by trying harder or being more resourceful. A bachelor is, by definition, not married. There is nothing anyone can do about that. The analogous claim about knowledge is that knowledge of the future is somehow a contradictory concept, and so there cannot be any such knowledge. But, on this alternative, this is not any particular weakness of people. It is not as if some smarter sort of being could have knowledge of the future.[2]

A second form of skepticism about the future is a view about the capacities of actual people:

SF2.   No one is able to know anything about the future.

(SF2) is comparable to claims such as

3.   No one is able to run a mile in 2 minutes.

(3) is true, but not because there is a contradiction involved in the concept of people running a mile that fast. It is just that as a matter of fact, people do not have that ability and no amount of training is going to get anyone to do it. It is beyond their capacities. Similarly, (SF2) says that knowledge of the future is beyond our capacities.

The least extreme form of skepticism merely says that we lack knowledge, leaving open the possibility that we can have knowledge. Applied to knowledge of the future, it is the thesis that

SF3.   No one does know anything about the future.

Most of the arguments about skepticism are best interpreted as arguments about our capacities, and thus about versions of skepticism like (SF2). The hard questions concern arguments about some kinds of local skepticism concerning our capacities. As we will soon see, it is not so hard to find reasons to think that people are not able to know things, or at least not able to know much about the world around them.

II. WHAT SKEPTICS CLAIM

This section will review two potential misunderstandings of *The Skeptical View*.

A. Truths We Do Not Know

People are sometimes said to be skeptical about the existence of life on other planets, but skepticism of this sort has little to do with the epistemological skepticism under discussion here. People who are skeptical about life on other planets doubt that there is life on other planets. So, of course, they doubt that anyone knows that there is life on other planets. Their fundamental claim, however, is not about our lack of knowledge. Their fundamental claim is about what exists in the universe. They might even think that if there were life on other planets, we could and would know it. The same sort of point can arise in a more puzzling case.

Suppose you think that we cannot have knowledge about ethical matters: We cannot know what is right and wrong. This would be a kind of ethical skepticism. There are two very different versions of ethical skepticism.

ES1.   There are ethical truths, but we cannot know what they are.

According to (ES1), there are facts about what is right and what is wrong, but they are beyond the limits of our modest cognitive powers. You might think that knowing what is right or wrong requires knowing the mind of God and that people cannot know this. Or you might think that to really know what is right or wrong you would have to know the consequences of actions out into the indefinite future, something also beyond our limited abilities.

A second kind of ethical skepticism holds that

ES2.   There are no ethical truths, so we cannot know any facts about ethics.

You might hold (ES2) because you think that ethical matters are matters of taste and preference. When we say that something is right or good, we are not asserting that it has some particular quality. Instead, we are expressing our approval of that thing. To say, "it was good that she contributed her old furniture to a charity", is to say something like "Hooray for her. She contributed her old furniture to a charity." And to say, "it was wrong for him to steal the furniture from the charity", is another way of saying "Boo for him. He stole furniture from a charity". On this view, ethical talk is simply an expression of attitudes. Compare cheering and booing at a baseball game. There are facts about the game that one might know or not know. But when your team wins and you cheer, cheering itself does not report some fact. It just expresses your attitude about what has happened.

(ES2) might be described as skepticism (or doubt) about the existence of ethical truths. It is analogous to "skepticism" about the existence of life on other planets. It is not a view about any epistemological issue. If there are no facts of a certain sort, then, obviously, we cannot know facts of that sort. The debate about this is *not* fundamentally a debate about an epistemological matter.

In contrast, (ES1) really is an epistemological thesis. It holds that our ways of forming beliefs about ethical matters cannot yield knowledge. We might argue, partly on epistemological grounds, that these skeptics are mistaken about what it takes to have knowledge or about the merits of our reasons for ethical judgments. The key point to grasp is that defenders of (ES1) think that there are facts of which we are ignorant. That is the sort of skepticism under discussion here.

We are mainly interested in skeptical views analogous to (ES1). These are views that hold there are truths in some domain, but we cannot or do not know what they are. We are interested in skeptics who contend that there are facts about the past, or the future, or the world around us, but, for one reason or another, we cannot know what those facts are. If you like, you can say that skeptics are skeptical about the existence of knowledge. But they are not skeptical about the existence of facts about the world. They contend that we do not or cannot know what they are. Thus, *The Skeptical View* is that there are truths, but we are unable to know what they are.

B. Skepticism, Truth, and Justification

Skeptics think that we cannot have knowledge (about some topic or other). If they are right, then there must be some condition for knowledge that is not satisfied in the relevant cases. It is easy to become confused about which condition that is. In this section, we will clarify this issue by examining a simple argument for skepticism. Although this argument for skepticism fails, discussion of it will make clear just what it is about knowledge that skeptics are (or should be) saying.

People sometimes say things like this:

> If you say that the ancients didn't know that the earth was flat because they were wrong about that, then you must also say that we don't know that the earth is (approximately) round, because we might be wrong about that.

This is an argument about arguments. The idea is that if one argument—one about the ancients—is a good argument, then so is another argument—one about us. The argument about the ancients is as follows:

Argument 6.1:   The Ancients on the Shape of the Earth

    1-1.   The ancients' belief that the earth was flat was false.

    1-2.   Therefore, the ancients did not know that the earth was flat. (1-1)

The allegedly analogous argument about us is:

Argument 6.2:   The Moderns on the Shape of the Earth

    2-1.   Our belief that the earth is round might be false.

    2-2.   Therefore, we do not know that the earth is round. (2-1)

The argument about these two arguments can be displayed this way:

Argument 6.3:   The Ancients and Us
    3-1.   If Argument 6.1 is sound, then Argument 6.2 is sound.
    3-2.   Argument 6.1 is sound.

    3-3.   Therefore, Argument 6.2 is sound. (3-1), (3-2)

The idea behind (3-1) is just that the two arguments are on a par: If one is a good argument, then so is the other. And (3-2) seems clearly right—the ancients were mistaken, so they surely did not have knowledge. But Argument 6.3 is unsound. (3-1) is false. The two arguments are not on a par. To see why, notice what the unstated assumption of Argument 6.1 is:

    1-1½.   If S's belief in p is false, then S does not know p.

This premise depends upon the fact that one of the conditions for knowledge is truth. If knowledge does require truth, as it surely does, then (1–1½) is true. Given this, and the fact that the ancients were wrong about the shape of the earth, Argument 6.1 is a good one.

    Now consider Argument 6.2. Notice that (2-1) does not say that we *are* wrong about the shape of the earth. Rather, it says that we *might* be wrong. To get from (2-1) to the conclusion of Argument 6.2, we need a different assumption, namely:

    2-1½.   If S's belief in p might be false, then S does not know p.

Notice the difference between these two premises

    1-1½.   If S's belief in p *is* false, then S does not know p.
    2-1½.   If S's belief in p *might be* false, then S does not know p.

These assumptions differ significantly. Premise (2-1½) does not say that there is no knowledge when the truth condition is not satisfied. It says that there is no knowledge when the truth condition *might not* be satisfied. This is enough to enable us to see that Argument 6.2 is not on a par with Argument 6.1. We can reject (3-1) of the main argument.

    You might think that Argument 6.2 is still a good argument. You might think that even if (2-1½) is different from (1-1½), it is still a reasonable premise. The idea that you do not have knowledge if you might be wrong does have some plausibility. But this should make you see that skepticism is not about whether we satisfy the truth condition for knowledge. Skeptics are not saying that our ordinary beliefs are false. If skeptics wanted to say that we failed to satisfy the truth condition, they would have to make claims about what is actually true. For example, if they wanted to argue that we do not know that the earth is approximately round on the grounds that our belief is false, they would have to say that the earth is not approximately round. But skeptics typically want to avoid making claims like that. They would say they just do not know what shape it is.

This leads us to a very important conclusion: Skeptics are not saying that we lack knowledge because our beliefs are uniformly false. Instead, what they are saying is that our beliefs might be false, and this shows that we are not well-enough justified in our beliefs to have knowledge. In the next section we will examine in detail several arguments intended to support skepticism.[3]

III. FOUR ARGUMENTS FOR SKEPTICISM

Almost all arguments for skepticism make reference to seemingly ridiculous possibilities—we are being deceived by an evil demon, life is just a dream, we are brains in vats. You might propose psychoanalysis, rather than philosophical reflection, for anyone who worries about these possibilities. However, advocates of *The Skeptical View* do not suffer from paranoid delusions. They think that these possibilities help us to see something about the nature of our evidence and provide the basis for strong reasons to think that *The Standard View* is mistaken. We will formulate four of their arguments in this section.

A. The Possibility of Error Argument

Consider the following passage from Descartes's *Meditations.*

> At the same time I must remember that I am a man, and that consequently I am in the habit of sleeping, and in my dreams representing to myself the same things or sometimes even less probable things, than do those who are insane in their waking moments . . . At this moment it does indeed seem to me that it is with eyes awake that I am looking at this paper; that this head which I move is not asleep, that it is deliberately and of set purpose that I extend my hand and perceive it; what happens in sleep does not appear so clear nor so distinct as does all this. But in thinking over this I remind myself that on many occasions I have in sleep been deceived by similar illusions, and in dwelling carefully on this reflection I see so manifestly that there are no certain indications by which we may clearly distinguish wakefulness from sleep that I am lost in astonishment.[4]

In this passage Descartes raises the possibility that he is dreaming. Elsewhere he mentions the possibility of being deceived by an evil demon who causes him to have the sensory experiences he has. The contemporary analogue of this is the possibility of being a mere brain in a vat of liquid—a skeptic tank—connected to a computer that is sending electrical impulses that cause impressions as if there is a world around you. The world you think you live in might be entirely artificial. For almost anything about the world that you believe, it is possible that you are mistaken because you are the victim of some such illusion or deception. This provides the basis for *The Possibility of Error Argument.*

> *Argument 6.4:   The Possibility of Error Argument*
>
> > 4-1.   For (almost) any belief any person has about the external world, that belief could be mistaken.

4-2.   If a belief could be mistaken, then it is not a case of knowledge.

4-3.   Therefore, (almost) any belief any person has about the external world is not knowledge (i.e, no one knows anything, or more than very little, about the external world). (4-1), (4-2)

This argument is about "almost" any belief, not strictly all beliefs. The reason for this is that some beliefs are exempt from the possibility of illusion or deception. "I exist" is the most famous example, and it appears in Descartes's famous saying, "*Cogito ergo sum*" ("I think, therefore I am"). The idea is that if Descartes, or you, are around to mistakenly think things—to dream, to be deceived by the demon or the computer—then Descartes, or you, must at least exist. Nonexistent things cannot dream or make mistakes. So your belief that you exist could not be mistaken.

Some people think even more is exempt from the possibility of error. Perhaps simple mathematical beliefs are exempt from this sort of error. Cartesian foundationalists think that beliefs about the contents of one's own mind are exempt from the skeptical worries provoked by this argument. Whatever exactly is left out by the "almost" in (4-1), a lot is included. The lack of "certain indications" to distinguish dreams from reality, or an evil demon's deceptions from reality, show that we could be mistaken about an awful lot, including much of what *The Standard View* says that we know. It seems, then, that (4-1) is clearly true, even though there is some question about exactly what falls under it. All external-world beliefs are included in the "almost." So, this argument is designed to support external-world skepticism. And that is skepticism enough to worry about.

The key premise of this argument is (4-2). The idea behind it seems to be that if you could be mistaken about something, then you are not justified in believing it and thus do not have knowledge. We will discuss this premise after stating the other arguments.

B. The Indistinguishability Argument

The skeptical scenarios involving dreams, evil demons, brains in vats, and the like reveal the possibility that things could seem just as they actually do while external things vary greatly. In other words, the world would seem to a brain in a vat just as it seems to an ordinary person in the ordinary world (a brain in a head). Somewhat more mundane and realistic examples reveal similar possibilities.

Example 6.1:   The Investigation[5]

Detective Jones is investigating a crime. She has perfectly comparable evidence that two people, Black and White, are innocent of the crime. This is very compelling evidence, the sort of evidence *The Standard View* says is adequate for knowledge. But it is not absolutely conclusive evidence—there is a possibility of error. In spite of this evidence, White actually is guilty. White has paid off witnesses to lie in his behalf and fabricated additional evidence to indicate his innocence.

Consider:

>   a.   Black is innocent.
>   b.   White is innocent.

From Jones's perspective, (a) and (b) are perfectly on a par. Each seems very clearly true, and not because of any bias or mistake on her part. She has excellent reasons to think that they are true. (If it helps, suppose that she has good reason to think that some third person is guilty.) According to an indistinguishability principle, it would be absurd to say that she has knowledge in one case but not the other. The idea is that cases of knowledge must seem different from cases of nonknowledge. In other words, a case in which you do know something cannot be "introspectively indistinguishable" from a case in which you do not know something. This principle implies that either Jones knows both (a) and (b) or she knows neither (a) nor (b). But since (b) is not true, she definitely does not know (b), so she does not know (a) either.

Two main ideas are used in this argument. One is the idea of *fallible evidence*. Fallible evidence for p is evidence that is logically compatible with the falsity of p. In the example, because it is possible for White to be guilty in spite of Jones's evidence, it follows that her evidence is fallible evidence for (b). Because her evidence for (a) is comparable to her evidence for (b), it too is fallible evidence.

The second idea used in the argument of this section is the idea of *introspectively indistinguishable* cases. These are cases that from the subject's point of view seem exactly alike. There are two variations on this idea. We can imagine two possible cases in which Jones believes (a) on exactly the same grounds, but in one case (a) is true and in the other it is false. These are introspectively indistinguishable cases in which her belief has different truth values. Another application of the idea applies to her beliefs about White and Black as the example was originally described. Although there is a difference in these beliefs— they are about different people—we are assuming that there is no internal ground for favoring one belief over the other. From her perspective, they are perfectly on a par. Such cases are also introspectively indistinguishable.

As we saw in earlier chapters, our evidence for almost everything is fallible. The skeptical scenarios show how we can be wrong about almost everything, in spite of our reasons. And this also shows that there are possible cases in which there are false beliefs that are introspectively indistinguishable from normal cases in which our beliefs are true. The normal case in which we get things right will be introspectively indistinguishable from a possible case in which we are deceived in one way or another.

These are the materials for the next skeptical argument:

Argument 6.5:   The Introspective Indistinguishability Argument

>   5-1.   If a person can have knowledge on the basis of fallible evidence, then there can be cases of knowledge that are "introspectively indistinguishable" from cases of nonknowledge.

5-2. But there cannot be cases of knowledge that are introspectively indistinguishable from cases of nonknowledge.

5-3. A person cannot have knowledge on the basis of fallible evidence. (5-1), (5-2)

5-4. But all the evidence we have for any propositions about the external world is fallible.

5-5. We cannot have any knowledge about the external world. (5-3), (5-4)

It is important to see that (5-1) is surely true. (5-2) is the indistinguishability principle. (5-3) follows from (5-1) and (5-2). (5-4) is surely true. And the conclusion follows from (5-3) and (5-4). (5-2), then, is the key premise of this argument.

C. The Certainty Argument

Perhaps the simplest of all arguments for skepticism is *The Certainty Argument*:

Argument 6.6:   The Certainty Argument

6-1. If S knows p, then S is absolutely certain of p.

6-2. No one is ever absolutely certain of anything about the external world.

6-3. No one knows anything about the external world. (6-1), (6-2)

In thinking about this argument it is helpful to distinguish psychological certainty from epistemic certainty. Psychological certainty concerns how one feels, the strength of one's conviction. Absolute psychological certainty is feeling as sure as possible that something is true. Epistemic certainty concerns the strength of one's reasons. Absolute epistemic certainty is having maximally strong reasons. The argument is about the latter. If the argument were about psychological certainty, the first premise would say that if a person knows something, then the person feels absolutely certain of it. And the second premise would say that no one feels absolutely certain of anything about the external world. But perhaps some people do *feel* certain about some things. That fact hardly undermines the intended skeptical argument. The point of the argument is that this feeling of certainty is not warranted or justified. No one is epistemically absolutely certain of anything about the external world.[6]

As we are understanding this argument, then, (6-2) says that no one is epistemically absolutely certain of anything about the external world. The skeptical scenarios seem to show that this is true. They introduce some grounds for doubt about propositions about the external world. That is enough to show that (6-2) is true.

This leaves (6-1) as the key premise of this argument. Does knowledge require absolute epistemic certainty?

D. The Transmissibility Argument

Yet another argument for skepticism has recently attracted considerable attention from philosophers.[7] This argument relies on the entirely plausible premise that if you know one thing, and you know that some second thing definitely follows from the first, then you can know that second thing. This principle, together with the skeptical scenarios, provide the basis for a fourth argument for skepticism. The gist of the argument is this: The things we ordinarily believe imply that the skeptical scenarios are false. So, given the principle just mentioned, if we realize this, and we have knowledge in the ordinary cases, then we can then deduce, and thus know, that the skeptical scenarios are false. But, according to the argument, we do not know that the skeptical scenarios are false. Do you *know* that you are not a brain in a vat, etc.? How could you know any such thing? If not, then you do not know the ordinary things you take yourself to know.

Here is how this line of thought applies to a specific example. Recall Brian from Example 5.8, *The Brain in the Vat*. Suppose Brian is (or at least seems to himself to be) an ordinary person in the world. Consider some skeptical hypothesis:

BIV.   Brian is a mere brain in a vat connected to an artificial life machine.

The word "mere" in (BIV) is intended to signify that Brian is just a brain, not a complete body. If Brian is a mere brain, then he does not have arms. Now, consider some ordinary proposition, such as

BA.   Brian has arms.

If Brian knows (BA), he knows on the basis of the ordinary sorts of experiences we all have. Suppose that he did know (BA). Suppose Brian also knows enough logic to realize that (BA) implies that he is not a mere brain in a vat. In other words, it implies that (BIV) is false. Brian can then use his knowledge about his arms, plus his knowledge of logic, to deduce that (BIV) is false. But, a skeptic will say, he cannot know that (BIV) is false, at least not in this way. It must be, therefore, that he does not know (BA) after all.

The line of thinking just presented can be generalized. Let (O) be any ordinary external-world proposition that *The Standard View* says we know. Let (SK) be any skeptical hypothesis inconsistent with (O). (O) will then imply that (SK) is false. Let S be any ordinary person who knows that (O) implies that (SK) is false.

Argument 6.7:   The Transmissibility Argument

    7-1.   S cannot know that (SK) is false.

    7-2.   (O) implies that (SK) is false, and S knows this.

    7-3.   If S knows that (O) is true, and that (O) implies that (SK) is false, then S can know that (SK) is false.

    7-4.   S does not know (O). (7-1)-(7-3)

Premise (7-2) is clearly true, given the way we set the example up. It is important to understand that even if S is a mere brain in a vat, he can still know about the logical connections between propositions. So the logical knowledge attributed to S in (7-2) is not threatened by the possibility that he is a brain in a vat. Premise (7-3) is a transmissibility principle.[8] It says that knowledge can be transmitted through known logical implication. Although there are details about this principle that may be somewhat questionable, the basic idea seems right. If you know one thing, and you know that it implies some other thing, then you can know that latter thing by inferring it from the former. Premise (7-1) seems right, at least to many epistemologists. We will discuss it more carefully later.

IV. RESPONDING TO SKEPTICISM

Each of the four arguments for skepticism has a conclusion that radically undermines *The Standard View*. If any one of them is sound, then *The Standard View* is mistaken and we know much less than we were inclined to think we know. We turn next to responses to these arguments.

A. The Skeptical View is Self-refuting

A tempting line of response to *The Skeptical View* begins by taking note of an unusual feature of a skeptic's overall position. The feature can best be brought out by constructing a dialogue between a skeptic and an antiskeptic.

> Antiskeptic:
>> Do you know that the premises of your skeptical argument are true? Do you know, for example, that almost any of our beliefs could be mistaken? Do you know that our evidence for almost all our beliefs is fallible?

> Skeptic:
>> Yes, I do know that my premises are true.

> Antiskeptic:
>> You say that you know these facts about our beliefs. But these are facts about the world. You claim we lack knowledge of all facts of this sort. Hence, in defending your argument you show that you do not consistently believe the consequences of your own conclusion. Your assertion of skepticism is a sham.

> Skeptic:
>> I guess you are right. My own arguments show that I do not know my premises to be true. I grant that I do not know them.

> Antiskeptic:
>> You cannot establish the truth of something on the basis of premises you do not know to be true. So, if you do not know that your premises

are true, then you do not know anything on the basis of your premises. In particular, you do not know that your skeptical conclusion is true. So you have not proven that skepticism is correct.

This dialogue raises several questions, but we will focus on just one of them here. Suppose we grant to the antiskeptic the claims made in this discussion. It is surely true that skeptics cannot consistently claim to know that no one knows anything about the external world. Compare:

4. I know that no one knows anything.

There is no way that (4) could be true. For if it were true, then, given what it says, I do know something, namely that no one knows anything. But if I knew that, then the proposition (4) says I know would be false, because I would know something. Skeptics who defend arguments such as those presented in Section III may appear to be in a similar predicament. They claim that no one knows anything about the external world, yet they seem to do so on the basis of claims about the external world.

These considerations show that there is something odd about skepticism. In asserting their arguments, skeptics seem to be implicitly claiming to know their premises to be true. Yet that is inconsistent with their conclusion. Furthermore, in living their lives, they are likely to do all sorts of things that suggest that they think they know things. For example, they will enter into conversations with others. Doing so seems to presuppose that they think they know that there are other people present and that they know what those other people are saying. For another example, they will get out of the way of oncoming trucks, suggesting that they know that walking in front of a moving truck is dangerous.

There is reason to doubt that skeptics really must think that they know things. Recall that skeptics are not claiming that our ordinary beliefs are *false*. They are claiming that we do not know them to be true. Thus, they can believe that moving trucks are dangerous but deny knowing any such thing. So, perhaps if they are very careful, skeptics could get by without ever claiming to know anything or doing anything that implies they think they know anything.

But suppose the critics of skepticism are correct in charging that skeptics do always explicitly or implicitly contradict themselves. Suppose it is true that they assert that no one knows anything, but at other times, they say, think, or presuppose that they themselves know things. This tells us something about the stability or overall consistency of skepticism, or of skeptics. Maybe no one can really consistently advocate *The Skeptical View*. But this leaves a puzzling question unanswered: What is wrong with the arguments for skepticism? They are valid arguments. This means that if their premises are true, then their conclusions are true. And their premises all seem right. Showing that skeptics somehow contradict themselves is of no help in figuring out where these challenging arguments go wrong, or even whether they go wrong at all. And that, at least according to many, is the central philosophical issue posed by skepticism.

One way to clarify the point just made is to distinguish two goals that one might have in thinking about skepticism. One of the goals is more rhetorical or dialectical. It amounts to convincing skeptics that they are wrong or showing that they do not really believe what they say or showing that they contradict themselves. The other goal is less about skeptics and more about their arguments. It amounts to figuring out what, if anything, is wrong with the premises of the arguments for skepticism. Our focus here is the second goal. This is not to say that there is anything wrong with having the first goal. However, accomplishing that goal—showing that skeptics contradict themselves—would fail to resolve a central question: Is the conclusion of the skeptical arguments true?

Avoiding the dialectical challenge of refuting or convincing skeptics has another advantage. Suppose one were to take on the goal of trying to convince an intransigent skeptic that we do know things. No matter what you do, a clever skeptic will resist. Your attempted proof will always make use of some premise or other. A clever skeptic will deny knowing that the premise is true. If you attempt to back it up, you will only appeal to additional premises. Like a child who endlessly asks "why?," a clever skeptic will never concede to you any premise that will establish your antiskeptical conclusion. It is a good idea to avoid getting into this sort of battle with a skeptic in the first place.

All of these dialectical issues leave open the questions with which we began: What should we say about the arguments for skepticism? Are their premises reasonable?

B. The Moorean Response

G. E. Moore was an influential philosopher of the first half of the twentieth century. His philosophical writings often included defenses of common sense from complicated philosophical objections. His response to skepticism was characteristic. After a detailed statement of an argument similar to one of the arguments just stated, Moore writes:

> Is it, in fact, as certain that all these four assumptions [the premises of the argument under consideration] are true, as that I *do* know that this is a pencil and that you are conscious? I cannot help answering: It seems to me *more* certain that I *do* know that this is a pencil and that you are conscious, than that any single one these four assumptions is true, let alone all four.[9]

Applied to the four skeptical arguments, the Moorean response is that it is more certain—more reasonable to believe—that we do have knowledge of the external world than that any of these arguments is sound. Because the arguments are valid, each must have a false premise. So the reasonable thing is to conclude that each has one or more false premises.

Even if you agree that Moore is right about this, it is clear that this response fails to explain what is wrong with the arguments. It does not help us to see where the arguments go wrong or what the underlying error in them might be. The Moorean response to skepticism, at least as presented here, simply says that it is reasonable to think that something or other is wrong with the arguments for skepticism. It does not tell us what.

In another much discussed lecture, Moore attempted to prove that there was an external world. He held out one of his hands and said, "Here is a hand" and, holding out his other hand, he said, "Here is another one." And from these premises he concluded that there is an external world.[10] There is something appealing about Moore's proof. His premises seem clearly true. His conclusion follows from his premises. It is difficult to identify a defect in his argument. Nevertheless, many readers are disappointed with Moore's response. Some think that, in one way or another, it fails to engage the arguments for skepticism. Perhaps the best way to put the complaint about the Moorean response is to say that it does not explain what is wrong with the arguments for skepticism.[11] His view implies, quite plausibly, that there is something wrong with them. It is desirable to have an explanation of just what is wrong with them.

C. Fallibilism

One prominent reply to the arguments for skepticism is that they all presuppose unreasonably high standards for knowledge. The charge is that the arguments rely, either explicitly or implicitly, on the assumption that knowledge requires absolute certainty, whereas in fact knowledge requires merely very good reasons (plus true belief, and whatever condition is needed to deal with the Gettier examples). This view is *fallibilism*. The details of fallibilism will emerge from consideration of fallibilist responses to each of the arguments for skepticism.

C1. Knowledge and Absolute Certainty The fallibilist response to skepticism is most easily appreciated in connection with *The Certainty Argument*. Fallibilists deny what was earlier identified as the key premise of that argument:

6-1.   If S knows p, then S is absolutely certain of p.

We are absolutely certain of very few propositions. But, according to fallibilists, this is not a problem because knowledge does not require absolute certainty. For example, when there is a table in front of you, the lighting is good, your visual system is working properly, and you believe as a result of your visual impression and your background information that there is a table in front of you, then you can have knowledge that there is a table there. While there is, from your perspective, some remote chance of error, there is no reason at all to think that you are making an error, and excellent reason to think that you are not making an error. If your belief is true, then you do have knowledge.

Notice that fallibilists are not saying that you can know something that is false. If there is no table in front of you, then you do not know that there is a table there. But if there is a table there, and you believe for excellent but not logically perfect reasons that there is a table there, then you do have knowledge.

Fallibilists think that skeptics manage to make us worry about skepticism by applying impossibly high standards for knowledge. There is some linguistic evidence that supports the fallibilist view that there is a difference between knowledge and absolute certainty. Consider an example in which two people are driving away from their house. One of them asks the other if he knows that he locked the door as they went out. He replies that he does. The first then asks if he is "absolutely certain" that he locked it, so certain that nothing could be more certain. He might sensibly reply that he is not. He has not thereby gone back on his first answer. If this is right, it is because the second question—the one about absolute certainty—was a new question, raising an issue not raised by the original question about knowledge. If so, then knowledge does not require absolute certainty. Similarly, we seem to be saying something different, and stronger, when we claim to "know with complete certainty" than when we merely claim to "know" something.

There are also some practical considerations that provide modest support for the fallibilist outlook. Suppose we agreed that knowledge required absolute certainty. In that case, we would have to concede that we do not know much and that *The Standard View* is radically wrong. But now reconsider the list of things *The Standard View* says that we do know. Having agreed with skeptics that knowledge requires absolute certainty and that we are not absolutely certain of many of the things on our original list, we must admit that we do not know those things to be true. But we should not thereby concede that our position with respect to those items is just like our position with respect to things for which we only have modestly good reasons. We might say that we "almost know" the things on our list, whereas we do not almost know the outcome of next year's World Series or even next month's election. We should also say that we do not "almost know" in examples such as those Gettier made famous. We could then ask what the difference is between Gettier cases and cases that are cases of almost knowing. We might even develop a discipline—"almost epistemology"—in which we study exactly the things studied here. In other words, if we agree with skeptics that "knows" applies only in cases of absolute certainty, we could introduce the phrase "almost knows" that would apply in the range of cases that fall short of absolute certainty but that are regularly classified as knowledge. Fallibilists think that "knows" is just used in this way in the first place, so that there is no need to concede that word to skeptics and introduce the phrase "almost knows" to do its job. To do that is just needlessly confusing.

There are, then, persuasive but perhaps not conclusive reasons to accept fallibilism. It will be helpful to see what fallibilists say about the other arguments for skepticism.

C2. Knowledge and the Possibility of Error   *The Possibility of Error Argument* had as its key premise:

5-2.   If a belief could be mistaken, then it is not a case of knowledge.

Fallibilists reject this. They think that knowledge is compatible with the *possibility* of error. It is important to be clear about what they are saying. Fallibilists are not saying that knowledge is compatible with actual error. They are not saying that you can know something that is not true. Nor are they saying that you can have knowledge when you have a positive reason to think that you are making an error. They are saying that knowledge requires strong justification and truth. Thus, if you believe something on the basis of excellent reasons, it is true, and if there is no Gettier-like funny business, then you have knowledge. If you believe something on the basis of those same excellent reasons, and it turns out that it is false because you are the victim of some sort of hoax or hallucination, then you do not have knowledge.

Rejecting (5-2) is closely connected to rejecting the view that knowledge requires absolute certainty. The assumption that knowledge requires certainty is equivalent to the assumption that if you are not certain of something, then you do not know it. And this assumption is central to the best reason for thinking that (5-2) is true. The defense of (5-2) goes like this: If you can be mistaken about something, then you are not absolutely certain of it. If you are not absolutely certain of something, then you do not know it. So, if you can be mistaken about something, then you do not know it. Once the assumption that knowledge requires certainty is rejected, as fallibilists say it should be, this defense of (5-2) fails.

One thing that could cause confusion here is that (5-2) is difficult to interpret. "If–then" sentences are often problematic, and when they have words like *could* in them, they are even more troublesome. One potential source of confusion can be exposed by considering some related sentences. First, notice that (5-2) is equivalent to

5-2a.   If S knows p, then S could not be mistaken about p.

Now consider an if–then sentence similar in structure to (5-2a):

5.   If S is a bachelor, then S could not be married.

(5) may seem correct to you, but there is something puzzling about it. This can be brought out by the following considerations. Suppose that you are dividing people into two groups: those who could be married and those who could not be married. You might say of a 3-week-old baby that he could not be married. At that age, he could not legally participate in a marriage ceremony and he could not do or say things necessary for being married. In contrast, a normal 30-year-old man who has chosen not to marry is in the group of people that could be married, even though he is not married. This should make you see that there is a difference between

5.   If S is a bachelor, then S could not be married.
5a. If S is a bachelor, then S is not married.

(5a) is true. Indeed, it is necessarily true. It is not some contingent and reversible truth. It is true partly as a result of what the word *bachelor* means. But (5) is not true. It is not the case that if a person is a bachelor, then the person is in the group of people who could not be married. Plenty of bachelors are people who could be married; they just are not married.

Analogously, compare:

5-2a.   If S knows p, then S could not be mistaken about p.
5-2b.   If S knows p, then S is not mistaken about p.

(5-2b) is true. Moreover, it is a necessary truth, because it follows in part from the meaning of *knows*. But it would be a mistake to think that this supports (5-2a). Thus, fallibilists accept (5-2b). They even agree that there are no possible circumstances in which (5-2b) is false. But they reject (5-2a), and with it (5-2) of *The Possibility of Error Argument*. To accept (5-2a) is to say that to know something requires that it be the sort of thing that you could not be mistaken about. (Comparable to saying, as in (5a), that to be a bachelor is to be the sort of thing that could not be married.) Few propositions meet this very high standard. The few that meet it are unusual. For example, no one can mistakenly believe that there are beliefs. No one can mistakenly believe what he or she would express with the sentences "I exist" and "I have a belief."[12]

C3. The Introspective Indistinguishability Argument The key premise of this argument was

6-2.   There cannot be cases of knowledge that are introspectively indistinguishable from cases of nonknowledge.

Fallibilists reject this. They hold that knowledge is not a pure "mental state." Whether a person knows depends upon both what her mind is like—what she believes and why—and what the world is like. If knowledge requires merely extremely good reasons, and not perfect reasons, then (6-2) is false. Take any case in which one has extremely good reasons, and one has a true belief and does have knowledge. Because the reasons are merely extremely good, but not perfect, it follows that there will be other possible cases in which one has those very same reasons, yet one's belief is false and one lacks knowledge.

One way to think of things is as follows: On the fallibilist view, knowledge results from a kind of cooperation between the world and the believer. When the believer does her part by believing in a proper way, she has done all she can toward having knowledge. When the world cooperates, by making it not be one of the unusual cases of a justified false belief or a Gettier-like case, then it is knowledge. When the world fails to cooperate, it is not knowledge. Because knowledge depends upon this sort of cooperation, there can be cases in which the person does her part and the world fails to cooperate. Such cases are introspectively indistinguishable from cases in which the world does cooperate. Hence, (6-2) is false.

If knowledge required absolute certainty, there might be a good case for premise (6-2). Absolute certainty is a kind of internal mental state that guarantees truth. Beliefs of which we are certain are introspectively distinguishable from beliefs that are not certain. So if knowledge required certainty, it would follow that knowledge requires a kind of mental state that guarantees truth, that is a kind of mental state introspectively distinguishable from false belief. Because, according to fallibilism, knowledge does not require absolute certainty, this line of support for (6-2) fails.

Notice that whatever we say about knowledge, there can be cases of "believing truly" and "believing falsely" that are introspectively indistinguishable. True beliefs do not have a brighter "glow" than false beliefs. There is not a blinking "T" before your mind's eye when you have a true belief. There is no internal feature that accompanies all and only true beliefs. Thus, there can be a case in which you believe something and your belief is true, and there are other possible cases that seem exactly alike, yet the belief is false. True beliefs are not introspectively distinguishable from false beliefs.

This is not to say that you cannot tell when you have good reasons for believing something and when you do not. You usually can tell that. Perhaps you always can. So perhaps justified beliefs are introspectively distinguishable from unjustified ones. That is, no justified belief is introspectively indistinguishable from an unjustified belief.[13]

One might think that this discussion fails to do justice to the thinking behind *The Indistinguishability Argument*. To see the point, consider an analogy. Suppose that you cannot tell the difference between two kinds of trees, say cypress and cedar. Seeing one and seeing the other are, at least as far as you can tell, introspectively indistinguishable. You might conclude from this that you can never know that you are seeing a cedar rather than a cypress. Analogously, it might be claimed that you can never know that you are seeing a real tree rather than merely dreaming that you are seeing a tree, or being caused by an evil demon to have a tree image, because these latter states are introspectively indistinguishable from seeing a real tree. Hence, you cannot know that you are seeing a real tree.

But, at least according to fallibilists, this thinking is mistaken. Even if seeing a cedar and seeing a cypress are introspectively indistinguishable for you, you can know that you are seeing one rather than the other. You might know because a tree expert has told you. Or you might know because you have independent compelling evidence that no cedars grow in your area. There are any number of good reasons you might have for believing that you see one rather than another. If knowledge requires absolute certainty, then none of these reasons is good enough for knowledge. However, as we have seen, fallibilists have some good reasons to reject that assumption. Similarly, then, you can have good reason to think that you are seeing a tree rather than being deceived by an evil demon, even if the two experiences are introspectively indistinguishable. (Further discussion of this point will appear in subsection C4 and in Chapter 7.)

People sometimes say that if fallibilism is right, then you never can tell whether you know anything.[14] That is, they argue:

Argument 6.8:   The Knowing That You Know Argument

8-1.   If fallibilism is true, then a person can never tell whether or not she has knowledge (i.e., she never knows that she has knowledge).

8-2.   Fallibilism is true.

8-3.   So a person never knows that she has knowledge. (8-1), (8-2)

Fallibilists accept (8-2). While (8-3) is not impossible or self-contradictory, it would be a very odd thing for fallibilists to accept: Why would you be able to know all sorts of things, but not that you know something? Among the things fallibilists will say one can know is that someone else knows something. How could it be that you can know that others have knowledge, but not yourself? So fallibilists will want to find a good basis for rejecting (8-1).

Fortunately, fallibilists can sensibly reject (8-1). Understanding why will make fallibilism clearer and more appealing. The fallibilist view is that knowledge about knowledge is relevantly like knowledge about other things. A person can know that the lights are on by having a justified true belief that the lights are on and not being in a Gettier case. Similarly, a person can have knowledge that she knows this fact by having a justified true belief that she knows that the lights are on. And she does have excellent reasons for thinking that she knows this: She is believing it on the basis of her observation of the lighting and not on a whim, she is usually right about this sort of thing, and so on. The key point is that her knowledge that she knows things is, like all knowledge, fallible. She is not absolutely certain that she has knowledge. Her reasons for thinking that she has knowledge are not logically perfect. They are merely extremely good. And that is all it takes to know. The key idea is that if you are a fallibilist about knowledge of ordinary propositions, then you should also be a fallibilist about knowledge about knowledge.[15]

C4. The Transmissibility Argument A more general statement of the key premise of *The Transmissibility Argument* is

7-1.   People cannot know that skeptical hypotheses are false.

Here fallibilists say that we do know that the skeptical hypotheses are false. Your reasons for thinking ordinary things such as that you have arms also provide you with excellent reasons for rejecting skeptical hypotheses such as that you are a brain in a vat. There is no reason to think that there are any brains in vats at all, nor that you are one of them. It is an hypothesis that you have excellent reasons to reject. True, those reasons are not logically perfect, but you no more need logically perfect reasons in this case than you need them in any other case. The same goes for the other skeptical hypotheses.

If knowledge required absolute certainty, then perhaps there would be better reason to accept *The Transmissibility Argument*. We cannot be absolutely certain that we are not brains in vats or that the other skeptical hypotheses are false. But, according to fallibilism, knowledge does not require certainty, and this defense of the key premise of *The Transmissibility Argument* fails.

Skeptics, of course, may deny what fallibilists say here. (We will consider in Chapter 7 one reason some skeptics might give for this.) But, unlike the other arguments for skepticism considered in this chapter, *The Transmissibility Argument* uses our lack of knowledge as a premise. The argument itself does not provide reasons to think that we do not know that skeptical hypotheses are false. In contrast, the other arguments considered in this section provided reasons for thinking that we lacked knowledge, reasons having to do with the possibility of error and the like. So, while skeptics may not like it, it is difficult to see why fallibilists are not in good position to reject *The Transmissibility Argument.*

V. INTERIM CONCLUSION

One kind of skepticism is "high standards skepticism"—skepticism that relies on the premise that knowledge requires certainty, or the impossibility of error. The skeptical arguments considered here make that assumption. The assumption is explicit in the case of *The Possibility of Error Argument* and *The Certainty Argument,* and it is implicit in *The Introspective Indistinguishability Argument* and *The Transmissibility Argument.*

The Moorean response to skepticism contends that it is more reasonable to think that we do have knowledge than it is to think that any of these arguments is sound. That response has considerable appeal, but it fails to explain just where it is that the arguments go wrong.

Fallibilism provides a more complete response to the arguments for skepticism. According to fallibilism, knowledge requires very good reasons (plus true belief and not being a Gettier case). But knowledge does not require certainty. We are able to satisfy the fallibilist conditions for knowledge.

Considerations in favor of fallibilism are significant and powerful, but not decisive. They include linguistic considerations, simplicity, the fact that some of the appeal of arguments for skepticism turns on mistakes (for example, the confusions about "if–then" and "must"), and the fact that fallibilism does not have the mistaken conclusion concerning knowing that you know that was just discussed. Fallibilism thus appears to be a sensible view. And if fallibilism is correct, then each of the arguments for skepticism has a mistaken premise.

One way to summarize fallibilism is as follows:

> Our experiences provide us with very good evidence, but not absolutely conclusive evidence, for propositions such as the proposition that we really do see a book (and thus we are not dreaming, hallucinating, a BIV, etc.). This evidence is good enough to justify our ordinary beliefs and thus to satisfy the justification condition for knowledge. All the arguments for skepticism rely on the mistaken assumption that justification, and thus knowledge, requires conclusive evidence. Thus, all those arguments fail.

This is a widely accepted and seemingly sensible view. It fits well with the modest foundationalist view described in Chapter 4. Unfortunately, skeptical issues remain. We will turn to them in Chapter 7.

ENDNOTES

1. For discussion of this criticism of reliabilism, see Richard Fumerton, *Metaepistemology and Skepticism* (Lanham, MD: Rowman and Littlefield, 1995), Chapter 6.
2. If "anyone" in (SF1) is restricted to mere humans, then one might defend (SF1) on the grounds that it is impossible for a mere human to have knowledge even though it is possible for some superior being, e.g., an infinite god, to have knowledge. The idea is that knowledge itself is not impossible, but it is incompatible with something essential to being human.
3. Additional arguments for skepticism will be considered in Chapters 7 and 8.
4. *The Philosophical Works of Descartes,* translated by Elizabeth S. Haldane and G. R. T. Ross (Cambridge, U.K.: Cambridge University Press, 1973), pp. 145–6.
5. John Tienson discusses an example similar to this one in "On Analyzing Knowledge," *Philosophical Studies* 25 (1974): 289–93.
6. A variant of *The Certainty Argument* is developed by Peter Unger in *Ignorance: A Case for Skepticism* (Oxford: Oxford University Press, 1975), Chapter 3.
7. One main source for this argument is Fred Dretske, "Epistemic Operators," *Journal of Philosophy* 67 (1970): 1007–23.
8. It is sometimes called a "closure" principle. The idea is that the set of things you know is "closed" under implication. This means that if the set includes one proposition, it also includes those that are implied by it. Although some philosophers have questioned (7-3), we will not do so here.
9. G. E. Moore, "Four Forms of Skepticism," in *Philosophical Papers* (New York: Collier Books, 1959), pp. 193–222. The quotation is from p. 222.
10. See G. E. Moore, "Proof of an External World," in *Philosophical Papers,* pp. 126–49. The "proof" appears on p. 145.
11. It is also possible that there is a difference between giving a sound argument for a conclusion, as Moore may have done, and giving a "proof" of that conclusion. Perhaps a proof, in the context of a debate about skepticism, must have premises that meet some special condition, such as being accepted by all parties to the debate. Moore's premises do not meet this additional condition.
12. The argument here assumes that a person cannot be mistaken about a proposition provided the person cannot believe it and be wrong. The propositions listed do meet that condition. It is consistent with this, however, that a person could mistakenly disbelieve one of these propositions. Someone could overreact to the skeptical arguments and come to believe, mistakenly, that he does not exist. In a sense, then, it is possible for a person to be mistaken about whether he exists.
13. Of course, defenders of the nonevidentialist theories of justification discussed in Chapter 5 would reject this.
14. Some of the ideas presented in the next few paragraphs first appeared in "Fallibilism and Knowing That One Knows," *Philosophical Review* 90 (1981): 77–93.
15. I am grateful to Bruce Russell for helpful comments on this section.

CHAPTER SEVEN

Skepticism (II)

The arguments for skepticism discussed in Chapter 6 were all arguments for "high-standards skepticism." They relied on the assumption that the standards for knowledge are extremely high, and that we do not, or cannot, satisfy them. Fallibilism and modest foundationalism provide a sensible reply to all these arguments. This, however, is not the end of the discussion of *The Skeptical View*. Another kind of skeptical argument challenges the claim that our reasons for our ordinary beliefs are as good as fallibilists and modest foundationalists think they are. In other words, this kind of argument denies that we meet ordinary standards for justification. In this chapter we will examine two such arguments.

I. THE PROBLEM OF INDUCTION

A. Inductive Inferences

Inductive reasoning is at the heart of science and is crucial to common-sense reasoning as well. Very roughly, inductive reasoning is reasoning that relies on observed patterns to draw conclusions about what occurs in other cases. If you have gone to a restaurant several times and found the food to be very good, you are likely to believe that you will find it to be good the next time you go there as well. If a researcher finds that the patients he has seen with a particular disease always or usually recover when treated in a certain way, then the researcher may conclude that this same pattern will apply to future patients. These are simple examples of inductive reasoning. It is clear that *The Standard View* rests on the assumption that we can learn about the world through this sort of reasoning. The fallibilist response to skepticism defended in Chapter 6 clearly relies on the assumption that inductive reasoning can yield justification.

The most widely discussed general pattern of inductive inferences is

Argument 7.1:   Inductive Pattern

   1-1.   All As examined up till now have been Bs.

   1-2.   The next A to be examined will be B.

A standard example used to illustrate this sort of reasoning is the inference from the observation that the sun has risen every day in the past to the conclusion that it will rise tomorrow. To make this example fit the displayed pattern, we must take the stated premise—the sun has risen every day in the past—to mean that the sun has risen on every day that has been observed up till now.

Argument 7.2:   The Sun Rise Argument

   2-1.   All days examined up till now have been days on which the sun has risen.

   2-2.   The next day (tomorrow) will be a day on which the sun rises.

For present purposes, it is acceptable to take this premise to be true. This seems to be a good example of inductive reasoning.

Not all inductive inferences follow exactly this pattern. The stated pattern draws a conclusion about only the next case. But sometimes from the same premise people draw a general conclusion:

Argument 7.3:   The Sun Rise Argument (II)

   3-1.   All days examined up till now have been days on which the sun has risen.

   3-2.   All days will be days on which the sun rises.

Although the conclusion here is different, the reasoning is similar. In both Arguments 7.2 and 7.3, observed patterns in previous cases are used to predict the future.[1]

In the cases just mentioned, the premise is about *all* the observed As. But some very similar inferences are not. Suppose that every fall a gardener plants some lily bulbs in his garden. Some of the bulbs sprout and some do not. Suppose that over a period of many years the gardener has observed that about 80 percent of the bulbs have sprouted each year. If the gardener is not overly optimistic, he is likely to believe that the same will happen this year. The inference this gardener makes is

Argument 7.4: The Lilies Argument

4-1. 80 percent of the lily bulbs I've planted each year in the past have sprouted.

4-2. 80 percent of the lily bulbs I will plant this year will sprout.

Obviously, additional information might undermine such an inference. For example, if the gardener knows that the weather is predicted to be unusual in the coming months, or if he has purchased bulbs from a different and unknown source, then he might be less likely to draw the conclusion. Still, the general pattern of inference seems correct.

People sometimes think that all inductive inferences are inferences in which one draws a conclusion about the future from premises about the past. But not all inferences that rely on the same style of reasoning are exactly like that. Consider a modification of the lily example. Suppose the gardener is too busy to look in the garden all spring during the season they sprout. At the end of the spring, the gardener might make essentially the same inference, concluding that 80 percent of the bulbs he planted *have* sprouted. So now the inference is entirely about the past, but the reasoning is the same.

The central feature of inductive inferences is thus that they involve inferences from observed cases to unobserved cases. It is sometimes said that the principle upon which inductive inferences rest is that the future will be like the past. But the real principle is that unobserved cases are like observed cases.

It is clear that *The Standard View* and modest foundationalism rely on the epistemic merit of inductive reasoning. It is not just our predictions about what will happen in the garden that are at stake. The justification of your belief that your favorite chair will support you rather than eject you when you sit in it depends upon induction. Much of what we commonly take ourselves to know similarly depends upon the legitimacy of inductive reasoning. There is, however, a long-standing philosophical question about the merits of such reasoning. We turn next to it.

B. Hume's Problem

David Hume raised a question about the merits of inductive inferences that has long troubled philosophers. Stated most simply, Hume's problem (or question) is: Do we have any good reason to accept the conclusions of inductive arguments? Are these arguments any good?

One classic statement of Hume's problem is in the following passage:

> All reasonings may be divided into two kinds, namely demonstrative reasoning, or that concerning relations of ideas, and moral reasoning, or that concerning matters of fact

and existence. That there are no demonstrative arguments in the case seems evident; since it implies no contradiction that the course of nature may change, and that an object, seemingly like those which we have experienced, may be attended with different or contrary effects. May I not clearly and distinctly conceive that a body, falling from the clouds, which, in all other respects, resembles snow, has yet the taste of salt or feeling of fire?[2]

Here Hume says that the reasoning in inductive inferences is not *demonstrative*. That is to say, the conclusions could be false even though the premises are true. This is surely right. In the next passage he goes on to consider the possibility that inductive arguments involve "moral reasoning." By this he does not mean that they involve questions about morality, but rather that "these arguments must be probable only."[3] He writes:

. . . all our experimental conclusions proceed upon the supposition that the future will be conformable to the past. To endeavor, therefore, the proof of this last supposition by probable arguments, or arguments regarding existence, must be evidently going in a circle, and taking that for granted, which is the very point in question.[4]

The idea here seems to be that if you think that inductive inferences are good inferences because they have worked, then you are in this very argument relying on the supposition that the future will be like the past. You are thereby assuming in this argument the very thing at issue. The question was: Why think inductive inferences are any good? Why think that the future will be like the past? To make this assumption in arguing that it will is to assume the very thing at issue.

As noted earlier, inductive inferences are really inferences from the observed to the unobserved, and inferences from the past to the future are just a particular case of this. But they are clear and interesting instances of inductive reasoning, and it will be harmless to follow Hume's lead and discuss induction as if it always involved past-to-future inferences. Hume's idea, then, seems to be that inductive inferences turn on some version of a principle such as

PF.   The future will be like the past. (Or, somewhat more precisely, if x percent of the observed As have been Bs, then X percent of the unobserved As are Bs.)

We could also have formulated this as a uniformity of nature principle, since it says that patterns found to hold in nature will continue to hold. There are details about this principle that need attention. Obviously, a specific inference of this sort is stronger when many As in many different circumstances have been observed. Furthermore, the future will surely not be like the past in all respects. A 49-year-old approaching his next birthday might use (PF) to argue that because on all his birthdays up till now he has been under 50, he will be under 50 on his next birthday. Clearly, something goes wrong here. However, since Hume is challenging the idea that anything at all like (PF) is justified, we will set these details aside.

One way to interpret Hume's remarks is as follows. Inductive inferences depend upon principle (PF) or some variant of it. But (PF) is not a necessary truth; it cannot be proven by a demonstrative argument. And if we attempt to establish (PF) by means of any nondemonstrative (or moral) argument, we rely on (PF) itself. We thereby argue "in a circle" and fail to establish the principle. And there is no other argument for (PF) available. Hume's own view seems to be that the mind is such that we just make these inferences as a result of habit, but there is no real justification for them. That is a disappointing, and skeptical, conclusion. If it is true that science relies essentially on inductive reasoning, it follows that there is no good justification for scientific reasoning. If *The Standard View*'s contention that we do know a lot about the world depends upon the adequacy of inductive reasoning, then Hume's argument casts doubt on *The Standard View*. If modest foundationalism implies that inductive reasoning yields justified conclusions, then Hume's problem casts doubt on modest foundationalism. It is not surprising that many philosophers have tried to find an answer to Hume's problem.

We may set out a precise form of *Hume's Argument* as follows:

Argument 7.5: Hume's Argument

> 5-1.   If (PF) can be justified at all, then it can be justified either by a "demonstrative" argument or by a "moral" argument (an inference from observed facts).
>
> 5-2.   Only necessary truths can be justified by demonstrative arguments.
>
> 5-3.   (PF) is not a necessary truth.
>
> 5-4.   (PF) cannot be justified by a demonstrative argument. (5-2), (5-3)
>
> 5-5.   All moral arguments assume the truth of (PF).
>
> 5-6.   Any moral argument for (PF) would assume the truth of (PF). (5-5)
>
> 5-7.   Any argument for a principle that assumes the truth of that principle fails to justify that principle.
>
> 5-8.   (PF) cannot be justified by a moral argument. (5-6), (5-7)
>
> _____
>
> 5-9.   (PF) cannot be justified. (5-1), (5-4), (5-8)

This argument is valid. Lines (5-4), (5-6), (5-8), and (5-9) follow from previous steps. So the only legitimate responses will involve the rejection of one of the other premises: (5-1), (5-2), (5-3), (5-5), (5-7). Each of these premises seems quite reasonable. Perhaps we are stuck with Hume's surprising conclusion.

It deserves emphasis that Hume's problem is not dependent, at least not explicitly, on high-standards skepticism. He is not asking how we can be certain that (PF) is true. Instead, he is denying that we have any good reason at all to believe it.

C. Three Responses to Hume's Problem

C1. Inductive Defenses of Induction One might be tempted to respond to Hume's problem by pointing out that induction works. That is, we have done well making inductive inferences in the past, so it is reasonable to conclude that it will continue to work. As an argument for (PF), this thought might be formulated as follows:

> *Argument 7.6:   The Inductive Argument for (PF)*
>
> 6-1.   (PF) has been true in the past.
>
> ─────────────────────────────────
>
> 6-2.   (PF) will be true in the future. (6-1)

Perhaps from (6-2) we could go on to infer that (PF) is simply true, and thus that we are justified in making use of it. If Argument 7.6 does justify (PF), it must also expose some flaw in *Hume's Argument*. We will return to this point shortly.

Hume, of course, would think that Argument 7.6 is a version of the sort of argument that "goes in a circle" and takes "for granted . . . the very point in question." One way an argument could assume the point in question is by taking that very point as a premise. In this case, since the truth of (PF) is the point in question, an objectionable argument would have (PF) as a premise. But the premise of *The Inductive Argument for (PF)* is not (PF) itself. In addition, (6-1) seems to be quite well justified. Thus, *The Inductive Argument* seems not to take the point in question as a premise. One response to Hume, then, is that premise (5-5) of his argument is false. Argument 7.6 is a moral argument for (PF), but it does not assume the truth of (PF). The reason Argument 7.6 does not assume the truth of (PF) is that (PF) is not among its premises. And once (5-5) is rejected, the remaining steps of the argument are left without support. *Hume's Argument* seems to be undermined.

There is, however, a second way in which an argument can assume the point in question. One way is to have the rule as an explicit premise. This is what we have discussed so far. The other way is for the rule to be the one that connects the argument's premise(s) to its conclusion. This is what happens in the case of Argument 7.6. (PF) is a not a premise of the argument, but it is the rule of inference or the principle that connects the premise of Argument 7.6 to its conclusion. If some rule of inference is in question—if we are wondering whether we are justified in using it—then an argument that uses that very rule assumes the truth of that rule. (PF) is the very rule required to get from the premise to the conclusion of Argument 7.6, so that argument does assume the truth of (PF). Hence, premise (5-5) is true after all.[5] The argument fails to answer Hume's challenge.

The fact that Argument 7.6 does not provide an adequate answer to Hume does not show that the premise of Argument 7.6 is false or that inductive arguments are in general defective. The problem is that this argument does not establish the legitimacy of using (PF) in a circumstance in which the legitimacy of using it is in doubt.

C2. Pragmatic Defenses of (PF) Some philosophers have noted that inductive reasoning has certain advantages over any competing strategies for forming beliefs about unobserved things.[6] Two related analogies will bring out the idea. First, consider a situation in which a doctor is going to perform an operation on a patient. The doctor is not certain that the operation will work, but she does know that

> A.   If anything will work to save the patient, the operation will.

To take a second case, suppose that you are put in the following unfortunate situation:

> . . . you were forcefully taken into a locked room and told that whether or not you will be allowed to live depends on whether you win or lose a wager. The object of the wager is a box with red, blue, yellow, and orange lights on it. You know nothing about the construction of the box but are told that either all of the lights, some of them, or none of them will come on. If the colored light you choose comes on, you live; if not, you die. But before you make your choice, you are also told that neither the blue, nor the yellow, nor the orange light can come on without the red light also coming on. If this is the only information you have, then you will surely bet on red.[7]

In this situation it is true that

> B.   If any bet will be successful, then a bet on red will be successful.

Advocates of the pragmatic justification of induction contend that something similar is true of induction; They say

> C.   If anything will work to form accurate beliefs about unobserved things, induction will.

The reason (C) is true has to do with the self-correcting nature of induction. Suppose some rival to induction were being considered. Perhaps reading tea leaves provides an alternative way to form true beliefs about the future. If so, then this pattern will be discovered over time. And inductive reasoning will eventually sanction it. That is, induction will license an argument for the conclusion that predictions based on tea leaf readings are true. If any general policy for forming beliefs proves to work correctly, induction will eventually approve of it. This may take time, so the case for (C) is not exactly parallel to the case for (A) and (B), but it still does provide some sort of vindication of (PF).

The pragmatic response to *Hume's Argument*, then, is that there is another way to justify (PF) in addition to demonstrative and moral arguments. There is the pragmatic argument just given. Thus, premise (5-1) is false.

This justification of inductive reasoning may provide less than some would want. First, reconsider the analogies. Even though (A) is true, it does not follow that the operation has much chance to succeed. Even though (B) is true, there is no reason to think that a bet on red will be successful or is even likely to be successful. The operation and the bet may be nothing more than the best of some very bad options. It is not clear that this defense of induction implies that induction is any better than the best of a set of bad options.

Furthermore, the point about the self-correcting nature of induction is a bit misleading. If nature is uniform, then induction eventually will lead to good principles (presumably), but if it is not, then induction need not. There is no guarantee that induction will yield good principles for forming beliefs about unobserved things.

Finally, if what was sought is a case for the epistemic rationality of (PF), the defense seems to fall short. It does not show that we have good reason to believe that (PF) is true. At most, it shows that we are at least as well off using (PF) as we are using any alternative to it. And that is less than what was sought.

Therefore, these considerations suggest that there is no pragmatic justification of induction in the sense of "justification" intended by Hume. *Hume's Argument* has not been refuted.

C3. An *a priori* Defense of Induction *Hume's Argument* is about the past-to-future principle, (PF).

> PF.   The future will be like the past.

Hume says, correctly, that no "demonstrative" argument establishes (PF). It is not true by definition, and demonstrative arguments are the sort that prove that sort of thing. Hume says that any argument for (PF) based on experience is "circular," or takes for granted the very thing in question. And that seems right as well. In a chapter of *The Problems of Philosophy*, Bertrand Russell attempted to set out the same problem Hume had discussed, but, interestingly, he formulated the principle under discussion somewhat differently. A somewhat simplified version of the claim Russell discussed is

> PFR.   Knowing that things have been a certain way in the past gives you a good reason to believe that they will be that way in the future.[8]

The key difference between (PF) and (PFR) is that the latter is about what we have reason to believe. If (PFR) is true, then the premises of inductive arguments can provide us with good reasons to believe their conclusions. These reasons, of course, are not conclusive. One can have other reasons that defeat, or undermine, the conclusion of an otherwise good inductive argument. (The 49-year-old who thinks he will still be under 50 at his next birthday has such defeating reasons.) (PF) and (PFR) also differ in a way that is directly relevant to *Hume's Argument*.

Hume is surely right to say that (PF) is not true by definition and cannot be established by means of a "demonstrative" argument. Things could change tomorrow, as he says. (PF) is not a necessary truth. But that same fact does *not* establish that (PFR) is not true by definition.[9] One imperfect analogy illustrates why. Suppose there is a jar with 1,000 marbles in it. You know that 999 of the marbles are black and one is white. You have randomly selected one but not looked at it. You will think you have picked a black one, and that is a reasonable belief. Now compare:

M1.   If there are 1,000 marbles in a jar, 999 are black, 1 is white, and 1 has been randomly selected, then the one selected is black.

M2.   If you know that there are 1,000 marbles in a jar, 999 are black, 1 is white, and 1 has been randomly selected (and you have no other relevant information), then it is reasonable for you to believe that the one selected is black.

(M1) and (M2) are related to one another in much the same way (PF) and (PFR) are related to one another. (M1), like (PF), says that if one condition obtains, then another will obtain. (In the case of (PF), the first condition is that some regularity has held in the past, and the second is that it will hold in the future.) (M2), like (PFR), says that if you know that the first condition obtains, then you have good reason to think that the second obtains. (M1) is not necessarily true. Indeed, there are situations in which (M1) is false. It is false in the case in which you select the white marble. In contrast, (M2) may well be necessarily true. Quite plausibly, the definition or nature of the concept of being reasonable makes it true. There is no possible situation in which the situation in the antecedent could be true, yet you would not be reasonable in believing that the selected marble is black.[10] (M2) is something we can know to be true *a priori;* that is, we can know it simply by understanding the concepts involved. We do not have to observe cases and infer its truth.[11]

Analogously, according to the present response to Hume's problem, (PFR) is true by definition and thus knowable *a priori*. It is part of the concept of being reasonable to use past cases as one's guide to the future. There is no possible situation in which the condition it mentions—knowledge that things have been a certain way in the past—could fail to give you a good reason to think that they will be that way in the future. There may be cases in which that belief is false, and there may be cases in which that good reason is overridden by other reasons (as in the example about the 49-year-old predicting his age on his next birthday). But there are no cases in which information about past regularities fails to provide some reason for beliefs about the future. That is just how being reasonable works.

The response to *Hume's Argument*, then, is that the argument as formulated is sound. (PF) cannot be proven. However, the epistemic merit of inductive reasoning does not depend upon the truth of (PF). Instead, inductive reasoning depends on the truth of (PFR). And, according to the present response, (PFR) is a necessary truth. If *Hume's Argument* were reformulated to be about (PFR), it would have a version of premise (5-3), modified to be about (PFR). That premise would say

5-3*.   (PFR) is not a necessary truth.

This premise is false. *Hume's Argument* is not sound when modified to be about (PFR).

Notice that this response to Hume does not rely on the assumption that everyone knows that some principle along the lines of (PFR) is true. The claim is not that, in order to know things by inductive inference, people have to study epistemology and come to see that (PFR) is true. Rather, (PFR) is true, and, because it is true, everyone (including those who haven't thought about it) is justified in believing the conclusions of good inductive arguments. In other words, if you are justified in believing the premise of an inductive argument, and have no defeating evidence for its conclusion, then you are justified in believing its conclusion.[12]

D. Induction and Tea Leaves

Critics may think that the solution to Hume's problem just advanced is no better than merely stipulating that induction is reasonable. It might be charged that defenders of any other practice for forming beliefs about unobserved objects could defend their practice in a similar way. For example, if a person's practice is to believe the first thing that pops into his head about unobserved objects, that person might argue that some analogue of (PFR) concerning that method of belief formation is reasonable. Or, to take a more colorful case, consider a tea leaf reader, Madam Malarkey.

Example 7.1:   Madam Malarkey, The Tea Leaf Reader

Madam Malarkey uses the configuration of tea leaves to form beliefs about unseen objects. If you want to know something about some object, Madam Malarkey will look into the tea leaves, and by means of some secret formula, use what she sees in them to form a belief about the unseen object. Critics object that her methods are irrational nonsense. Some attempt to challenge her, asking if she has found that her beliefs have proved to be correct. She replies, of course, that to worry about track records and past performance is a sheer prejudice of irrational inductivists. The tea leaves tell her that the tea leaves are the way to proceed. And, when further challenged, she offers an *a priori* defense of her approach. She says that there is a principle that is true by definition:

> TLR.   Knowing that the tea leaves predict that p will be true provides good reason to believe that p will be true.

Madam Malarkey's defense is, surely, pure malarkey. But is the *a priori* defense of induction any better? Is Madam Malarkey on as good grounds as we are? Perhaps not. There are a few things to be said in behalf of induction.

First, suppose it turns out that we cannot offer a proof that (PFR) is true. It is a mistake to infer that it is false or that our inductive reasoning is not reasonable. Suppose you have some premises (or evidence) and believe something on that basis. It is one thing to say that the conclusion is reasonable only if the evidence supports the conclusion. It is another to say that the conclusion is reasonable only if you can "show" or "prove" that the evidence supports the conclusion. It is difficult to see why the latter, more demanding, requirement is correct.

Second, we must admit that Madam Malarkey may be unimpressed by our response. But we should be careful to distinguish two projects: convincing intransigent skeptics or fools and seeing if there is a sensible view according to which our ordinary beliefs are reasonable ones. Hume was neither intransigent nor a fool. But it is plausible to think he conflated two principles, (PF) and (PFR). Perhaps he would find some merit in the *a priori* response, even if Madam Malarkey would not.

Third, and most important, there is a good reason to think that the *a priori* defense of induction is superior to Madam Malarkey's defense of (TLR). The reason is based on a distinction between fundamental principles and derivative principles. Some principles are, if true, true only derivatively or as a result of something more fundamental. If someone proposed, as a fundamental principle, that it is reasonable to believe the things reported in a specific newspaper, that claim should surely be rejected. Even if the newspaper is in fact worthy of trust, any principle specifically about the newspaper is a derivative principle. The same is true of (TLR). One can imagine, just barely, situations in which it would be true. Perhaps there are some possible, though unrealistic, situations in which something observable about tea leaves is regularly connected to properties of unobserved objects one is inquiring about. Were such patterns discovered, it would be reasonable to accept (TLR), or some variant of it. But that is not the case in the actual world. In the actual world we have good reason to think tea leaves are not reliable predictors. In any case, (TLR) is the sort of thing that, if true, is at best contingently true. And, in fact, we don't have evidence that it is true. In contrast, (PFR) is not in the same way derivative or contingent. When properly understood, there is no situation in which it is not reasonable to use past patterns (of the appropriate sort) as guides to future results.

Finally, it possible that the idea of inference to the best explanation, to be discussed later in this chapter, can be of some help here. We will return to this point at the end of the chapter.

E. Conclusion

The *a priori* defense of induction provides a plausible response to the problem Hume set for inductive reasoning. The key to the response requires seeing the problem not as one of proving that the future will be like the past, but rather as one of defending the idea that past (or observed) cases are reasonably used as evidence about future (or unobserved) cases. The response relies on the idea that it is an *a priori* fact about the nature of evidence, not a contingent fact about how things are in the actual world, that it is reasonable to use observed cases as evidence.

This defense leaves open many hard questions about inductive reasoning. As noted, it is not true that the future will be like the past in all respects, nor is it reasonable to believe that it will. We know that we will be older in the future than we were any time in the past. Determining exactly which observed patterns it is reasonable to believe will continue to obtain is an exceedingly difficult problem.[13] Nevertheless, the *a priori* defense of inductive reasoning does at least provide a suitable response to Hume's problem. It is safe to conclude that *Hume's Argument* does not undermine scientific reasoning and *The Standard View*.[14]

II. ORDINARY-STANDARDS SKEPTICISM AND BEST EXPLANATIONS

A. Alternative Hypotheses and Skepticism

Advocates of *The Skeptical View* have another argument for their view. The argument can be brought to light by raising a simple but difficult question:

> What, exactly, is the feature of your evidence that gives you such good reason to think, for example, that you really do see a book rather than that you are dreaming, hallucinating, a BIV, etc.?

Here, the question is not one of certainty. Skeptics who raise this question admit that we need not have certainty in order to have knowledge. However, they contend that if our evidence is good enough to give us knowledge, then our evidence must be good enough to provide good reason to think that our ordinary beliefs are true and the skeptical alternatives are false. However, they claim, when one looks at one's evidence, it is not so clear that our reasons are that good.

The issue can be formulated somewhat more precisely as follows. At any moment, one's current observations are one's present experiences and apparent memories. I now seem to see a computer on a desk, seem to remember seeing the same sort of desk yesterday, and so on. More generally, as I now seem to remember and experience things, my experiences follow patterns. The objects I experience either stay still or move around in relatively smooth ways. Objects do not simply appear and disappear in a random or disorganized way. Furthermore, places look similar over time, or they change in regular ways. My office looks today approximately the way it looked yesterday. When I go home, my house will look similar to the way it looked when I left. The plants in my garden change gradually in regular ways. Things appear in just about the way relatively stable and persisting objects would appear to a perceiver with a relatively stable perceptual system. We can sum this up as follows:

> O. I have memory and perceptual experience that are regular and orderly.

The commonsense explanation of (O) is

> CS. There is a world of enduring and relatively stable physical objects. My experiences are typically caused by these objects stimulating my sense organs.

Of course, (CS) can be fleshed out in many ways. In fact, one can regard many of the results of scientific investigation as spelling out the details of this bare-bones "theory." There are alternative explanations one might offer for (O). They include:

BIV.   I am a brain in a vat connected to a powerful computer. The computer stimulates my brain, giving me sensory experiences. The computer has been programmed to make my experiences regular and orderly.

DR.   All my experiences are dream experiences. My dreams are (usually) relatively systematic and orderly.

EG.   My experiences are caused by an evil genius. This genius causes me to have regular and orderly experiences in order to trick me into believing (CS).

These alternative explanations are also incomplete. It seems possible that they too can be filled out in ways that provide more detailed explanations of (O).

The question raised by ordinary-standards skepticism is, "Why believe (CS) when there exist these alternative explanations of our fundamental data?" Behind the question raised by ordinary-standards skepticism is a final argument for skepticism. The main idea in the argument is that the evidence we have does not provide good reason to believe the commonsense propositions we all do believe rather than the skeptical alternatives mentioned. The argument can be formulated as follows:

Argument 7.7:   *The Alternative Hypotheses Argument*

7-1.   The evidence people have, (O), does not provide better reason to believe ordinary external-world propositions and (CS), than to believe the rival skeptical hypotheses, such as (DR), (BIV), and (EG).

7-2.   If one's evidence does not provide better reason to believe one hypothesis than to believe some rival hypothesis, then one is not justified in believing that hypothesis.

7-3.   People are not justified in believing (and thus do not know) ordinary external-world propositions and (CS). (7-1), (7-2)

This is a valid argument and, once again, the conclusion asserts a significant skeptical thesis. So any defender of *The Standard View,* and modest foundationalism, must find a good response to the argument. To find reason to deny (7-1), one must uncover reasons to think that our evidence really does support our commonsense beliefs over the rivals. To find reason to deny (7-2), one must find reason to think that our beliefs can be justified even if they are not better supported than their rivals.[15]

Modest foundationalism, as discussed in Chapter 5, holds that our ordinary perceptual beliefs are "proper" responses to perceptual stimuli. It is plausible to view *The Alternative Hypotheses Argument* as a challenge to that view. The responses to be considered in the next section, then, are all ways of spelling out the modest foundationalist response to the argument.

B. Three Responses

B1. Epistemological Conservatism Epistemological conservatism is the view that one is justified in retaining an existing belief provided one's evidence does not provide better support for some rival belief.[16] This view is an epistemological analogue of what seems to be a fairly reasonable practical principle. Suppose one is considering replacing some material possession, such as a house, a car, or a computer. In general, it would be foolish to purchase the replacement if what one ended up with was exactly as good as what one had before the change. Making a change makes no sense unless it is an improvement, in one way or another, on what one already has. One might sensibly replace an older car by a newer car of the same model, thereby gaining increased reliability and added features. One might replace an existing house by a smaller and less expensive one if one's family or financial circumstances indicate that one will be better off by so doing. So the principle does not say that it always best to buy bigger and more expensive things. It just says that it is sensible to make a change only when something is gained by so doing. Perhaps a reason for this is that there is always some cost—financial or otherwise—in making the change. It is foolish to incur these costs to end up in exactly as good a situation as one is already in.

An implication of this practical principle is worth noting explicitly. Suppose that there are two very similar cars, A and B. You might be in the following situation. Given the similarity of the cars, if you already own A, then it is reasonable to stick with A and unreasonable to switch to B. But if you already owned B, it would be reasonable to stick with B and unreasonable to switch to A. Even though the one you have is not better than the other, sticking with what you already have is more reasonable than switching. It is this preference for sticking with what one already has that makes this principle conservative.

Epistemological conservatism says that a principle somewhat analogous to the one just described holds for believing as well. When your evidence supports a couple of theories equally well, then if you already believe one of those theories, it is reasonable to stick with that belief rather than switch. In effect, the fact that you already believe one of them is a tiebreaker. Applied to *The Alternative Hypotheses Argument*, epistemological conservatism says that (7-2) is false: It is reasonable to retain our commonsense beliefs even though they are not better supported by our evidence than their rivals are.

Epistemological conservatism is subject to an important objection. To begin, there is a significant way in which the analogy between believing and practical actions breaks down. Suppose that you already own a car and are considering keeping it or replacing it. As we are understanding this example, all your options include owning some car or other. Perhaps you could choose not to have one at all, but that, we may assume, is a terrible option for you. In the belief examples, however, you do have the option of suspending judgment about the propositions in question. To see the significance of this, consider the following example:

Example 7.2:   Two Suspects

Detective Jones has definitively narrowed down the suspects in a crime to two individuals, Lefty and Righty. There are good reasons to think that Lefty did it, but there are equally good reasons to think that Righty did it. There is conclusive reason to think that no one other than Lefty or Righty did it.

What should Jones think? Under these circumstances, it clearly would be unreasonable for him to think that Lefty did it and Righty did not. It would be equally unreasonable for him to think that Righty did it and Lefty did not. Clearly, he should suspend judgment about whether Lefty did it and, equally, he should suspend judgment about whether Righty did it. Furthermore, the mere fact that he already believes that one of them, say Lefty, did it, is of no epistemological significance whatsoever. Suppose Jones came upon the evidence about Lefty first and so reasonably came to believe that Lefty did it. Once he learns that there is equally good evidence for the proposition that Righty did it, he should stop believing that Lefty did it. Returning to the practical matter of the car, when a person owning one car learns that there is another equally good car, even one that he could trade for at no cost, it is not true that he should get rid of the already owned car. Part of the reason for this is that there is no analogue of suspending judgment.

It may be that there are some costs involved in changing beliefs. At the very least, it can be cognitively disruptive. There may be other beliefs that have to be changed when the one under consideration is changed. This might lead you to think that there are factors to be weighed against the evidential considerations and that these other considerations might alter the outcome in some cases. But in thinking along these lines one is allowing practical considerations to enter into epistemological evaluations. As we saw in earlier chapters, there can be practical considerations relevant to beliefs, but such considerations do not affect the epistemic evaluation of beliefs.

It is possible that defenders of epistemological conservatism can find a way to modify their theory to avoid the objection raised. Perhaps there is some relevant difference between the beliefs of the detective in the example just given and our ordinary beliefs that a suitably modified conservative principle could appeal to. But until such a difference is established, it is best to look beyond epistemic conservatism in developing a response to *The Alternative Hypotheses Argument*.

B2: Immediate Perceptual Justification One might think that our experiential evidence really is better evidence for the proposition that there are things as we seem to experience them than for the proposition that we are dreaming that there are such things, or that we are being deceived by an evil demon or a computer into thinking that there are such things, or any other specific skeptical alternative. Advocates of this view will reject premise (7-1) of *The Alternative Hypotheses Argument.*

One statement of this view can be found in the work of Roderick Chisholm. In his *Theory of Knowledge,* Chisholm proposes as fundamental epistemological principles such principles as the following:

> If S believes that he perceives something to have a certain property F, then the proposition that he does perceive something to be F, as well as the proposition that there is something that is F, is one that is *reasonable* for S.[17]

Notice that the antecedent of this principle requires that S believe that he perceives something to be F, not merely that it be true that he seems to see something F. So this principle may not fit our situation exactly, because the modest foundationalist view we are considering takes the fundamental evidence to be perceptual experiences, not beliefs about them. Still, Chisholm's view is close enough to be relevant here.

What bears emphasis is that Chisholm does not derive this principle from some other, more fundamental truths. One can imagine a skeptic producing a rival principle, say, that when one has an experience and believes that one is dreaming or that one is being tricked by an evil demon, one is reasonable in those beliefs. Chisholm's view would be that his own principle is correct and these others are wrong. He might defend his view in part by noting that his principle can explain how we have knowledge of the external world. Chisholm's approach bears some similarity to Moore's view discussed earlier.

Another philosopher who defends a view along these lines is James Pryor. He writes:

> My view is that whenever you have an experience as of *p,* you thereby have immediate *prima facie* justification for believing *p.* Your experiences do not, in the same way, give you immediate *prima facie* justification for believing that you are dreaming, or being deceived by an evil demon, or that any of the skeptic's other hypotheses obtain.[18]

Pryor's idea is that our perceptual experiences make it seem as if there are certain things external to us, things such as trees, houses, other people, and so on. He thinks that we are justified in taking things to be as they seem, provided we do not have defeating evidence. That is why he says the justification is merely *prima facie.* This means that the evidential support can be defeated by other evidence. In the typical case, it is not.

Pryor acknowledges that one might like to have a more informative explanation of why our experiences justify our commonsense beliefs. He rejects a number of potential explanations of this. For example, his view is *not* that our commonsense beliefs are justified by our experiences because there is a reliable connection between them.[19] One might try to get some mileage out of the fact that our perceptual beliefs seem to be *irresistible* in the light of our experiences, but Pryor denies that this carries any epistemic significance.[20] Nor does he give any weight to the "best explanation" account, which will be covered in the next section. The best he gives in defense of his view is that our experiences have a kind of "phenomenal force": When we see a table, it "feels as if" there really is a table there. And this, he thinks, is significant.

The immediate perceptual justification thesis can thus be summed up in the following principle:

> IPJ.   Whenever a person has an experience as of p's being the case, the person has immediate *prima facie* justification for believing p.

Since this justification is merely *prima facie,* it is possible for it to be defeated. It is also possible, of course, for a person to have a second source of justification for a proposition that has justification of the sort described in (IPJ). Thus, the proposition that there is a table in front of me might be justified in this way, and it might have additional justification from the fact that I've heard someone else say that there is a table there.

One difficulty for (IPJ) is that it seems somewhat *ad hoc.* This can be brought out by imagining a defender of the evil genius theory. Such a person can equally well assert that our experiences "just are" evidence for propositions about the evil genius rather than for propositions about ordinary objects. Furthermore, it is possible that the idea that our experiences make it "feel as if" there are external objects is a mistake. Perhaps our beliefs result in part from training or indoctrination. Perhaps they result from a built-in bias. It would be good to have some more general defense of our preferred position. Thus, one might agree with Pryor's claim that our experiences do give us reason to believe commonsense propositions and not skeptical alternatives, but one might also think that there must be some more general theoretical account of reasonable belief that explains this fact.

It is possible that defenders of (IPJ) will defend their view by appeal to considerations similar to those used in defense of inductive reasoning. The idea there was that using observed cases as the basis for drawing conclusions about unobserved cases was simply part of the idea of good reasoning. Analogously, defenders of (IPJ) might claim, believing commonsense external-world propositions on the basis of perceptual experiences just is good reasoning. Yet, to many, the cases seem importantly different. There must be, the critics contend, some explanation of why the experiences we have justify the beliefs they do. Unlike (PFR), principles such as (IPJ) and Chisholm's principle about perception are not fundamental principles.

There is a second, and possibly related, difficulty for (IPJ). The principle makes use of the idea of a person having an experience as of p's being the case. This idea may seem reasonably clear. When you look at a table, you have an experience as of its being the case that there is table there. When you see a book, you have an experience as of its being the case that there is a book before you. However, there is a difficult question about this idea, as is brought out by the following example:

> *Example 7.3:   Three People in a Garden*
>
> Three people, Expert, Novice, and Ignorant, are standing in a garden looking at a hornbeam tree. They have a clear and unobstructed view of the tree. The visual appearance present to each of the three people in the garden is exactly the same. (Minor differences due to their slightly different positions are irrelevant to the example.) Expert knows a lot about trees and can easily identify most trees, including this one, immediately. Novice knows a little about trees but is unfamiliar with hornbeams. Ignorant does not know anything about trees. He does not know which of the things in the garden is a tree and which is a flower.

A question a defender of (IPJ) must face is this: What do these people experience? That is, do they all have an experience as of its being the case that there is a hornbeam tree before them, or that there is a tree before them, or that there is a green and brown object before them? Or do they have experiences that differ in content?

If defenders of (IPJ) say that they all have an experience as of there being a hornbeam there, then their theory seems to yield the incorrect result that even Novice and Ignorant are justified in believing that there is a hornbeam there. If they say that they all have an experience as of there being a tree there, then the theory seems to yield the incorrect result that even Ignorant is justified in believing that the thing he is looking at is a tree. Perhaps, then, defenders of (IPJ) should say that the experience is just as of its being the case that there is something partially green and partially brown there. While not obviously unacceptable, this makes the content of what's immediately justified more limited than defenders of the theory seemed to have in mind.

It is possible for defenders of (IPJ) to argue that background information and prior experiences can affect what one's experiences are like. Thus, even though Expert, Novice, and Ignorant all have visually identical experiences, Expert has an experience as of its being the case that there is hornbeam tree before him, while neither Novice nor Ignorant have an experience as of that proposition being true. Novice (and, presumably, Expert) have an experience as of its being the case that there is a tree there, but Ignorant does not.

Thus, defenders of (IPJ) can spell out the application of their view to this example in a way that may yield the desired results. But it must be admitted that the idea of what it is for one to have an experience as of its being the case that p is far from clear. Some better account of how all this works is needed. One has the sense that defenders of this view are simply saying whatever they must to achieve the desired results. A more general theoretical basis for their view is desirable.

These considerations are by no means decisive. They do not refute the idea some perceptual beliefs enjoy immediate *prima facie* justification. Perhaps the idea could be extended to memory as well: Memory beliefs also have immediate *prima facie* justification. If so, we have a response to premise (7-1) of *The Alternative Hypotheses Argument* and some hope that *The Standard View*, and modest foundationalism, can be vindicated. However, the two considerations just raised do show that there is some unclarity in the idea of what it is for a person to have an experience as of its being the case that p and that it is at least reasonable to wonder why our experiences provide evidence for our commonsense beliefs rather than their skeptical alternatives. We will turn next to a view that attempts to provide the desired explanation.

B3: Inference to the Best Explanation A third response to *The Alternative Hypotheses Argument* shares with the second the claim that premise (7-1) of the argument is false. But the third response holds that it is not a simple or fundamental fact about perceptual experience that it supports our commonsense beliefs. Rather, according to this view, perceptual beliefs are supported by our experiential evidence in much the way theories in science can be supported by the relevant experimental evidence. Very roughly, the idea is that there can be a number of alternative theoretical explanations of a particular event or pattern of events. That is, each theory provides an explanation of why things happen as they do. But, on this view, there can be theoretical grounds for thinking one explanation is a better explanation than another, and that this better explanation is therefore more reasonable to believe than the other.[21]

The general idea of what counts as a best explanation is reasonably familiar. Nevertheless, it proves extremely difficult to spell out the idea in any precise way. An example will illustrate the idea.

Example 7.4:   The Variable Colleague

You work in an office and have a colleague who works with you every day. You notice that your colleague's behavior is quite variable, although not bizarre or extraordinary. Some days he is in a good mood, other days he is not. You can come up with two potential explanations of your observations. Explanation 1 is that your colleague's mood, and consequently his behavior, varies with how well he sleeps. This explanation can be filled out with accounts of why he sleeps better some nights than others and explanations of how sleep affects behavior. Explanation 2 is that your "colleague" is really two different people, identical twins with markedly different personalities. They never go out in public together and never let anyone know that they are twins. They tell each other everything that happens every day, so there are no revealing episodes in which they appear to be ignorant of the things they should remember from previous days.

Each explanation is consistent with your observations. Each does, in some sense, provide an explanation of why you observe the variations in behavior.

There may be something exotic or intriguing about Explanation 2. Nevertheless, it seems highly unreasonable to accept it. Explanation 1 is a much better explanation. One thing that makes Explanation 1 better is its simplicity in comparison to Explanation 2. Explanation 2 is pointlessly complex. It introduces two people, with odd motivations and habits, and a complex scheme for tricking people, when no such complexity is needed to explain the data. It is far more reasonable to believe the mood variation story. Perhaps a second virtue of Explanation 1 is that it better fits with our background information about people. They just do not undertake the complex schemes that Explanation 2 introduces.

A second example may help to clarify the idea. Suppose we see footprints in the sand along the beach. The footprints are in the shape of boots commonly worn by people, though not typically worn by people at the beach. We might wonder why these prints are on the beach. There is an obvious explanation and a host of alternative explanations. The obvious one and one alternative are

T1.   People wearing boots recently walked along the beach.
T2.   Cows wearing boots and walking on their hind legs recently walked along the beach.

Both (T1) and (T2), when suitably filled out, do explain the prints you observed. But (T1) has the virtue of simplicity. It does not introduce the pointless complexity that (T2) introduces. (T1) is the better explanation.

It must be admitted that it is very hard to spell out in detail just what a best explanation is. Simplicity and conforming to background information are two characteristics mentioned previously. However, as Peter Lipton points out in a book-length discussion of inference to the best explanation, there are cases in which explanations that seem to be simple are nevertheless quite unreasonable.[22] For example, some conspiracy theorists propose unified explanations of numerous salient assassinations and other significant political events. They propose some international organization behind all of them. There is a kind of simplicity to this, in contrast to the diverse and independent explanations that most experts regard as much more plausible. Perhaps the conspiracy theory is complex in that it attributes a complex set of behaviors and motivations to one organization, even though it manages to unify the explanations of many events.

Lipton briefly states the application of inference to the best explanation to skepticism:

[As] part of an answer to the Cartesian skeptic who asks how we can know that the world is not just a dream or that we are not just brains in vats, the realist may argue that we are entitled to believe in the external world since hypotheses that presuppose it provide the best explanation of our experiences. It is possible that it is all a dream, or that we are really brains in vats, but these are less good explanations of the course of our experiences than the ones we all believe, so we are rationally entitled to our belief in the external world.[23]

The response to *The Alternative Hypotheses Argument,* then, is that (7-1) is false. We can set this out as a formal argument:

Argument 7.8:   The Best Explanation Argument

8-1.   Our experiential evidence is better explained by (CS) than by (DR), (BIV), (EG), or any other available alternative.

8-2.   If one explanation better explains one's evidence than any other available alternative, then one's evidence better supports that explanation than any of those alternatives.

8-3.   Our evidence better supports (CS) than it supports (DR), (BIV), (EG), or any other alternative (so (7-1) of *The Alternative Hypotheses Argument* is false). (8-1), (8-2).[24]

In support of (8-1) we can point to the fact that the alternative explanations do bring in a kind of complexity—amazingly sophisticated computers, evil geniuses monitoring our thoughts, implausibly orderly dreams. These explanations seem *ad hoc,* complex, and ridiculous. *The Best Explanation Argument* thus seems promising.

Still, there are difficult problems. There are, as noted, questions about exactly what in general counts as a best explanation. There is, further, some question about exactly why the evil genius hypothesis is such a bad explanation anyway. In a certain sense, it is elegant and simple. Rather than a complex world of enduring objects, it poses one all-purpose cause of everything. There is something simple about it. So (8-1) is not obviously true.

Finally, there is a hard question about (8-2). As formulated, this premise says that a person is justified in believing a proposition when it is a better explanation of the relevant data than its rivals. The hard question is whether it is enough for the explanation in fact to be the best explanation, or does the person have to realize that it is the best explanation? Example 7.3 can be used to illustrate the basis for thinking that (8-2) should be revised to include the requirement that the person realize that the explanation is best. In that example, Expert, Novice, and Ignorant were looking at what was in fact a hornbeam tree. Novice was unable to identify the tree by the way it looked. But suppose Novice wondered why the tree looked the way it did and why it had leaves of the particular shape it had. In one use of the phrase "best explanation," it seems to be true that the best explanation of Novice's experience was that there was a hornbeam tree in front of him. After all, nothing else would look just like that. But then, by (8-2), Novice is justified in believing that he sees a hornbeam. But this is the wrong result.

We might get around this problem by revising (8-2), requiring of a justified explanation not merely that it be the best explanation but that the believer have reason to believe that it is the best explanation. Novice, in the example just considered, does not satisfy this condition. So the new principle would have the right results.

This suggests that *The Best Explanation Argument* needs revision, perhaps along the following lines:

> *Argument 7.9:   The Best Explanation Argument (Revised)*
>
> 9-1.   We are justified in believing that our experiential evidence is better explained by (CS) than by (DR), (BIV), (EG), or any other alternative.
>
> 9-2.   If we are justified in believing that one explanation better explains one's evidence than any other explanation, then one's evidence better supports that explanation than any of those alternatives.
>
> ───────────────────
>
> 9-3.   Our evidence better supports (CS) than it supports (DR), (BIV), (EG), or any other alternative (so (7-1) of *The Alternative Hypotheses Argument* is false). (9-1), (9-2)

Perhaps (9-2) avoids the problem proposed for (8-2). And perhaps (9-1) is acceptable as well, at least for those of us who have thought about these matters. But there is a question to worry about here. If the best explanation view is adequate to defend *The Standard View*, and modest foundationalism, then it must be that considerations about best explanations justify the beliefs of people who have not given a moment's thought to skeptical issues and the comparative merits of these explanations. Thus, if this approach is to account for everyone's knowledge, then, apparently, even those who have never thought about any of this must be justified in believing that (CS) explains their observations better than its rivals. Perhaps this is true, but it is likely that critics would have reservations about this view. Thus, they might be more inclined to accept (8-1) than (9-1).

There is, then, a dilemma for defenders of the best explanation response to skepticism. Premise (8-1) seems more plausible than (9-1), at least if the "we" in (9-1) includes ordinary people who have not thought about skepticism. But premise (9-2) is considerably more plausible than (8-2), given the objection based on Example 7.3. The best option for defenders of the best explanation view is to claim that (9-1) is true and to claim that typical people, who have not thought about these matters, are nevertheless justified in believing that (CS) is the best explanation of their experiences.[25]

C. Conclusion

The three responses to *The Alternative Hypotheses Argument* covered in this section do not exhaust the possibilities, but they do give a good indication of the range of responses. Epistemic conservatism seems to be subject to decisive objections. The idea that many commonsense beliefs enjoy immediate *prima facie* justification has some plausibility, but there is a crucial unclarity in the view and it leaves unanswered what seems like a perfectly sensible question: Why do our experiences justify our commonsense beliefs rather than their rivals? Best explanationism attempts to answer this question. Although there are difficult questions about the details of this view, it survives as a plausible response to ordinary-standards skepticism.

One might wonder whether we are justified in believing that best explanations are always true. One can imagine a critic raising questions analogous to those Hume raised about induction. And the response may well be the same: It is not the case that, necessarily, best explanations are always true. But it is the case that, necessarily, one is justified in believing what one knows to be a best explanation. This may even lend some support to the response to Hume's problem advanced earlier in this chapter. One reason to believe that observed regularities will continue to obtain is that this is part of the best explanation of one's experiences.

We have, then, a plausible, though not decisive, response to ordinary-standards skepticism. One might have hoped for a more clear-cut refutation of skepticism. The difficulty of providing that refutation is distressing and reveals the power of the intellectual challenge posed by *The Skeptical View*.

APPENDIX: CONTEXTUALISM

A widely discussed view in recent epistemology is *contextualism*. Some philosophers think that it provides the basis for a good response to skepticism while at the same time giving *The Skeptical View* its due respect. In this section we will briefly examine contextualism.

Contextualism is fundamentally a view about the way the word "knows" functions. The central idea is that the standards for applying the word "knows" vary from one context to another. Sometimes the standards for its application are very high, and in those settings what we express by saying "S knows that p" is usually false. But in other settings the standards are more easily met, and what we express by uttering those same sentences may be true.

The contextualists' idea can best be appreciated by considering a relatively uncontroversial analogy. Suppose you go to the zoo with a young child. The first few animals you see are monkeys and birds. You then go into the elephant area and see a baby elephant. You say to the child, "Look at that elephant. It is big." You then go through the rest of the zoo and see the adult elephants, among other large animals. On your way out, you see the baby elephant again, now standing near the adults. Pointing at the same baby elephant, you say, "Look at the baby elephant. It is so small. It's not big."

An obnoxious onlooker might charge you with contradicting yourself. He might ask you to make up your mind and decide whether the baby elephant is big or not big. "It can't be both," he might say. But you have a sensible reply to this charge. The response draws on a fact about the way the word "big" functions. Whenever we say that something is big, we are comparing the thing in question to the members of some comparison class. We often do not explicitly state what that class is. Instead, the conversational background or the context help determine the comparison. In your first remarks about the elephant, you were comparing the baby elephant to the general group, animals at the zoo. Relative to that group, the baby elephant is big. Later, you were comparing the baby elephant to a more restricted group, elephants. Relative to that group, the baby elephant is not big. You did not contradict yourself. The context in which you used the word "big" changed.

Contextualists in epistemology think that the word "knows" is in some ways like the word "big". In different settings, the word has different standards for application. In ordinary settings, when we talk about the world and make claims about what we know, ordinary standards are in effect. We often can satisfy them. Sometimes, however, we raise the standards for the application of the word "knows". Contextualists typically say that this happens when we discuss arguments about skepticism. Under those circumstances, they say, the skeptics are right. We do not meet the high standards in place in those contexts.

Contextualists claim that their theory has a strength that the theories we have discussed up until now have all lacked. The strength is that it can explain our varying reactions to claims about knowledge. In ordinary settings, we accept a variety of knowledge claims without reservation. They seem plainly correct. And then skeptical arguments come along and many people deny that they know things. Yet, later on, these people will once again confidently claim to have knowledge. Contextualists claim that people are right each time: In the ordinary settings, their claims to knowledge are correct; and in the skeptical contexts, their denials of knowledge are also correct. There is no contradiction involved here, just as there is no contradiction in the things said at the zoo.

There are a variety of ways in which contextualists can work out the details of their view. Evidentialist contextualism accepts an evidentialist view about justification and can even accept much of what modest foundationalism says about knowledge.[26] According to this approach, when we attribute knowledge to someone, how well justified the person has to be for our attribution to be true varies from one context to another. Ordinarily, ordinary standards obtain. We can satisfy those standards. But sometimes the standards are higher. And sometimes, as when we are discussing skepticism, the standards are so high that we do not meet them. In those contexts, attributions of knowledge are typically not true.

Nonevidentialist contextualism typically makes use of an account of knowledge that is closer to some of the nonevidentialist theories discussed in Chapter 5. One such view is the *relevant alternatives* theory.[27] According to this view, a person knows a proposition to be true just in the case the person can "rule out" or "eliminate" all relevant alternatives to that proposition. But what counts as a relevant alternative depends upon the context of the person attributing (or denying) knowledge (and not the context of the person being talked about). In ordinary contexts, only ordinary alternatives are relevant. But in some contexts, such as when skepticism is at issue, a broader range of alternatives count as relevant. With respect to many propositions, we can rule out ordinary alternatives, but not some of the more exotic ones. Hence, in ordinary contexts it is true that we have knowledge, but in other contexts it is not.

An example will make the idea clearer. Suppose Jones sees Smith down the hall. In commenting on this, you say that Jones knows that he sees Smith. This is because Jones can rule out the alternatives to its being Smith that he sees. The alternatives are that he sees, say, Black or White. But he can tell, by the person's size and shape, that it is Smith and not Black or White. So, in this setting, when you say that Jones knows that he sees Smith, what you say is true.

But now suppose the conversation turns to skepticism. Now there are new relevant alternatives. Maybe Jones is having a hallucination. Maybe Smith's previously hidden identical twin is down the hall. Jones cannot rule out these alternatives, because things would appear just the same if they were the case. So now, according to the theory, it would not be correct to say, "Jones knows that he sees Smith."

A question defenders of the relevant alternatives theory must face concerns their use of the phrase "rule out" or "eliminate." They claim that we cannot rule out alternatives such as those just mentioned. This is because these alternatives are consistent with our experience.[28] In other words, Smith cannot rule out the alternative that he sees Jones's twin on the grounds that he has never heard that Jones has a twin and, because he knows Jones well, he would have heard about any twin he had. And he cannot rule out the hallucination alternative on the grounds that it is an inferior explanation of his observations. The relevant alternatives theory is, therefore, committed to extremely high standards for knowledge. It holds that you can rule out an alternative when, and only when, that alternative is inconsistent with your observations.

However exactly the details of contextualism are spelled out, the theory has certain attractions. It implies that a great many of our ordinary attributions of knowledge are correct. If, upon arriving at class one morning you say, "I know that I brought my book with me," contextualists can agree that what you say may well be true. In contrast, skeptics would say that you were wrong. But contextualism also can explain the appeal of *The Skeptical View*. It holds that in the contexts in which we discuss skepticism, skeptical arguments are good arguments. In those contexts, the conclusions skeptics draw are correct. This is because discussion of skepticism causes us to be in conditions in which the standards for knowledge are very high, so high that we cannot meet them.

Contextualism has some liabilities as well.[29] For one thing, it concedes a great deal to skeptics, perhaps more than is correct. Many people, especially fallibilists of all sorts, think that skeptics are wrong when they say that people do not have knowledge. They think that there are defects with the arguments for skepticism. But contextualism, at least in the forms discussed here, implies that in the settings in which skepticism is discussed, the claims of the skeptics are correct. As we have seen, there are some reasonably good replies to skepticism, so it is difficult to see why so much should be conceded to skeptics.

Furthermore, it is far from clear that the word "knows" does shift its standards in the way contextualists claim. In the case of the words that most obviously vary with context, such as "big," it is very easy to see that apparent contradictions need not be genuine contradictions. Thus, when you are told in the preceding example that you first said that the baby elephant is "big" and later said that it is "not big," you probably would not feel as if you had contradicted yourself. If you are moderately sophisticated about these matters, you might simply explain that you meant "big for an animal" and "not big for an elephant." You would not find your first statement called into question by your second. In contrast, if you

find yourself moved by the skeptical arguments, you probably think that your ordinary claims are called into question. This suggests that "knows" differs cru-
cially from words like "big" and casts some doubts on the contextualist analysis.

Finally, it is worth noting the similarity of what evidentialist versions of contextualism say about skepticism to what modest foundationalists say about skepticism. Recall that evidentialist versions of contextualism say that we have good
reasons to believe many of the things we ordinarily believe, reasons good enough
to yield knowledge. Relative to ordinary standards, we also have good reason to
deny that we are brains in vats. In light of *The Alternative Explanations Argument*,
these contextualists must have some account of why these reasons are good
enough to give us knowledge (by ordinary standards). They will, presumably,
have to appeal to one of the views along the lines of those we discussed in response to that argument. Contextualism by itself—the mere view that the standards for attributions of knowledge vary—does nothing to explain why it is true
that we meet ordinary standards. This is not an objection to contextualism.
Rather, the point is important because it reveals that the evidentialist version of
contextualism as a partial response to skepticism depends upon the adequacy
of one of the other previously discussed responses.

The adequacy of the nonevidentialist version of contextualism previously
mentioned, the relevant alternatives theory, as a response to skepticism depends upon the merits of the idea that to have knowledge is to be able to rule
out, in the special sense of "rule out" that the theory uses, alternatives. This is,
in its own right, a controversial theory. One difficulty it seems to face is that it
is hard to see how it can account for knowledge based on inductive reasoning.
This is because the falsity of an inductive conclusion is never ruled out by one's
evidence, and it is hard to see why the falsity of the conclusion is not a relevant
alternative in any case of inductive reasoning.[30] Contextualism could also be developed in ways that draw on the other nonevidentialist theories discussed in
Chapter 5. It would, however, inherit the difficulties of those theories.

ENDNOTES

1. This ignores special cases in which you have reason to think that the As will be Bs
   for the near future but will cease being Bs later on. In such a case, you might have
   good reason to think that the next A will be a B but that not all As will be Bs.
2. David Hume, *Enquiry Concerning Human Understanding*, 2nd ed., edited by L. A.
   Selby-Bigge (Oxford: Oxford University Press, 1962), Section IV, Part II, p. 35
3. *Enquiry Concerning Human Understanding*, Section IV, Part II, p. 35.
4. *Enquiry Concerning Human Understanding*, Section IV, Part II, pp. 35–6.
5. It is possible that a defender of the inductive justification of induction would object
   instead to premise (5-7). The claim would be that the inductive justification does
   appeal to (PF) (in the way described in the text) but that the argument can still
   justify the principle. The considerations presented in the present paragraph would
   seem to undermine this response as well.
6. See Hans Reichenbach, *Experience and Prediction* (Chicago: University of Chicago
   Press, 1938).
7. Brian Skyrms, "The Pragmatic Justification of Induction," *Choice and Chance*, 2nd ed.
   (Belmont, CA: Wadsworth, 1975), p. 43.

8. Bertrand Russell, *The Problems of Philosophy* (Oxford: Oxford University Press, 1959), p. 65. Russell goes on to formulate explicitly a somewhat different, and more detailed, principle.

9. The idea presented here is based on the proposal made by Peter F. Strawson in *Introduction to Logical Theory* (New York: John Wiley & Sons, 1952).

10. Assuming, of course, that you do not have defeating evidence about its color.

11. The topic of *a priori* knowledge is a complex and controversial one. The claim here is simply that (PFR) is the sort of thing that can be known simply through understanding, in much the way it can be known that all bachelors are male or all mothers are parents. For more on *a priori* knowledge, see Chapter 8.

12. In light of this, one might want to reexamine what was said earlier about the inductive defense of induction.

13. This problem is often called "The New Riddle of Induction." The classic formulation of the puzzle is in Nelson Goodman, *Fact, Fiction, and Forecast* (Cambridge, MA: Harvard University Press, 1955).

14. In Chapter 8 we will consider extending the *a priori* defense of induction to questions about perception and memory.

15. The discussion here focuses on the best explanation of our overall experiences. More narrowly focused versions of the same issues could be developed. These would examine the best explanations of the specific experiences one is having at a particular time. Essentially, the same points would apply.

16. For a critical discussion of this view, see Richard Foley, "Epistemic Conservatism," *Philosophical Studies* 43 (1983): 165–82.

17. *Theory of Knowledge* (Englewood Cliffs, NJ: Prentice Hall, 1966), p. 45.

18. "The Skeptic and the Dogmatist," *Nous* 34 (2000): 517–49. The quotation is from p. 536.

19. "The Skeptic and the Dogmatist," endnote 6.

20. "The Skeptic and the Dogmatist," endnote 37.

21. An interesting defense of this response to skepticism can be found in Jonathan Vogel, "Cartesian Skepticism and Inference to the Best Explanation," *Journal of Philosophy* 87 (1990): 658–66. For critical discussion, see Richard Fumerton, *Metaepistemology and Skepticism* (Lanaham, MA: Rowman and Littlefield, 1995), pp. 207–14.

22. *Inference to the Best Explanation* (London: Routledge, 1993). See especially Chapter 4.

23. *Inference to the Best Explanation*, p. 72.

24. (8-3) denies premise (7-1) of *The Alternative Explanations Argument*. But (8-3) does not imply that we are justified in believing (CS). (8-3) leaves open the possibility that (CS) is merely the best of a bad set of explanations, and thus not justified. To use the kind of view under consideration here to support the claim that our commonsense beliefs are justified, rather than just to refute (7-1) of the argument, it would be necessary to defend a stronger claim: (CS) is not only better than the rivals but is a very good explanation. Defenders of modest foundationalism who appeal to best explanationism are likely to defend this stronger claim as well.

25. This is not to say that they justifiably believe (i.e., have a well-founded belief) that (CS) is the better explanation; it is just to claim that their evidence does support that proposition.

26. For a defense of this kind of contextualism, see Stewart Cohen, "Contextualism, Skepticism, and the Structure of Reasons," *Philosophical Perspectives* 13 (1999): 57–89.

27. A version of this theory is defended by David Lewis in "Elusive Knowledge," *Australasian Journal of Philosophy* 74 (1996): 549–67.

28. This is the view David Lewis defends in "Elusive Knowledge."

29. The material in this section is drawn from Richard Feldman, "Skeptical Problems, Contextualist Solutions," *Philosophical Studies* 103 (2001): 61–85.

30. For discussion of this point, and additional objections to the relevant alternatives theory, see Jonathan Vogel, "The New Relevant Alternatives Theory," *Philosophical Perspectives* 13 (1999): 155–80.

CHAPTER EIGHT

Epistemology and Science

This chapter examines *The Naturalistic View*. *The Naturalistic View* is not a single thesis about the conditions for knowledge and justification. Instead, it encompasses a general view about the proper role of science in epistemology. It holds that science should play a much more significant role in epistemology than advocates of *The Standard View* have traditionally given it. We will examine two issues arising out of *The Naturalistic View*.[1] The first issue concerns the implications of some research results that seem to show that people systematically reason badly and, perhaps, know less than *The Standard View* suggests. The second issue arises because epistemologists usually defend and discuss *The Standard View* without paying attention to scientific results. Naturalists think that this is a methodological mistake.

I. EVIDENCE OF HUMAN IRRATIONALITY

On the basis of a large body of research into the ways people form beliefs, some philosophers conclude that people are systematically irrational.[2] The charge is that people have a deeply rooted tendency to make a variety of logical blunders, errors concerning probability, mistakes involving causation, and so on. Although results such as these are not likely to support skeptical conclusions as broad and general as those discussed in Chapters 6 and 7, they do call into question the extent of our knowledge. If we make as many errors as the critics say we do, then perhaps we do not have knowledge even when we manage to get things right. If we make as many mistakes as some critics charge, then it is unlikely that we know as much as *The Standard View* says we do.

A. Examples of Alleged Irrationality

This section will review a few of the examples frequently discussed in the philosophical literature on empirical evidence about rationality. Readers are encouraged to give their own answers to the questions before reading the explanations in the following section.

A1. The Questions

Question 1: The Selection Task In this experiment subjects are shown four cards. They are told that each card has a letter of the alphabet on one side and a number on the other side. They can see only one side of each card, and they see a vowel, a consonant, an even number, and an odd number.

E	K	4	7
Card 1	Card 2	Card 3	Card 4

They are asked to identify which cards they must turn over to examine the other side in order to find out if there are any violations of the rule:

> If a card has a vowel on one side, then it has an even number on the other side.

Question 2: Linda, the Bank Teller A second, much discussed example asks people to rank the likelihood of several propositions about a person given an initial description of that person.[3] The description is as follows: Linda is 31 years old, single, outspoken, and very bright. She majored in philosophy in college, and she was heavily involved in issues concerning discrimination and social justice. Given this description, they are asked to rank, in order of the probability that they are true, the following statements:

a.   Linda is active in the feminist movement.
b.   Linda is a bank teller.
c.   Linda is a bank teller and is active in the feminist movement.

Question 3: Frequencies of letters A third example reveals something about memory.[4] Suppose a word is chosen randomly from an English text. Order the following from most probable to least probable (1 = most probable, 4 = least probable):

R is the first letter.

K is the third letter.

R is the third letter.

K is the first letter.

These are only a small sample of the questions used to test human rationality. We turn now to the answers people commonly give to these questions.

A2: Answers and Common Responses

Answer to Question 1: Problems with Conditionals One author reports a study in which about 45 percent of the respondents said it was necessary to check cards 1 and 3, a somewhat smaller percentage said that only card 1 needed to be checked, and fewer than 5 percent said that cards 1 and 4 had to be checked.[5] This sort of result is, apparently, quite common.

Critics contend that this result reveals a tendency to commit a serious logical blunder. You do have to check card 1, because the rule would be shown to be false if there were an odd number on the other side. Similarly, card 4 must be checked. If there is a vowel on the other side, then this card falsifies the rule. However, the rule does not say what is on the other side of a card with a consonant. So it does not matter what is on the other side of card 2. There is no need to check it. Nor is there a need to check card 3. If there is a vowel, then this card conforms to the rule. If there is a consonant, then, as in the case of card 2, it is irrelevant. Thus, the correct answer is one given by very few people: cards 1 and 4 must be checked.

It is worth noting that people do better when faced with a logically identical problem using more realistic elements. For example, if the question concerns whether there are violations of the rule:

If a person is drinking beer, then the person is at least 21 years old

and the cards show what they are drinking (Coke or beer) on one side and their age on the other, people realize that they do need to check the age of the person drinking beer and the drink of the person under 21.

Answer to Question 2: The Conjunction Problem People typically answer (c), that Linda is bank teller and active in the feminist movement, is the most probable of the options. However, this answer violates a rule of probability: For any propositions A and B, $Pr(A\&B) \leq Pr(A)$. In other words, the probability of a conjunction cannot be greater than the probability of one of its conjuncts. Because (c) is a conjunction of the other two options, it cannot be the most probable option. Consider (b). There are two ways (b) could be true. One way is for (c) to be true; the other is for Linda to be a bank teller who is not active in the feminist movement. Call this option (d). The probability of (b) is thus the probability of (c) plus the probability of (d). As long as (d) has some probability, the probability of (b) must be greater than the probability of (c) Thus (c), The Common answer, cannot be correct. (Researchers are less interested in whether (a) or (b) is a better answer.)

Answer to Question 3: Selective Memory Problems Many people say that it is more probable that each letter is first than third. In fact, third is more probable. (The comparative frequencies of R and K are not of central interest here.)

B. The Argument for Human Irrationality

The examples described in Section A, and many more like them, illustrate ways in which people go wrong in their thinking. An argument for our irrationality can be formulated on the basis of the results described:

> *Argument 8.1:   The People Are Irrational Argument*
>
> 1-1.   People frequently give incorrect and unreasonable answers to questions such as those just described.
> 1-2.   If (1-1) is true, then people are significantly irrational.
> _____
> 1-3.   People are significantly irrational. (1-1), (1-2)

There are some obviously imprecise elements in this argument. There is no precise account of what counts as giving incorrect answers "frequently" or what counts as being "significantly" irrational. This lack of precision will not figure prominently in the discussion that follows. What is at issue is whether this argument establishes its conclusion. Because the argument is valid, critics must find a basis to resist one of the premises. Objecting to (1-1) requires arguing that the answers people give to the questions are not so bad, that they do not show irrationality even in these cases. Objecting to (1-2) requires arguing that failing on these questions is not evidence of significant irrationality. The idea would be that there is something special about these particular questions and that making mistakes here is not indicative of any general irrationality. (The second response may end up turning on just what counts as being "significantly" irrational.)

C. Defending Human Rationality

Some people are strongly inclined to think that whatever the examples described in Section A show, they do not show that people are in any general way irrational or unreasonable. They think that there must be something wrong with *The People Are Irrational Argument*. This section will review a few of these responses to the argument.

C1. Evolutionary Arguments One reply to *The People Are Irrational Argument* is based on the idea that people must be rational because they have survived, and, indeed, thrived in the evolutionary battle.[6] The idea behind this response is simple. People's beliefs guide their behavior, and if their beliefs were systemically mistaken, they would not be able to behave successfully. For example, if people were systematically wrong in their beliefs about such things as where to find food or how to avoid enemies, they would not survive. Thus, even if we make mistakes on the questions in the studies, we must not make mistakes on the broad range of issues that most affect our survival. As a result, (1-2) is false.

However, it is difficult to see in these evolutionary considerations any good basis for thinking that (1-2) is false. The fact that human beings have survived shows at most that people reason in some ways that are advantageous for survival. But that is far short of showing that the errors made in the experimental situation are not evidence of significant and widespread failures of rationality. There are several reasons for this. First, many beliefs are about theoretical and abstract matters that have little direct connection to survival. These beliefs could be irrational without undermining the chances for survival. Furthermore, beliefs that enhance survival need not be true or even reasonable. For example, if a person has just the slightest reason to believe that a particular kind of food is dangerous to eat, the person might irrationally leap to the conclusion that the food is dangerous. This will be part of an extremely cautious stance toward food sources. If there are plenty of other food sources around, this approach will work out well. But the beliefs involved may fail to be epistemically rational.[7] Finally, optimistic and self-serving beliefs can be beneficial to us even when they are not epistemically rational beliefs. Evolutionary pressures might promote such beliefs. As a result, there is little reason to think that evolutionary considerations establish that there is anything wrong in *The People Are Irrational Argument*.

C2. An Analogy to Language Another response to the argument relies on an alleged analogy between reasoning and language.[8] The rules of correct grammar for English derive, in some sense, from the way speakers of the language actually speak. Exactly how this works is a complicated matter that we will not address here. But the alternatives to this idea are highly implausible. One alternative would be that there is some committee that sets the rules, in somewhat the same way that the authorities in a professional sport set the rules for the games. But there simply is no governing body setting the rules for English. While some professors and analysts may wish they had that job, they simply do not.

A second alternative is that the rules for correct English usage are somehow set independently of all human activity in the way, perhaps, that rules of arithmetic are set. The rules of arithmetic seem to exist independently of anything anyone does. We could not make $2 + 2 = 5$ no matter what rules we established or how we chose to speak.[9] In contrast, the English language could have been different. Indeed, it *is* different than it used to be. The rules of the language change over time, as anyone reading English texts from long ago can easily see.

If the rules for proper English are neither abstract necessary truths in the way the rules of arithmetic are nor arbitrary conventions set by a governing body the way the rules of football are, then they are best seen as some kind of generalization from, and perhaps idealization of, the way people actually speak. That is, they are a function of how people speak. This is not to say that people never break the rules of English. Surely they do. Still, they cannot be completely incorrect either. If people by and large come to speak a certain way, eventually that becomes the correct way to speak.

If the rules of good reasoning are analogous to the rules of proper speech, then they too are a function of how people actually do reason. If that is the case, then people cannot reason incorrectly all the time, or even a great deal of the time. In some sense, people must have a general tendency to reason correctly.

Assume for the sake of discussion that the analogy between the rules of a language and the rules of reasoning is a good one. It is unclear whether this would provide any good reason to resist *The People Are Irrational Argument*. Even if how we speak somehow determines what correct English is, we still may routinely speak incorrectly. Perhaps it is our more considered and reflective utterances that determine correctness, and our common unreflective utterances depart from those standards. Something similar could be true in the case of reasoning: Our common and unconsidered judgments could be frequently irrational, even if rationality is determined by what we do when we are more careful. If the conclusion of the argument is just that we are, as a matter of fact, often irrational, the conclusion might still be true. Of course, if the conclusion is intended to assert something stronger, that we are systematically irrational even when we are more careful, then the analogy to language may serve to undermine the argument (perhaps by bringing the second premise into doubt).

There is, however, good reason to doubt that the analogy between reasoning and language is all that strong. Language is simply a social practice. Reasoning seems different. It is more like arithmetic. Our minds could be constructed in such a way that we have built-in tendencies to make significant logical errors. Perhaps we should not be blamed for those errors. And perhaps the standards for rational belief cannot assume capacities well beyond those any person could have. Still, it could be that people routinely make significant errors, even when they are careful. The idea that people routinely speak incorrectly does seem incoherent, but the idea that we reason incorrectly does not.

The view that an analogy to language provides the basis for a reply to *The People Are Irrational Argument* is not promising.

D. Rethinking the Examples

The arguments considered in Section C attempted to reply to *The People Are Irrational Argument* in a general way by trying to show that whatever the research showed about how people form beliefs, it could not show that they are significantly irrational. In this section, we will examine some responses that look more specifically at the examples and also at the concept of rationality, in an effort to show that the implications of the research are not as bleak as one might think.

D1. Language Problems One question about some of the examples concerns whether people understand the words in the same way as the experimenters intend. Consider again the example about Linda the bank teller. People are asked to rate the various alternatives for how "probable" they are. The conjunction rule that people violate is an uncontroversial rule about probability. However, it is not clear that people understand the word "probable" in the intended way. To grasp what people may be thinking about, consider a different example. Suppose that you go to a special screening of a movie. The movie tells the story about Linda during her college years, portraying her as a well-educated, politically active person. As the movie nears its end, you are told that you will see two descriptions of a closing scene and be given a choice of which one you will see. One option is that in the closing scene she will be a bank teller. The other option is that she will be a bank teller who is active in the feminist movement. You may choose to see the second option for the plausible reason that it is a more "likely" way for the story to go. That is, it is a better ending. It is true that the description of the first option leaves open whether Linda is active in the feminist movement. But by not including this key fact about her in its description, it may strike you as a worse ending, less in keeping with the story that preceded it. It is possible that when people give their answers to the question in this case, the question they take themselves to be answering is about which ending is a better ending to the story about Linda rather than a question about mathematical probability. And perhaps their answer to the question they have in mind is a sensible one.

If people are interpreting the question in the way just described, then it is not clear that they are making any error at all. If they are making an error, it is perhaps an error in interpreting the question. In this case, the example may illustrate one way in which people misunderstand one another, but it does not illustrate a sort of irrationality that calls into the question the justification of our beliefs.

D2. Lack of Information Reconsider next the example about the frequency with which letters appear in particular positions in words. Psychologists Nisbett and Ross describe people as giving "biased" estimates as a result of their use of "the availability heuristic" in cases like this one.[10] Thus, it seems that because people can think of more words that begin with a particular letter than words that have that letter in third position, they conclude that there are more words with that letter in first position than in third position. More generally, perhaps they typically conclude that there are more As than Bs when they can think of more As than Bs. In other words, they judge on the basis of the available information about As. And this can lead people astray. In this case, it is because it is easier for us to bring to mind words by which letter they have first than by which letter they have third.

If this is what people do, then the inference they make seems to be exactly the right one, given the premise they have. It is, roughly, an inference from a fact about the observed (or remembered) words to all words. This seems to be a standard inductive inference. Their conclusion may be wrong, but the inference is not unreasonable.

One might still complain about what people do in this case. The complaint would be that they should have realized that they had additional evidence that was relevant, evidence that would tend to discount (or "defeat") the evidence they thought of. That is, they should have thought of the fact that their memories work in the way they do.[11]

It is difficult to know exactly what to make of this charge. To evaluate their beliefs from an evidentialist perspective requires that we determine what evidence people "have" in this sort of case. Do they just have as evidence the probabilistic and frequency information they think of? If so, then they believe what their evidence supports. In that case, the example is no evidence of irrationality at all. Do they also have as evidence the other facts, the facts that show that their recalled data are likely to be biased? If so, then the example is evidence of irrationality: What they believe is not supported by their evidence. It is hard to say which view is correct. A restrictive notion of evidence possessed would lead to the result that people have only the limited evidence and that their beliefs are rational. A more expansive notion would not.

Thus, a plausible response to this alleged error is that it is not a case of unjustified belief or bad inference. Instead, it is a case in which people fail to bring to mind some information that, in some sense, they could have considered. In any case, merely getting the wrong answer does not show irrationality. And not knowing that one's memory works in a way that is apt to make what one remembers not representative does not show irrationality.

D3. Using Different Rules Consider again the example of Linda and the violation of the conjunction rule. Suppose that people are estimating probabilities (rather than interpreting the question differently). What rule do people use? It is likely that they estimate probabilities by means of similarity:

> The more like the typical A a thing is, the more probable it is an A.

When they are making comparative probability judgments, perhaps they use a rule such as

> If X is more like the typical A than it is like the typical B, then it is more probable that X is an A than that X is a B.

These rules often yield correct results and they are relatively easy to apply. They are far easier to apply than the more complex rules of probability that would get the correct results in the example about Linda.

These rules do lead to incorrect answers in some cases. For example, when there are a lot more Bs than As it can be more probable that a thing is an atypical B than a typical A. Suppose you saw an extremely tall 25-year-old man who appears to be physically fit. He looks like someone who might be a professional basketball player. But the odds are that he is not: Relatively few people who fit that description make it as professionals. The numbers of professional players are so small that resemblance to the typical one is not a good guide to probability.

Thus, a plausible account of this example is that people are using a different, fairly sensible, and easily applied rule. It is difficult to see why this makes for irrationality.

D4. Summary The cases considered so far are cases in which people often form mistaken beliefs, largely because they either do not have (or, possibly, fail to think of relevant evidence) or do not know relevant rules or interpret questions differently than was intended. It is not clearly correct to conclude that these are cases of irrationality, given that it is not clear exactly what beliefs fit the evidence people have in these situations. The examples are therefore less than decisive as cases of irrationality. Premise (1-1) of *The People Are Irrational Argument* is therefore called into question.

It is also unclear just how many of our beliefs might be contaminated by the sorts of errors discussed here. A full discussion of this would require an examination of a much larger sample of the alleged errors. Still, it is fair to say that errors such as those discussed here do not reveal systematic errors widespread enough to undermine *The Standard View* to a significant degree. Depending upon exactly how the sentence "people are significantly irrational" is interpreted, this shows that there is some doubt about premise (1-2)—which says that the results are evidence of significant irrationality—or it shows that the conclusion of the argument is consistent with *The Standard View*.

E. Another Basis for Charges of Irrationality

There is, however, another class of cases in which people more clearly violate evidentialist standards. These are cases in which people are guided by emotions rather than evidence. Wishful thinking illustrates this. Suppose that there is an accident and it is known that most of the people involved were killed or seriously injured. Sometimes in real cases of this sort, survivors, or their relatives, say in follow-up interviews that they believed all along that they would survive. If those reports are true, the beliefs were irrational. (They might be useful, but they are not epistemically rational beliefs. They do not fit the evidence.) Cases of the opposite sort occur as well. There may be such a thing as fearful thinking. For example, good students who have ample evidence of their competence sometimes believe that they will get bad grades. Nervousness and other psychological factors may contribute to this. And this fearful thinking may cause the students to study harder than they otherwise would. Still, the belief is not supported by the evidence. Many other beliefs illustrate similar points. People may be led to their beliefs as a result of their desire to be different or their desire to conform. Perhaps some people believe in occult phenomena with little evidence but as a result of the appeal those beliefs have for them. In addition, there are surely times when people form beliefs because they consider only part of their evidence, ignoring disconfirming evidence for one reason or another.

Thus, even if the rationality experiments show only departures from rules of probability and logic, rather than irrationality, it would be a mistake to conclude that people do not have irrational beliefs. Surely they do.

F. Conclusion

The general arguments, discussed in Section C, designed to show that people could not be irrational do not succeed. They failed to show that *The People Are*

Irrational Argument must be mistaken. It is also worth noting that those arguments did not say very clearly what was wrong with the argument anyway.

The responses discussed in Section D dealt with various examples in different ways. They show that there are explanations for people giving answers other than the intended ones without their being irrational. But these responses are far from conclusive. The present discussion only dealt with a few examples, and it is unclear whether similar responses would work for others. Furthermore, the discussion illustrated some complexities and obscurities in the concept of rationality. For example, it is not entirely clear what to say about cases in which people use simple and generally effective rules that, in certain cases, yield results incompatible with those yielded by the proper rules of logic. The idea that any violation of a rule of logic or probability constitutes a case of irrationality seems implausible. All of this adds up to reason to doubt (1-1) of the argument.

Finally, a stronger case for widespread irrationality comes from the fact that not all our beliefs are guided by our evidence. Sometimes we are guided by emotions. Sometimes we ignore part of our evidence. Sometimes we make mistakes about what our evidence supports. The resulting beliefs fail to be rational, even if they have other virtues. But this is no basis for any form of general philosophical skepticism. It does not show that people are incapable of having knowledge or reasonable belief. At most, it shows that in some range of cases, perhaps more cases than most of us would like to admit, our beliefs are not epistemically reasonable.

II. NATURALISTIC EPISTEMOLOGY

A. Background

Advocates of *The Naturalistic View* emphasize that there are important connections between philosophy and science generally and epistemology and psychology or cognitive science particularly.[12] One sort of connection is illustrated by our discussion of the alleged evidence for irrationality. Another idea about how science and epistemology are connected traces back to an extremely influential article by W. V. O. Quine.[13] In this section, we will examine two charges against *The Standard View* that can be extracted from the ideas of naturalistic epistemologists.

B. Psychology Instead of Epistemology

The first naturalistic charge against *The Standard View* amounts to the claim that traditional epistemology should be abandoned in favor of the empirical study of human cognition. This is not so much an argument for the conclusion that *The Standard View* is false as it is an objection to the way philosophers have traditionally defended and discussed that view.

Quine argues in the first part of his paper that Cartesian foundationalism has failed. In particular, he rejects the claim that our knowledge of the world, our scientific knowledge, can be derived from statements about our own sensations. As we saw in Chapter 4, Cartesian foundationalism held that anything we know about the world can be derived from such statements. It was argued in Chapter 4, and in Chapter 6, that such a view led inevitably to skepticism. So Quine's view concurs with those conclusions.

However, rather than looking for alternative accounts of knowledge, Quine goes on to say that the traditional effort to respond to skepticism fails, and he recommends what on the surface seems to be the abandonment of epistemology altogether. He writes:

> The stimulation of his sensory receptors is all the evidence anybody has had to go on, ultimately, in arriving at his picture of the world. Why not just see how this construction really proceeds? Why not settle for psychology?[14]

Quine seems to be recommending that we abandon the effort to show that we do in fact have knowledge and that we instead study the psychological processes that take us from sensory stimulations to beliefs about the world. He elaborates on this idea in a widely quoted passage:

> Epistemology, or something like it, simply falls into place as a chapter of psychology and hence of natural science. It studies a natural phenomenon, viz., a physical human subject. This human subject is accorded a certain experimentally controlled input—certain patterns of irradiation in assorted frequencies, for instance—and in the fullness of time the subject delivers as output a description of the three-dimensional external world and its history. The relation between the meager input and the torrential output is a relation that we are prompted to study for somewhat the same reasons that always prompted epistemology: namely, in order to see how evidence relates to theory, and in what ways one's theory of nature transcends any available evidence. . . . But a conspicuous difference between old epistemology and the epistemological enterprise in this new psychological setting is that we can now make free use of empirical psychology.[15]

If there is an argument here that should worry defenders of *The Standard View*, it is not an argument for the conclusion that they are wrong about the extent of our knowledge. Rather, Quine seems to be inferring the following thesis from the failure of Cartesian foundationalism:

N1. Philosophical thinking about knowledge should be abandoned in favor of the empirical study of how people actually go about forming their beliefs.

Although Quine's writings have been extremely influential, not many philosophers have accepted (N1). The failure of Cartesian foundationalism does not imply the failure of modest foundationalism, coherentism, reliabilism, or any other theory of knowledge. So it is difficult to see why epistemology ought to be replaced by psychology simply because Cartesian foundationalism is inadequate. There are other approaches to the same questions that are not thereby shown to be inadequate.

Moreover, Quine's contention that the study of the psychological processes that lead to belief amounts to "epistemology, or something like it" is misleading.

Jaegwon Kim points out a conspicuous difference between traditional epistemology and what Quine recommends: The two fields study strikingly different
topics.[16] The old epistemology studied questions about rationality, justification,
and knowledge. It focused on epistemic support and the question of whether our
basic evidence adequately supports our beliefs about the world. Cartesian foundationalism, with its excessively restrictive account of epistemic support, led to
skepticism. Other accounts do not. What Quine seems to propose requires ignoring these questions about epistemic support and investigating instead the
causal connections between our sensory evidence and our beliefs about the
world. Thus, if we follow the Quinean recommendation, we will study the same
relata—our basic evidence and our beliefs about the world. However, we will
study a different relation. Traditional epistemologists asked whether there was
an epistemic support relation between the data and the beliefs. Naturalistic epistemologists following Quine will study which experiences give rise to which beliefs. The original epistemological questions seem to be perfectly good questions,
well worthy of our attention. It is difficult to see, then, why the availability of this
other field of study, concerning how we reason, is a suitable replacement for
the evaluative questions that are at the heart of epistemology.[17]

Thus, there is little merit to the contention that traditional epistemology
should be replaced by psychology. The first thesis of naturalistic epistemology,
(N1), is without support.

C. Can Epistemological Questions Be Answered *a priori*?

A second, and less extreme, version of naturalism emphasizes the idea that epistemology can, and should, make use of empirical results. Naturalists contend that
traditional discussions of *The Standard View* have improperly ignored scientific
information. Understanding and evaluating this charge requires emphasizing a
distinction that has been prominent in the history of philosophy. This is the distinction between *a priori* knowledge and *a posteriori* knowledge.[18] A person is said
to know something *a priori* when that knowledge is "independent of experience."
In contrast, *a posteriori* knowledge is dependent on experience. Any proposed
examples of *a priori* knowledge are bound to be controversial, but an example
may illustrate the idea.

Contrast the propositions:

1. All bachelors are unmarried.
2. All bachelors eat poorly.

You can know that (1) is true without doing any research into the life styles of
bachelors. Sending out a questionnaire, for example, would be pointless. Suppose you did send out a questionnaire to thousands of people. One question
asked whether the respondent was a bachelor and another asked whether the
person was married. If some questionnaires came back with answers indicat-
ing that the respondent was a bachelor but was married, you would not con-

clude that (1) is false. You would instead conclude that there was an error in that response. No experiential evidence could lead you to think that (1) is false.

In contrast, to know whether (2) is true, you would have to find out what some bachelors eat. Upon learning this, you could decide about (2). Commonsense information, based on observation of a few bachelors as well as general information about people, probably leads you to be confident that (2) is in fact false. But knowledge of (2), or of the falsity of (2), depends upon such information in a way that knowledge of (1) does not. So (1) is the sort of thing that can be known *a priori*, whereas (2) is not.

There are complications. To know that (1) is true, you have to know what it is to be a bachelor and what it is to be married. And this knowledge, of course, comes from experience. But this knowledge is just what is required to grasp the concepts involved in (1). In contrast, you could, at least in principle, fully understand (2) without being in a position to know whether or not it is true. You could understand what a bachelor is and understand what it is to eat poorly,[19] yet not have information about the diets of bachelors.

A precise analysis of the concepts of *a priori* and *a posteriori* knowledge (or justification) would require considerably more work. But perhaps the brief discussion presented here will suffice for the discussion that follows.

The distinction between *a priori* and *a posteriori* knowledge is relevant to the discussion of naturalistic epistemology because some philosophers have suggested that philosophical claims generally, and epistemological claims in particular, are things that can be known *a priori*. And if that is correct, then it follows that scientific information is not needed to know philosophical truths in general or epistemological facts in particular. One of the ideas that can be extracted from Quine's essay on naturalistic epistemology is that science is relevant to epistemology, that epistemological facts cannot be known *a priori*.[20] Many recent philosophers have agreed with this Quinean thesis, arguing that empirical information about the ways people actually form beliefs and other facts about cognition are relevant to epistemology.[21] This leads us to the second charge of naturalistic critics of traditional epistemology. Again, the charge is not that *The Standard View* is false; rather, it is

> N2. Traditional epistemologists have discussed and defended their views without making adequate use of scientific information about how our minds work.

In the remainder of this chapter we will examine the merits of this charge.

There is little doubt that some philosophers have given the impression that their philosophical claims were impervious to any scientific refutation, or any refutation at all. One might associate this sort of attitude with responses to skepticism such as G. E. Moore's.[22] Here is a more recent statement of a view much like Moore's:

> In typical skeptical arguments, we invariably find that we are more certain of the knowledge seemingly denied us than we are of some of the premises. Thus it is not

reasonable to adopt the skeptical conclusion that we do not have that knowledge. The rational stance is instead to deny one or more of the premises . . . we "need not refute the skeptic—we already know that the skeptic is wrong."[23]

This sort of remark can give the impression that the author thinks that no information, empirical (scientific) or otherwise, could possibly show that skepticism is true or could undermine other epistemological claims. This suggests the view that we know *a priori* that we do have knowledge.

Recall also the discussion of immediate perceptual justification in Chapter 7. According to the view discussed there, it is a fundamental epistemological fact that perceptual experiences provide justifying evidence for the corresponding beliefs. This view seems to imply that our experiences do justify the related beliefs. No scientific information about the reliability of sense perception was appealed to in defending this claim. It seemed to be offered as something known *a priori*.

It should be conceded that the naturalists are right when they contend that epistemologists often proceed without paying attention to results in cognitive psychology. Indeed, Chapters 1–7 of this book proceeded with little reference to any results from scientific studies of how we think. All of this can give the impression that epistemology is an *a priori* subject matter, entirely independent of science.

Two ideas will figure prominently in the discussion that follows. The first is that there are a wide variety of claims traditional epistemologists make, and scientific results may bear more heavily on some of these claims than they do on others. The second main idea in the discussion that follows is that there is a three-way distinction among *a priori* knowledge, commonsense (or armchair) knowledge, and scientific knowledge.[24]

It will be helpful in the discussion that follows to identify a few claims traditional epistemologists are apt to make. The first two are modifications of the two claims, (SV1) and (SV2), that constitute *The Standard View,* which were set out in Chapter 1:

E1.   People have a great deal of knowledge of the world around them, including some knowledge of the past, their current surroundings, the future, morality, mathematics, and so on.

E2.   Some of our main sources of knowledge are perception, memory, introspection, testimony, and rational insight.

Some other claims traditionalists make have emerged in later chapters. The ones listed here are representative of other claims made throughout the text and by traditional epistemologists generally:

E3.   Knowledge requires justified true belief that does not essentially depend upon any falsehood.

E4.   A person is justified in believing a proposition when the belief fits the believer's evidence.

The contention of naturalists is that traditional epistemologists improperly assert things such as (E1)–(E4) as if they are *a priori* claims, ignoring scientific results that bear on them.

Consider next the distinction among *a priori*, armchair, and scientific knowledge. *A priori* knowledge was described earlier in this section. Armchair knowledge and scientific knowledge are both kinds of *a posteriori* knowledge. Armchair knowledge includes the things that ordinary people can know without any particular scientific expertise. It is the kind of thing you can know from your armchair. You do not have to go to the lab (or even read reports about what has been done in the lab) to have this knowledge. But armchair knowledge does depend upon experiences and observations of things in the world. It is thus not *a priori* knowledge. Scientific knowledge, as its name suggests, is knowledge that requires some special knowledge of scientific matters. This is knowledge that only those with special information have. The distinctions among *a priori*, armchair, and scientific knowledge are obviously rough, and many items of knowledge would be hard to classify. Still, this three-way classification is helpful in thinking about the naturalists' complaint about traditional epistemology.

When traditionalists such as Moore and his followers assert (E1) and claim to know that skepticism is false, it may seem that they are claiming that this is *a priori* knowledge. Naturalists are apt to think that any such claim is presumptuous. If they then think that such knowledge is not *a priori*, and they think of all non-*a-priori* knowledge as scientific knowledge, then they may conclude that scientific information is needed to argue against skepticism. But adding armchair knowledge to the mix may provide a way to put traditionalism in better light. Traditionalists do not, or, in any case, should not, say that anyone knows *a priori* that skepticism is false. They need not say that it is known *a priori* that we know the things *The Standard View* says we know. Instead, they can claim that this is armchair knowledge. We do not need to study science in order to find out that we know things, but we do have to have experiences in the world. More generally, the view suggested here is that much of the information traditional epistemologists rely on in formulating their theories is armchair knowledge.

Such a view has several advantages. First, its defenders can acknowledge what seems to be a plain fact: We do not have *a priori* knowledge that we know particular contingent facts about the world. We simply do not know *a priori* that we know things about the past or about the colors and shapes of the objects around us. Just as we have learned particular facts about the past or about the world around us, we have learned that we know those sorts of things. Things could have worked out differently. We could have failed to know those sorts of things. That we know them is not *a priori*. It seems equally clear, however, that we do not need to be cognitive scientists to know that we do have knowledge.

When Moore and other traditionalists say that they know that skeptics are wrong, they need not be committed to the implausible claim that no scientific information could possibly undermine *The Standard View*. It surely is at least possible that cognitive science will reveal that our perceptual systems are highly unreliable under certain circumstances and that some things that we take to be knowledge are false or that our beliefs about them are, if true, only coincidentally true.[25] Indeed, the combined force of a large body of results such as those canvassed in Section I of this chapter could lead to the result that we know far less than *The Standard View* implies. It would be a mistake to rule this out as impossible.

Thus, perhaps some of the controversy between traditionalists and advocates of *The Naturalistic View* is eliminated once armchair knowledge is clearly identified. One point some naturalists emphasize is that some epistemological claims are not *a priori*. This is correct. Our knowledge that we know quite a lot, and our knowledge of what we know, is not itself *a priori* knowledge. In other words, we do not know *a priori* that (E1), (E2), and *The Standard View* are true. What some traditionalists claim is that scientific information is not needed in order to know these truths. This, too, is correct. Our knowledge that *The Standard View* is true is armchair knowledge.

There are complications to notice in connection with the status of our claims about the status of the various sources of knowledge. In thinking about this, it will be helpful to bear in mind a distinction between fundamental principles and other, less fundamental, principles. Traditionalists may think that epistemological principles are knowable *a priori*. It was suggested in response to Hume's problem that a fundamental principle, such as (PFR), is knowable *a priori*.[26] Similarly, it is not implausible to hold that a principle about testimonial evidence is also knowable *a priori*. Perhaps something such as the following is an *a priori* truth about testimonial evidence:

> TE.   Knowledge that a particular source has been trustworthy with respect to a given topic in the past provides good reason to believe things that source testifies to on that topic in the future.

Perhaps claims like (E3) and (E4) are also knowable *a priori*. Scientific advances would not undermine claims like these. And even if science were to show that some of the things we firmly believed are false or that some of the sources we routinely trust are not worthy of that trust, general principles such as (E3), (E4), or (TE) would not thereby be called into question.

The claim that we can have *a priori* knowledge of a general truth such as (TE) should not be confused with claims to have *a priori* knowledge of facts about the trustworthiness of particular sources. Traditionalists need not claim that they have *a priori* knowledge of the trustworthiness of sources such as the well-regarded national newspapers, nor need they claim that we know *a priori* that the supermarket tabloids are less than trustworthy. All of this we have learned from experience. It is only the general principles, such as (TE), that can be known *a priori*.

A difficult puzzle about our knowledge of the reliability of perception and memory remains. Consider the claim

>   REL.   My perceptions and memories are reliable guides to the world
>   around me.

One view is that we have armchair knowledge of (REL). According to this view, we can have, without any special knowledge of the sciences, adequate justification for believing (REL). Of course, it is possible that scientific information will defeat this justification. And it is also possible for scientific information to add further confirmation of (REL). The puzzle about (REL) concerns how we could possibly come to learn that it is true. If we did learn any such thing, presumably it would be via a "track record" argument such as

Argument 8.2:   The Memory Argument

2-1.   I have memory beliefs M1, M2.
2-2.   Most of M1, M2, . . . are true.

2-3.   My memory is reliable. (2-1), (2-2)

Each person might use an argument like this one to establish the trustworthiness of his or her own memory. However, these track record arguments seem inadequate to establish their conclusions. If (2-3) is not already justified for me, it is hard to see how I could be justified in accepting (2-2). If I don't already know that my memory is trustworthy, how can I be justified in accepting the proposition that most of my memory beliefs are true? A similar argument for the reliability of perception could be construed. It would be open to a similar objection.

If track record arguments for the reliability of memory and perception do not work, one might attempt to offer an *a priori* defense analogous to the defense of induction offered in Chapter 7. But such an effort seems to be doomed from the start. It is simply not an *a priori* truth that our memories or our perceptions are reliable guides to the world around us. Even *The Standard View* acknowledges that they are not completely reliable. And surely it is possible for them to have been even less reliable than (we believe) they actually are. *A priori* arguments for the reliability of memory and perception therefore seem unpromising as well.

There is at least one other option. To begin to explore this option, notice that it is a mistake to think that people are justified in their memory or perceptual beliefs only if they have justified beliefs about the trustworthiness of memory and perception. To think that people must have these beliefs about the merits of their beliefs—metabeliefs—overintellectualizes what it takes to have justification. Children and others who have not thought about justification can still have justified beliefs. Thus, one does not first have to establish (REL), or anything like it, in order to have justified perceptual or memory beliefs.[27] Young children, for example, can know a great deal about the world around them on the basis of perception and memory, but they do not have to believe anything like (REL).[28] That requires a kind of sophistication they most likely lack.

If this is right, the complaint about track record arguments was incorrect. The complaint was that one needed prior justification for believing that memory was reliable in order to be justified in believing that M1, M2, etc. are true (where M1, M2, etc. are one's memory beliefs) and one needed prior justification for believing that perception was reliable in order to be justified in believing that most of one's perceptual beliefs are true. But this is not right. One's perceptual experiences can more directly justify the perceptual beliefs, and one's memories can more directly justify M1, M2, etc. One need not be able to group these beliefs together under the headings "perceptual beliefs" or "memory beliefs" in order for the individual beliefs to be justified. Thus, (2-2) and the comparable belief about perception could be justified without one realizing what kind of beliefs they are and thus without (2-1) and the comparable premise about perception being justified.

As we become more sophisticated, we learn to reflect on our beliefs. As this happens, we acquire justification for beliefs about the sources of our beliefs. We realize that some beliefs fall under the heading of perception and others under memory. Of course, this does not take enormous sophistication, and it surely does not take special scientific knowledge. Thus, over time, we come to learn that some of our beliefs arise from perception and memory. When we are able to put these points together, we can then use track record arguments to justify (REL).

Somewhat more complex defenses of (REL) may also be available. Recall *The Best Explanation Argument* from Chapter 7. The considerations supporting that argument may carry over to the present setting.[29] Our current reasons for thinking that perception and memory are reliable may be that this is part of the best explanation of our overall experiences. As epistemological naturalists would be quick to point out, scientific information can contribute to our understanding of these matters. That is, it can give us a much better understanding of just when our cognitive systems fail us and when they typically work well. It would surely be a mistake for traditionalists to claim that we know everything there is to know about perception and memory *a priori* or from our armchairs. We surely can get a more detailed and thorough understanding of the matter from careful research about cognition.

If something like this is right, then we can have armchair knowledge that (REL) is true. If traditional epistemologists suggested that (REL) was known *a priori*, then they were mistaken. And if advocates of *The Naturalistic View* contend that information available only to those familiar with scientific work can know (REL), then they, too, are mistaken.

Perhaps, then, we can have *a priori* knowledge of only a limited number of fundamental epistemological truths (and of the logical consequences of these truths). This would include principles such as (PFR), (TE), and a related principle about the reasonableness of believing the best explanations of one's data. Perhaps the general accounts of knowledge and justification can also be known *a priori*. Facts to the effect that we know specific things or that particular sources are in fact trustworthy, are best regarded as items of *a posteriori* knowledge. But this can be armchair *a posteriori* knowledge. It is for this reason that it was possible to conduct the discussion without attention to scientific results.

III. CONCLUSION

This chapter has reviewed two challenges to *The Standard View* based on the claims of proponents of *The Naturalistic View*. The first challenge derived from empirical studies purporting to show that people are systematically bad reasoners. If correct, this undermines much, though not all, of what *The Standard View* claims. The contention of the present chapter is that the empirical results may show a variety of errors, misunderstandings, and ignorance, but they do not show such widespread irrationality as to undermine *The Standard View*.

The second challenge is based on the arguments of naturalistic epistemologists. Their contention is not that *The Standard View* is false, but rather that traditional philosophical ways to discuss and defend it are inadequate. It may be that some traditional epistemologists have overstated what can be known *a priori*. And it may also be that they have incorrectly assumed that scientific results are irrelevant to all epistemological claims. It is also important for traditional epistemologists to carefully distinguish between what they can know *a priori* and what they can know from their armchairs. With these points in mind, it is safe to say that traditional epistemology is not undermined by the arguments of the naturalists.

ENDNOTES

1. In raising these questions we turn our attention to question (Q5) from Chapter 1.
2. Good summaries of the research results can be found in Richard Nisbett and Lee Ross, *Human Inference: Strategies and Shortcomings of Social Judgment* (Englewood Cliffs, NJ: Prentice Hall, 1980); Thomas Gilovich, *How We Know What Isn't So: The Fallibility of Human Reason in Everyday Life* (New York: Free Press, 1991); and Scott Plous, *The Psychology of Judgment and Decision Making* (New York: McGraw-Hill, 1993). For a detailed discussion of the empirical results and their philosophical implications, see Edward Stein, *Without Good Reason: The Rationality Debate in Philosophy and Cognitive Science* (Oxford: Clarendon Press, 1996).
3. This description of the example is taken from Stein, *Without Good Reason*, p. 1. The original example appeared, in somewhat different form, in Amos Tversky and Daniel Kahneman, "Extensional versus Intuitive Reasoning: The Conjunction Fallacy in Probability Judgment," *Psychological Review* 90 (1983): 293–315.
4. This example is described in Nisbett and Ross, *Human Inference: Strategies and Shortcomings of Social Judgment*, p. 19.
5. This experiment was originally reported by Peter Wason in "Reasoning" in Brian Foss (ed.), *New Horizons in Psychology* (Harmondsworth, U.K.: Penguin, 1966). The description provided here is from *The Psychology of Judgement, and Decision Making*, pp. 231–2.
6. For a detailed discussion of this argument, see Stein, *Without Good Reason*, Chapter 6.
7. Stephen Stich discusses this example in *The Fragmentation of Reason* (Cambridge, MA: MIT Press, 1990), pp. 61–3. The idea is adapted from the work of John Garcia et al., "Biological Constraints on Conditioning," in Abraham Black and William Prokasy (eds.), *Classical Conditioning* (New York: Appleton-Century Crofts, 1972).

8. One source for this argument is L. Jonathan Cohen's influential essay, "Can Human Irrationality Be Experimentally Demonstrated?" *Behavioral and Brain Sciences* 6 (1983): 317–70.

9. We could, of course, change the way we use words so that the symbol "5" meant 4.

10. *Human Inference: Strategies and Shortcomings of Social Judgment,* p. 19.

11. See *Human Inference: Strategies and Shortcomings of Social Judgment,* p. 20.

12. The material in this section draws on ideas first presented in Richard Feldman, "Methodological Naturalism in Epistemology," in *The Blackwell Guide to Epistemology,* edited by John Greco and Ernest Sosa (eds.), (Malden, MA: Blackwell, 1999), pp. 170–86.

13. "Epistemology Naturalized," in W. V. O. Quine, *Ontological Relativity and Other Essays* (New York: Columbia University Press, 1969).

14. "Epistemology Naturalized," p. 75.

15. "Epistemology Naturalized," pp. 82–3.

16. In "What is Naturalized Epistemology?" *Philosophical Perspectives,* Vol. 2 (1988): 381–406. See esp. p. 390.

17. For a defense of Quine, see Hilary Kornblith "In Defense of a Naturalized Epistemology" in *The Blackwell Guide to Epistemology,* pp. 158–69.

18. These concepts came up earlier, in connection with the problem of induction.

19. Nothing in the example turns on the vagueness of "eating poorly." Something far more precise could be substituted without affecting the point of the example.

20. Some philosophers contend that nothing can be known *a priori* or that the *a priori/a posteriori* distinction makes no sense. We will not take up this issue here.

21. See, for example, Philip Kitcher, "The Naturalists Return," *The Philosophical Review* 101 (1992), pp. 53–114; and Alvin Goldman, "Epistemic Folkways and Scientific Epistemology," reprinted in *Naturalizing Epistemology,* 2nd ed., edited by Hilary Kornblith (Cambridge, MA: MIT Press, 1994), pp. 291–315.

22. See Chapter 7.

23. John Pollock, *Contemporary Theories of Knowledge* (Totowa, NJ: Roman and Littlefield, 1986), p. 6.

24. Others have made similar distinctions in discussing this topic. See, for example, Susan Haack, *Evidence and Inquiry* (Oxford: Blackwell, 1993), Chapter 6; and Harvey Siegel, "Naturalize Epistemology and 'First Philosophy'," *Metaphilosophy* 26 (1995): 46–62, esp. p. 56.

25. That is, we are in Gettier cases more often than we would have thought.

26. To say that (PFR) itself is knowable *a priori* is not to say that the things we know through its application are also knowable *a priori.* Knowledge arrived at through the application of (PFR) requires the non-*a priori*-knowledge that things have been a certain way in the past.

27. Analogously, one does not have to prove that induction works in order to have any beliefs justified by inductive inference.

28. This is not to say that perception and memory are necessarily sources of justification. It is, perhaps, possible for people to have fleeting and disconnected perceptual experiences. Such experiences may not justify to any degree beliefs about the external world. However, the richer, more integrated experiences of normal people, including children, justify beliefs about the world without the believer being justified in believing anything as complex as (REL).

29. The liabilities of that response to skepticism carry over here as well. There is a question about why people who have not thought about these matters are justified in their memory and perceptual beliefs. See Chapter 7, Section V, for discussion. Of particular relevance here are the last paragraphs of Subsection B3.

CHAPTER NINE

Epistemological Relativism

A final set of questions about for *The Standard View* emerges from consideration of *The Relativistic View.* Like *The Naturalistic View,* and unlike *The Skeptical View, The Relativistic View* suggests not so much that *The Standard View* is false, but rather that it is incomplete and that it fails to take important considerations into account. The starting points for *The Relativistic View* are the observations that there is a great deal of cognitive diversity and that seemingly reasonable people can have substantial disagreements. *The Standard View* seems to ignore this. This chapter will examine these points and their implications.[1]

I. UNCONTROVERSIAL FORMS OF RELATIVISM

Harvey Siegel (a critic of relativism) describes relativism as follows:

> Epistemological relativism may be defined as the view that knowledge (and/or truth) is relative—to time, to place, to society, to culture, to historical epoch, to conceptual scheme or framework, or to personal training or conviction—so that what counts as knowledge depends upon the values of one or more of these variables.[2]

There are a variety of different ideas that one might extract from Siegel's characterization of relativism. We will begin with some simple and uncontroversial formulations. Consider the following claims:

R1. What one person knows might differ from what another person knows.

R2. What one person knows at one time might differ from what that person knows at another time.

R3.   What is generally known in one society might differ from what is generally known in another society.

R4.   What is generally known in one society at one time might differ from what is generally known in that society at a different time.

No one, at least no one who is not a skeptic, would disagree with any of these theses.

One point about the meaning of (R1)–(R4) should be clarified. Consider (R1). One thing that makes it true is the fact that each of us has secrets, things about ourselves that no one else knows. As a result, each of us knows things that others do not know. There is no implication here that one person can know something incompatible with something another knows. (R1) does not imply that I can know that it is raining in a particular place at a particular time and you can know that it is not raining at that time and place. It just says that we can know different things. Similar points apply to (R2)–(R4).

Theses analogous to (R1)–(R4) are true about reasonable or justified belief. Different people can reasonably believe different things, and the widely held reasonable beliefs in one society might differ from those of another. Reasonable beliefs can change over time as well. Furthermore, in the case of reasonable belief, it is not controversial to admit that there can be direct conflicts in what is reasonably believed. We have seen this point at various places earlier in this book. The ancients may have had reasonable beliefs about the shape of the earth that differ from what we reasonably believe about that topic now. None of this is particularly controversial. Nor does it call into question anything associated with *The Standard View*. These are not relativistic theses, or, if they are, then these forms of relativism are entirely uncontroversial. Presumably, in characterizing relativism as he did, Siegel had something else in mind.

II. SERIOUS RELATIVISM

A more striking relativist thesis, and probably one that Siegel had in mind, is a thesis about the relativity of the standards for knowledge or reasonable belief. Stephen Stich proposes such an account of relativism in the following passage:

> An account of what makes a system of reasoning or belief revision a good one is relativistic if it is sensitive to facts about the person or group using the system. It may then turn out that one system is best for one person or group, while a quite different system is best for another.[3]

The idea here is that there are no uniquely correct standards of rationality or knowledge, that somehow whether something counts as rational or as knowledge is in some way or other relative to a set of standards that can vary from one setting to another. We can formulate this version of relativism this way:

R5.   The correct (or reasonable) system (or principles) for forming beliefs for one person or group can be different from the correct (or reasonable) system for another.

Relativism is often contrasted with "absolutism," according to which there is only one correct system, applicable to all people.

This statement of relativism is unclear enough to make assessment of it problematic. A simple example will help to bring out the issues.

Example 9.1: Two Teachers

Professor Expert is a distinguished scholar in her field. In her classes she presents detailed and accurate lectures on the course material. Students listen carefully to things she says and, unless something highly unusual occurs, accept her word. Professor Provocative is also a distinguished scholar in his field, but in his classes he typically says outrageous things in order to provoke students into thinking through the material. Students listen carefully to things he says and, unless something highly unusual occurs, they reject what he says.

The students in the two classes in Example 9.1 follow different principles of belief formation in their two classes. One group of students follows the rule: Believe what the teacher says. The other group follows a contrary rule. It would be a mistake to say that one rule is uniquely correct. Each group of students, we might say, is using a rule or standard that is appropriate for its circumstances.

Differences in rules can be on a much grander scale than the one in Example 9.1. For example, for a great many propositions, we take visual evidence to be particularly important. Thus, if you want to know whether there is an apple in the refrigerator, visual evidence would be more significant than your memory of what was there earlier or what is on the list next to the refrigerator. But people whose vision is extremely poor will not give visual evidence the same priority; they will follow different rules. And, for another example, people brought up in vastly different societies, where the value of scientific studies is given far less credence than many contemporary cultures give it, will follow different rules as well.

If differences of the sort illustrated by these examples are sufficient to make (R5) true, then this form of epistemic relativism is almost surely true. This kind of relativism is relatively uncontroversial. The rules that work out best for one person or group may differ from what works out best for another person or group. If that is all relativism implies, it is surely true.

Relativism of the sort so far described is no threat to *The Standard View*. It is consistent with the points raised in the past few paragraphs that we do know the things that *The Standard View* says we know and that the sources of knowledge it identifies are indeed sources of knowledge. Furthermore, the modest foundationalist account of knowledge and justification is also consistent with relativism.

There is reason to wonder, however, whether the relativistic theses so far described reveal the heart of *The Relativistic View*. One reason for doubt about this is that everything asserted so far is also consistent with what one might plausibly take to be an absolutist view about epistemic matters. Unless absolutism is a naively simplistic, and plainly unsatisfactory, doctrine, it also implies that different principles ought to be applied in different circumstances. To disagree with what we have described as the relativist assessment of Example 9.1, an absolutist would have to say that either all students ought always to believe what their teachers say or that no students should do so. Obviously, however, no one would say that. In fact, the policies of the students in the two classes seem to fall under a single, more general principle to the effect that one ought to believe the things said by sources one has reason to trust.[4] Similarly, absolutists would have to be extraordinarily misguided to deny that people with different perceptual capacities can reasonably treat perceptual evidence differently. Once again, it is likely that a suitable, more general principle will cover all the cases. Relativism, if it is noteworthy, must imply something more than this. It must imply something absolutists might want to deny.

There is a much more questionable thesis that at least many philosophers associate with relativism.[5] It is difficult to state this thesis precisely. The following passage presents one statement of the view:

> For the relativist there is no sense attached to the idea that some standards or beliefs are really rational as distinct from merely locally accepted as such. Because he thinks that there are no context-free or super-cultural norms of rationality he does not see rationally and irrationally held beliefs as making up two distinct and qualitatively different classes of things.[6]

The key claim here is contained in the first sentence. It will serve as our next statement of relativism:

> R6.   No "standards or beliefs are really rational as distinct from merely locally accepted as such."

(R6) does seem to imply something much more controversial. In thinking about Example 9.1, we assumed that it really was rational for the students in Professor Expert's class to believe the things she told them and that it really was rational for the students in Professor Provocative's class to reject the things he told them. Moreover, it was not the fact that the students actually had these different practices that made them rational. One could imagine unduly harsh students in Professor Expert's class not accepting what she said. They might have that critical practice, yet (at least according to the sort of view applied previously) not be reasonable in disbelieving her statements. Similarly, excessively gullible students in Professor Provocative's class could have the practice of unreasonably accepting the outrageous things he says. Our previous discussion thus seemed to assume that there was a fact about what was really rational. (R6) denies this. Apparently, defenders of (R6) think that there is nothing more to rationality than local standards. Thus, if one group adopts one standard (e.g., believe what the professor says) and another group in descriptively identical circumstances adopts a different standard (e.g., deny what the professor says), each group is rational.

(R6) is difficult to interpret and assess. Presumably its defenders think that rationality is in some sense special and that other properties "really" do apply to objects. It is difficult to see why they would bother to say that things are not "really" rational if they also thought that things are not "really" square and not "really" human and not "really" composed of atoms. Relativism about these matters seems plainly absurd. To take another example, if the people in some society are suffering from an unusual disease, it would be a mistake to think that there is no fact about what really is causing the disease but only local beliefs about that matter. If one group thinks it is a virus and another thinks it is contaminated food, they really do disagree and they cannot both be right.[7] A reasonable question, then, is why relativists think that rationality is in this way special.

One might be led to think that there is nothing that is "really" rational because everyone who thinks about the matter will address the issue from his or her own perspective or context. There is no privileged vantage point from which to view things. Whatever you think about rationality will be affected by your experiences, your culture, and other factors. Something like this may well be true. We can do things to try to overcome some of our biases, but we will then view things from whatever perspective or point of view we then have. However, it is hard to see any reason to think it follows that there is no truth to the matter. When we make judgments about any topic, including the shapes of objects or the causes of diseases, we must make them from our own point of view. Again, we can do a great deal to avoid biases, but our conclusions will always be affected by our perspectives or points of view. It does not follow that objects do not "really" have shapes or that diseases do not really have causes.

Finally, it is difficult to see why someone who defends (R6) is not committed to a form of absolutism anyway. Such a person thinks that all there is to rationality is local standards. Why not say, then, that what is really rational for a person is whatever is demanded by local standards. That is, (R6) seems to be equivalent to

> A1.   It is always really rational for a person to conform to the locally accepted standards of rationality.

(A1) is a highly implausible rule: Local standards could embody foolish rules. But that is not crucial for present purposes. What is crucial is that even this last form of relativism seems, upon analysis, to turn into a kind of absolutism.

The conclusion so far is that there are versions of relativism that are entirely uncontroversial, such as (R1)–(R5). These forms of relativism are not incompatible with things most absolutists claim, and they are not incompatible with anything implied by *The Standard View*. Another form of relativism is expressed in (R6). But this version of relativism is implausible and poorly defended. It too is equivalent to an implausible kind of absolutism. No doubt other versions of relativism could be developed, and it remains possible that a better version will be developed.

None of this should be taken to discount the observations of cognitive diversity that lead some to *The Relativistic View*. People are diverse, and it would be a mistake to deny this or to arrogantly assume the superiority of one's own views.

However, it is difficult to extract any significant epistemological doctrine from these observations, at least no doctrine that undermines *The Standard View.*

III. REASONABLE DISAGREEMENTS

It is not uncommon for a conversation about a controversial subject to end with the declaration that reasonable people can disagree about the issue in question. Advocates of *The Relativistic View* are eager to allow that this remark can be true. It is made in political, religious, philosophical, and sometimes scientific discussions. Perhaps it is hoped that this allows for respectful disagreement and greater tolerance of opposing views. Nothing in what follows is intended to minimize the value of being respectful and tolerant. Instead, the question to be addressed concerns the extent to which it is possible for reasonable people to disagree. Perhaps relativists and absolutists differ over how much reasonable disagreement there can be.

A. Uncontroversial Cases of Reasonable Disagreement

It will be best to begin by clarifying the issue. This can be done by identifying and setting aside two kinds of situation that might seem to involve reasonable (or rational) people disagreeing but which are beside the point under discussion here.

First, one might think that a reasonable person is one who has a general tendency to have reasonable beliefs. Just as an honest person might tell an infrequent lie, a reasonable person might have an occasional unreasonable belief. When he has such a belief, the reasonable person would disagree with another reasonable person who has similar evidence but is not suffering from this lapse of rationality. This is clearly not what the remark "reasonable people can disagree" is intended to convey. Rather, the claim is that both points of view are reasonable in the same circumstances.

A second way in which it is uncontroversial that reasonable people can disagree turns centrally on what counts as a disagreement. Suppose I like vanilla ice cream and you prefer chocolate. We disagree, in a sense, about something. Yet there is nothing unreasonable about either preference. Perfectly reasonable people can have nonintellectual disagreements like this. Of course, in this sort of case there is no particular proposition such that one person thinks that it is true and the other thinks that it is false. And it is the existence of reasonable disagreements about the truth value of a proposition that is under discussion here.

These two examples suggest that the real point of asking whether reasonable people can disagree is to ask whether it can happen that one person believes a proposition and the other person believes the denial of that proposition, yet both people are reasonable in their beliefs. Again, however, it is easy to see that the answer to this question is uncontroversially affirmative. Examples such as the one about ancient and modern beliefs about the shape of the earth establish the point. However, the sort of case that often prompts the remark that reasonable people can disagree differs from this one. Let us assume that the ancient people's beliefs were based on the best observational and theoretical information available to them. That is what made their belief reasonable. We are in a clearly superior position to them with respect to this particular issue. We have observations and information that go well beyond what they had. We are aware, at least in a rough way, of the information they had and a lot more. That enables us to say, correctly, that they were reasonable in their belief, yet they were wrong, and that our belief in a competing proposition is reasonable as well.

The relationship between the ancients and us on these matters is in an important way asymmetrical: We know about them, but they did not know about us. There was no conversation in which they heard our view, we heard their view, and then we both reasonably came to (or stuck with) our different views. In contrast, the sort of situation envisioned at the beginning of this section was one in which two people engage in a dialogue, hear and express defenses of the various views, and then come to the conclusion that rational people can disagree about the matter at hand. In this case, there is a sharing of information, yet different conclusions are reached. This is a more puzzling sort of case. When this happens, can the two parties both be reasonable?

B. Maintaining Beliefs in the Light of Disagreement

One form of our question asks whether it is reasonable to maintain your own beliefs when you know that there are other people who are just as intelligent as you who have beliefs that conflict with yours. The question is most challenging when it comes to beliefs that arouse the most passion among people, such as their moral or religious beliefs. Is it reasonable to maintain your own beliefs when you know that there are other people, as intelligent and well-informed as you, who believe things in stark contrast to what you believe? Can you sensibly think that your own beliefs are reasonable, yet the beliefs of those who disagree with you are reasonable as well? Here the idea is that there is no asymmetry, or at least no obvious asymmetry, as there was in the case of the ancients and us. In these cases, you and those with whom you disagree know all about each other's views. To say that your own beliefs are reasonable yet their competing beliefs are reasonable as well, is to say (assuming an evidentialist perspective) three things:

    a.   You have good reasons for your beliefs.
    b.   They have good reasons for their competing beliefs.
    c.   You are right and they are wrong.

Is this combination of beliefs defensible?

You might think that the situation under discussion is not one in which you must accept element (c). But if there is a real disagreement, then there is something you believe and the others deny. And if you believe p and you know that someone else believes ~p, then you think that the other person is wrong. You might not want to put the point so boldly, but that is what consistency demands that you think. If you think that they could be right at the same time you are right, then you think that you really do not disagree at all. Where there is real disagreement, element (c) is present.[8]

Some people have tried to interpret apparent disagreements over important issues in ways that make them not real disagreements. That is to say, they have attempted to interpret some issues in ways in which point (c) does not apply. For example, some people have attempted to interpret apparent differences about religious matters as something other than genuine disagreements. One might say that apparently conflicting religious views are really cases in which people use different language to say essentially the same thing. Or one might take religious talk not to be descriptive of facts but rather ways of expressing one's allegiance to particular ways of life. We will not enter into these disputes about the nature of religious language here.[9] Our question is about genuine disagreements. If religious disagreements are genuine disagreements, then what is said below applies to them.

Our question, then, is whether a person can reasonably accept all of (a)–(c) in the case of a genuine disagreement about some factual matter. Perhaps this is a point about which relativists and absolutists disagree. In other words, maybe advocates of *The Relativist View* accept, and absolutists deny, a principle such as

> R7.   It is possible for a person to be justified in believing p while also being justified in believing that other people are justified in believing ~p.

(R7) seems to be what the person who ends a conversation with "reasonable people can disagree" has in mind. She's saying, "I'm reasonable in my belief, but you are reasonable in your competing belief."

It is clear, however, that absolutists would have no trouble accepting (R7). As a first step toward seeing why, consider the following example:

Example 9.2:   Effective Treatments

Dr. J does a careful study to examine the effectiveness of drugs X, Y, and Z for treating some disease. The study indicates that X works best. Dr. J. has no other information relevant to the preferability of the three medications. Meanwhile, Dr. K has done a similar study and it indicated that Y works best. Neither researcher knows anything about the other's results, or even of the existence of the other study. Neither researcher is at all negligent for failing to know about the other's study. Each has good reason to think that his study was effectively designed and carried out.

At this point, we can accept each of the following:

1.   Dr. J is reasonably well justified in thinking that X works best.[10]
2.   Dr. K is reasonably well justified in thinking that Y works best.

In its present form, this example does not provide support for (R7). To establish (R7), it is not enough that (2) is true. What is needed is that Dr. J is justified in thinking that (2) is true.

Suppose we add to the story that Dr. J learns about Dr. K's results. If we can also add factors to this story that make Dr. J justified in thinking that he is right and Dr. K is wrong, then we will have an example of establishing (R7). It is not difficult to do so. Suppose that Dr. J also knows about flaws in Dr. K's study, flaws that Dr. K has no way of knowing about and do not involve errors of reasoning. The fact that Dr. K has no way of knowing about these flaws and has not made errors of reasoning makes it true that she (Dr. K) is justified in her belief. The fact that Dr. J has found these flaws shows that he does have reason to discount her results and to believe that he is right and she is wrong.[11] He is still justified in thinking that X works best. We thus have a case establishing (R7). The example turns on the fact that Dr. J knows more than Dr. K does. He is able to explain away her conflicting results. Thus, you can have good reasons for your belief, know that other people have good reasons for their competing belief, and still be justified in retaining your own.

It turns out, then, that relativist thesis (R7) is true. But this in no way establishes anything absolutists would wish to deny. The principles of reasoning could be as absolute as one could imagine, and the example just described would establish (R7).

As described so far, the example of Dr. J and Dr. K involves an asymmetry. Dr. J knows more than Dr. K about the situation. In this respect, it is like the example about the ancients and us on the shape of the earth. But we can modify the example to eliminate this feature. Suppose that the two doctors exchange all their information about the two experiments. Then they have exactly the same evidence about the research results. And suppose that they maintain their original beliefs. Dr. J still thinks X works best and Dr. K still thinks Y works best. Perhaps relativists want to say that each of them would be justified and that each would be justified in believing that the other is justified. They could reasonably disagree about the best medicine. If relativists say this, they are defending a principle such as

> R8.   It is possible for a person to be justified in believing p, and justified in believing that other people are justified in believing ~p, and not have any reason to believe that his or her own reasons (or methods) are superior to those of the other people.

To accept (R8) is to accept a significant thesis. This may be what those who advocate the possibility of reasonable disagreements have in mind. For (R8) is a way of saying, "I have my belief, you have yours, we are both justified, and our epistemic situations are comparable." This allows for disagreement without the assumption of a superior position on the part of either party to the disagreement.

Absolutists will deny (R8). Evidentialists seem to be committed to the view that the two doctors in our example cannot be justified in believing different things on the basis of the same evidence. They will deny (R8). Thus, perhaps (R8) is a point of contention between relativists and absolutists.

There is good reason to favor the absolutist side in this dispute. For each doctor to maintain his or her belief in their situation is to give special status to his or her own study for no good reason. This is a failure to treat like cases alike. They should both suspend judgment about which drug is most effective. There is no reason to accept the relativist claim that each of them is justified in maintaining his or her original belief. It is best to reject (R8).

A related idea is as follows. Sometimes you have a particular belief and you know that other people, just as intelligent as you, have beliefs that conflict with yours. It may be comforting and friendly to think that they are justified in their belief and you are justified in yours. But if you genuinely and reasonably think that they are justified in their belief, then, if you are to be reasonable in maintaining your belief, you need some good reason to think that, for one reason or another, they have a justified false belief. That is, you need some information comparable to what we have in the case of the ancients and us. Lacking that, you are not justified in maintaining your belief.

This is a troubling outcome. Many people are inclined to think that their philosophical, political, religious, and other views are reasonable but that those who disagree with them are reasonable as well. They want to be tolerant and inclusive. They want to maintain their own views but concede that those who differ with them have their good reasons as well. The upshot of our discussion is that, in cases in which all the evidence on both sides has been shared, this combination of views is not reasonable. You cannot reasonably think that your beliefs are justified by that evidence and that the others' competing beliefs are also justified by that evidence. And further, even if you have not shared all the evidence, once you concede that others have good reasons for their views, you must have good reason for thinking that they are mistaken if you are to be reasonable in maintaining your original beliefs. Reasonable disagreements are harder to come by than defenders of (R8) might think.

C. Two Objections

The argument of the previous section denies that there can be reasonable disagreements of the kind relativists describe. This section examines two replies.

C1. Differing Attitudes Toward Risk

Example 9.3: Risky and Cautious

Risky and Cautious examine the evidence concerning a proposition, P, and they find that the evidence slightly supports it. Risky concludes that this is good enough evidence to believe P and believes it. Cautious concludes that believing on that amount of evidence is too risky. Cautious does not believe p. But each recognizes the legitimacy of the other's policy. They decide that each has a reasonable attitude toward p.

If Risky and Cautious are right in thinking that each of them is reasonable, then we seem to have a case of reasonable disagreement of the kind being sought. This example, if correct, shows that there is not a unique reasonable attitude to take toward a proposition, even with a fixed body of evidence. This seems to undermine absolutism.

The sort of disagreement involved in Example 9.3 differs from what was present in the cases considered earlier. This is not a case in which people really disagree about p; that is, it is not a case in which one believes it and the other disbelieves it. Instead, one believes it and the other merely suspends judgment about it. And there is no way to modify the case so that Cautious would come to believe ~p on the basis of the evidence, unless they had a far more substantive disagreement about the nature of that evidence. So, even if correct, this is not a case of reasonable disagreement of the sort we have been seeking.

It might even be that the case only arises because we have been talking about belief as if it is an "all or nothing" attitude. But it might be that we should distinguish degrees of belief, or that we should acknowledge differences between cautious acceptance, full conviction, and a range of attitudes in between. Arguably, then, some weak form of belief is justified in the example under consideration. In this view, suspension of judgment is justified only when the evidence concerning a proposition is really counterbalanced—when it does not even modestly support the proposition. If that is the case, then differing attitudes toward risk do not seem to justify even the more modest sort of disagreement involved in Example 9.3.

Examples such as Example 9.3 thus do not support any significant abandonment of the absolutist view. Perhaps they show that there is room for some reasonable differences in how much evidence is required in order to reasonably form a belief. But this does not come close to showing that there can be reasonable disagreements of the sort envisioned by (R8).

C2. When Choice is Required

Example 9.4:   The Fork in the Road

Lefty and Righty are driving in separate cars to an important meeting. They drive at different times so that they do not see one another. There is a fork in the road. Each must take one of the forks. The directions did not mention the fork, they have no map or cell phone, and there is no one around to ask. Turning back is not an option. They must make a choice. Lefty chooses the left fork. Righty chooses the right fork. Later, upon hearing what has happened, Lefty says that Righty made a reasonable choice, although he, Lefty, was reasonable as well. Neither thinks his own choice was better than the other's.

Lefty and Righty had exactly the same information when they made their decisions. They made different decisions, and, at least at the later time, they each know that the other has made a reasonable decision. This shows that reasonable people can disagree, even when all the evidence is shared. This may seem to support (R8) and to refute absolutism.

In thinking about examples such as this one, it is important to separate questions about belief from questions about action. We can grant that it is reasonable to take the left fork and that it is reasonable to take the right fork. One has to take one of the forks—we are assuming there is no other option—and there is no basis for concluding that one fork is better than the other. Thus, taking either is acceptable. But this does not show that reasonable disagreement of the sort characterized earlier is possible. And no objection to absolutism about reasonable belief is brought out by this case. It is reasonable to take the left fork. It is equally reasonable to take the right fork. But it is not reasonable to *believe* that the left fork is the better route. Nor is it reasonable to *believe* that the right fork is the better way to go. The justified attitude toward these propositions is suspension of judgment. A reasonable person would think, in this situation, "I have no idea which way is best. But I will go this way." The choice of a way to go will be arbitrary.

Suspension of judgment is an option always available in the case of believing. In some cases of action, the option of doing nothing—which is in some ways the analogue of suspending judgment—is either not available or is a clearly inferior option. But in all the kinds of cases under consideration here, suspending judgment about the controverted propositions is at least a candidate for the reasonable attitude. And it may well be that in many of the cases in which people think that reasonable people can disagree, what is really true is that reasonable people will suspend judgment about the topic. And this may be true even if some related action must be taken. Dr. J, in the final version of the example, would, if he were reasonable, suspend judgment about which drug is best. And he would suspend judgment even if he must give some medication to a patient in need of a cure.

This suggests an important point that may apply to some real-life cases in which people want to say that reasonable people can disagree. If you think that either of the two conclusions is equally well supported by the evidence, then suspension of judgment is the rational attitude to take. This may be disappointing, in that it may feel better to have a belief. The beliefs in question may even make a real difference to your life. Still, the conclusion of the present line of thought is that in such cases suspension of judgment is the epistemically rational attitude. At the same time, it may be best to act in such cases, as the example about the fork in the road shows.

Consistently following evidentialist principles, then, may require taking a more humble stance than some would like. Suspension of judgment may be the reasonable attitude toward many difficult issues.

IV. CONCLUSION

This chapter has examined *The Relativist View* and its implications. It turns out to be difficult to formulate exactly what the relativist position is. Some versions of the doctrine, such as (R1)–(R4), merely assert that there are differences in the things known by different people or groups. Such versions of relativism are entirely innocuous. Other versions, such as (R5), assert that there are differences in the principles of reasoning that people can reasonably use. Suitably interpreted, this too is true and hardly controversial.

Other versions of relativism, such as (R6), assert that there are no real truths about what is reasonable; there are merely varying local standards. It is difficult to understand exactly what this means, except perhaps that the unique proper standard is to follow whatever the local customs dictate. This amounts to a fairly implausible absolutist thesis. There is, then, nothing in these relativist doctrines that is both plausible and controversial.

Another idea associated with *The Relativist View* is suggested by the common expression, "Reasonable people can disagree." This expression can be interpreted in a variety of ways, but the one of greatest interest applies to situations in which two people have shared all their relevant information and come to different conclusions about a topic. They each claim to be reasonable in drawing their conclusion, but perhaps out of a desire to be respectful and tolerant, acknowledge the rationality of the other. (R8) formulated the relativist principle along these lines.

If (R8) is true, then two people in a conversation can share all their evidence and reasonably come to different conclusions, in full knowledge of the position of the other. This would amount to a violation of evidentialist standards. Although it does not directly conflict with *The Standard View*, it does conflict with the absolutism implicit throughout our discussion. The conclusion drawn here is that (R8) is not true, that there are no cases of the sort it describes. In the situations most plausibly thought to be cases of reasonable disagreement, suspension of judgment is the reasonable attitude to take toward the disputed proposition.

The Relativist View poses a set of interesting and puzzling issues. The existence of cognitive diversity may provide a basis for reduced confidence in some things some people believe. But there is nothing in the considerations advanced in this chapter to cast doubt on *The Standard View*.

ENDNOTES

1. In raising these issues we turn to question (Q6) from Chapter 1.
2. Harvey Siegel, "Relativism," in Jonathan Dancy and Ernest Sosa (eds.), *A Companion to Epistemology* (Oxford: Blackwell, 1992), pp. 428–30. The quotation is from pp. 428–9.
3. Stephen Stich, "Epistemic Relativism," Routledge Encyclopedia of Philosophy Online, (2000). General Editor: Edward Craig. http://www.rep.routledge.com/.
4. See principle (TE) in Chapter 8.
5. I am grateful to Harvey Siegel for helpful comments on this chapter, and especially this section. For an excellent discussion of the topic, see his "Relativism," in I. Niiniluoto, M. Sintonen, and J. Wolenski (eds.), *Handbook of Epistemology* (Dordrecht: Kluwer, 2001).
6. B. Barnes and D. Bloor, "Relativism, Rationalism and the Sociology of Knowledge," in M. Hollis and S. Lukes (eds.), *Rationality and Relativism* (Cambridge, MA: MIT Press, 1982), pp. 27–8.

7. Of course, there could be a combination of factors causing the disease.

8. Some relativists might deny this. We saw in Section II of this chapter, in connection with (R6), that some people contend that nothing is really rational and that there are just local standards about that matter. A relativist who extended that view to other topics might say that in all apparent disagreements, there is no real truth and thus no real disagreement.

9. For discussion of these issues, see Philip L. Quinn and Kevin Meeker (eds.), *The Philosophical Challenge of Religious Diversity* (Oxford: Oxford University Press, 2000).

10. This is not to assume that the belief is well enough justified to meet a justification condition for knowledge. It has some lesser, but positive, epistemic status.

11. It is worth noting that the evidence for the flaws in the competing study is not evidence that drug X is effective. It is, rather, evidence that serves to undermine a defeater for this proposition. The defeater is the original information about the other studies.

CHAPTER TEN

Conclusion

We began with *The Standard View*. This involved two main claims:

SV1.   We know a large variety of things, including facts about our immediate environment, our own thoughts and feelings, the mental states of others, the past, the future, mathematics, and morality.

SV2.   Our primary sources of knowledge are perception, memory, testimony, introspection, reasoning, and rational insight.

In an effort to spell out more fully what *The Standard View* amounts to, we asked what knowledge is, what justification is, and what the connection is between epistemic justification and moral, prudential, and other types of justification. These were questions (Q1), (Q2), and (Q3), respectively.

The *Traditional Analysis of Knowledge* held that knowledge is justified true belief. This initially plausible analysis is shown to be false by the Gettier-style examples in which a person has a justified true belief in which the truth of the belief is, in some hard-to-specify sense, not connected to the person's justification. That the belief is true is coincidental. Explaining just what this amounts to proved to be remarkably difficult. Our best effort is captured in the *No Essential Falsehood* account, according to which

EDF.   S knows p = df. (1) p is true; (2) S believes p; (3) S is justified in believing p; and (4) S's justification for p does not essentially depend on any falsehood.

The heart of our response to (Q2), the question about the nature of justification, is found in *evidentialism*. This view is spelled out in the following pair of principles, which identify two distinct aspects of epistemic justification:

EJ.   Believing p is justified for S at t iff S's evidence at t supports p.

BJ.   S's belief in p at time t is *justified (well-founded)* iff (i) believing p is justified for S at t; (ii) S believes p on the basis of evidence that supports p.

According to evidentialism, what's justified for a person depends only on the evidence the person actually has, not on what evidence the person could have had or what evidence the person has practical or moral reasons to obtain. This construal of evidentialism depends in part upon the proposed answer to (Q3), according to which questions of epistemic justification are entirely independent of questions of prudence, morality, and the like.

There are, of course, hard questions about the details of evidentialism, and many philosophers find nonevidentialist theories, such as reliabilism and the proper function theory, preferable. The heart of these rival theories is that justification is, in one way or another, a matter of the right sort of causal connection obtaining between a belief and the facts in the world that make it true. The theories differ greatly over the details of this connection, and the debate over these theories continues to be a lively one. It was argued here, however, that each of these nonevidentialist theories has serious liabilities. There can be justification without any of the specified causal relations obtaining, and the causal relations can be present when justification is absent.

Foundationalism and *coherentism* are the two traditional accounts of the structure of justifying evidence. They are ways of filling out the general evidentialist picture. Coherentism holds that justification is entirely a matter of the internal coherence of beliefs. Fanciful, but convincing, examples cast doubt on coherentism. Furthermore, it turns out to be remarkably difficult to spell out in a clear way just what internal coherence amounts to.

Foundationalism comes in a variety of forms. The traditional form held that there were basic beliefs whose justification did not depend upon any other beliefs. These foundational beliefs were, according to Cartesian foundationalists, propositions about our own mental states. The rest of our knowledge, it was said, was what could be deduced from these certain foundations. Cartesian foundationalism runs into insuperable difficulties, at least if *The Standard View* is true. We are not completely certain of, or infallible about, the things it says are basic. And the rest of what we know cannot be deduced from these things anyway.

A more contemporary, and more plausible, form of foundationalism is *modest foundationalism*. This view holds that our basic beliefs include not merely the unusual beliefs about our own internal states the Cartesians focused on, but rather ordinary beliefs about objects in the world around us. The rest of what we know is what can be inferred from these basic beliefs. But again, modest foundationalists relax the Cartesian's demand for logical certainty in these inferences.

The hardest problem in formulating the details of modest foundationalism is identifying which of our responses to experiences actually are justified. We settled, in Chapter 4, on the idea that only those beliefs which constitute a "proper response" to experience are justified. This aspect of the view received more attention in Chapters 7 and 8, in response to skeptical challenges. Modest foundationalism is, at least according to the arguments presented here, the most promising account of justification available to support *The Standard View*.

The Standard View is not without rivals. We examined three. One rival, *The Skeptical View*, defends one or another of the arguments for skepticism, the view that we are unable to know much at all about the world around us. (Q4) asked whether there was any good response to these arguments. It was argued that *fallibilism* (of which modest foundationalism is a leading example) provides the best response, because many of the arguments for skepticism rely on the mistaken assumption that knowledge requires certainty or the impossibility of error. But fallibilism by itself provides a response only to those skeptical arguments that invoke high-standards skepticism, arguments that make use of the assumption that the standards for knowledge are extraordinarily high. Ordinary-standards skepticism challenges *The Standard View's* implication that we meet even the lower, fallibilist standards. In effect, it challenges the claim that we meet the standards for justification and knowledge set by modest foundationalism.

Ordinary-standards skepticism finds its support in Hume's famous argument about the epistemic merit of induction and *The Alternative Explanations Argument*, which contends that we have no good reason at all to believe the things we do believe instead of any of a number of alternative hypotheses equally compatible with our experiential data. Responding to these arguments is among the most difficult challenges faced by evidentialist defenders of *The Standard View*. The present working out of that view appeals to *a priori* principles of reasoning in response to Hume on induction and to the *a priori* rationality of inference to the best explanation in response to *The Alternative Explanation Argument*. The response to the latter also depends upon the debatable contention that our ordinary explanations are better explanations of our experiences than their skeptical alternatives are. There is little doubt that difficult questions about these issues remain unanswered.

The two remaining alternatives to *The Standard View* do not explicitly deny the truth of (SV1) and (SV2). *The Naturalistic View* is the view that empirical results concerning the nature of human thinking are of great importance to epistemology. (Q5) asked whether this is true and whether this view constituted a challenge to *The Standard View*. One prominent line of thought within *The Naturalistic View* draws on results from cognitive psychology that seem to call into doubt the accuracy of some of the purported sources of knowledge identified in (SV2). This challenge, if sound, possibly undermines some of the most extravagant claims proponents of *The Standard View* might make. But it does not amount to a full skeptical challenge. It was argued here that although these results may call into question the rationality of some of our beliefs, it may be that our apparent errors result from such things as lack of information or different interpretations of language, and these failures (if, indeed they are failures at all) do not amount to irrationality.

The Naturalistic View also challenges traditional defenders of *The Standard View* on the grounds they defend their claims without proper regard for empirical information that is essential to their assessment. This charge may have some merit, as it is true that some defenders seem to contend that things such as (SV1) and (SV2), and their consequences, are *a priori* truths. They are, however, at best contingent *a posteriori* truths, and any knowledge we have of them comes from experience. This fact, however, does not show that the sciences that study human reasoning, despite their enormous value, have a great deal to contribute to the philosophical questions that are at the heart of epistemology. Some of these questions are conceptual questions that can be answered *a priori*. Others are not, but the empirical information needed to answer them is not, in general, detailed scientific information but rather information available to us in our armchairs. This is not to say that scientific results cannot ultimately refute things that we reasonably believe from our armchairs. It can, and it has. Still, the central philosophical questions do not depend for their answers on those results.

The final set of questions, (Q6), are prompted by *The Relativist View*. This view is prompted by the recognition of cognitive diversity and the variety of beliefs and principles sensible people endorse. Advocates of *The Standard View* can, and many do, acknowledge this starting point. It is surely true that there are differences in what people know, and there can be direct conflicts in what people rationally believe. There can also be differences in the derivative principles they apply to their varying circumstances. *The Standard View*, when properly spelled out, can accept all of this. Thus, either relativism is innocuous, or relativism goes the beyond claims so far described. It proves to be remarkably difficult to identify exactly what it is, beyond these claims, that relativists wish to assert. Nothing along these lines that challenges *The Standard View* has emerged from investigations of relativism.

Our final conclusion, then, is that *The Standard View* is correct after all. However, its defense leads to surprisingly difficult conceptual issues and questions, many of which remain unanswered.

Index